CHRONICLES OF
GINGER FARM

CHRONICLES OF GINGER FARM

*Daily Life on a Small Canadian
Farm During Times
of Great Global Change
1929–1962*

Gwendoline P. Clarke

Published in 2009 by
BPS Books
Toronto, Canada
www.bpsbooks.com

A division of Bastian Publishing Services Ltd.
www.bastianpubserv.com

ISBN 978-1-926645-02-5

Cataloguing in Publication Data available from
Library and Archives Canada.

Design and typesetting: Greg Devitt, Greg Devitt Design

Printed by Lightning Source, Tennessee. Lightning Source paper, as used in this book, does not come from endangered old growth forests or forests of exceptional conservation value. It is acid free, lignin free, and meets all ANSI standards for archival-quality paper. The print-on-demand process used to produce this book protects the environment by printing only the number of copies that are purchased.

Photographs on pages i and ii: The author's foster son, Johnny, at the controls of the farm wagon; the author at her desk, composing a Ginger Farm column.

TABLE OF CONTENTS

INTRODUCTION

If you live in Southern Ontario, chances are you have driven on Highway 401 over the Highway 25 cloverleaf dozens, if not hundreds, of times. Even if you have visited or moved to the province from some other part of the country, you most likely have had to pass that way. Perhaps you have exited the 401 there, taking a break at various restaurants. While gazing out over your burger, you may have noticed the correctional facility on the other side of the road. This piece of land once supported a hundred-acre farm. It was like thousands of other farms, most of which have disappeared, their ways remembered only in children's storybooks. The life of this particular farm, however, *has* been extensively chronicled, from a more realistic perspective.

My maternal mother, Gwendoline P. Clarke, published a weekly record of life on this farm and of the surrounding community from 1929 to the early 1960s. She wrote her column for the *Acton Free Press*, a newspaper serving nearby farming communities, including Milton, the town closest to her farm.

Gwen and "Partner," her husband (my grandfather), valiantly worked their farm through forty years of good if hard times. Their one hundred acres became known to a wide and appreciative audience as Ginger Farm. It was so named, she wrote, because it takes "ginger" — and lots of it — to run a farm.

Once a week Grandma traveled — at first by horse and wagon and later in her unreliable Ford "Coach," characteristically dubbed "The Optimist" — from the countryside into Milton. There she dispatched her column to the *Free Press*. She wrote these columns in what time she could snatch from her many responsibilities as farm-woman or farm-wife (her terms) as well as mother, civic volunteer and officer of her beloved Scotch Block Women's Institute. She clearly enjoyed every bit of it, the writing perhaps most of all.

The passages in this book, which have been edited lightly for consistency and clarity, are only ten percent of those she wrote over those nearly three decades. Years that saw great changes in Canada, from the hardships of the Great Depression to the Second World War to the Cold War. In the midst of the anxieties of those times, Grandma shared her knack of finding joy in day-to-day life. A favourite saying of hers, and one she lived by, was, "The blue of heaven is greater than the cloud."

Grandma was fascinated with history. "Where is the person, past the colt age, who doesn't long to know something abut his ancestors — their home, their farm, their country and the conditions in which they lived?" she wrote. Not only that, she believed that preserving family and community history was everyone's responsibility. She encouraged her readers to play their part, and, if at all possible, to write their own chronicles. "Remember, what happens to-day is the history of to-morrow," she wrote, noting that "in time (your chronicles) would become a priceless personal possession."

As for my grandparents' own history, Grandma was born Gwendoline Fitz-Gerald in Sudbury, Suffolk, England. She married my grandfather, Lancelot Clarke, in 1918, when he was on leave in England during the First World War. He had been born in the same area of England, but had moved to Canada after clerking in London between the ages of fifteen and eighteen. He had worked as farmhand near Milton, Ontario, and as a cowboy and on a harvesting crew in the West, until 1914, when he joined the 28th Regiment of the Canadian Army for the fight in Europe.

The newly married couple left England for Canada in 1919 and took a half section of land (three hundred and twenty acres) at Chaplin, near Moose Jaw, Saskatchewan. They built a sod, or earthen, house and farmed there until 1923. Their children, Dorothy (my mother) and Uncle Bob, were born in 1920 and 1922, respectively. The foursome moved to Milton in 1923. One year later they bought what became Ginger Farm. In 1958 they sold the farm, by this time operated primarily by their son, Bob, to the government, which was putting Highway 401 through their area. They then moved to Cooksville, Ontario, where Grandma died, in 1966, and Grandpa, in 1975. I loved them dearly.

When I was a very young boy, my mom and dad would load us in the Chevy and we'd leave Toronto for a brief visit to paradise. I was able to enjoy the chickens, pigs, cows, cats and dogs of those storybook farms, but for real. However, eventually the farm was sold, Grandma got a stove she didn't have to heat with wood, the government built their highway and our own lives went through changes.

My father died in a car accident when I was eight. After that my grandfather filled a big hole in my life, and until my late teens we used to share lots of stories, the ones we couldn't tell my mom.

The neighbours and community of Ginger Farm loved my grandmother's columns for their insights and her joyful touch. The quality of those insights remains intact — perhaps they are even more relevant today in what we mistakenly believe is a more complex time. My hope is that this book will give you many enjoyable moments as it helps you reconnect with our country roots as citizens of the twenty-first century.

David Patchell-Evans

DEDICATION

We wish to dedicate this book to Gwendoline Clarke's daughter, Dorothy — our mother.

Mom has enjoyed an exciting life: the Great Depression, running a munitions factory during the Second World War, being an early version of a liberated woman and bringing up three less than angelic boys on her own. She later became matriarch to seven more kids and supportively touched the lives of dozens more. By her eighties the once freelance bookkeeper had become a director of a major company and an experienced globetrotter. Jeep excursions in Bali and ransacking castles in Japan predated cruises on the Caribbean.

Throughout the vicissitudes of her and our lives, Mom has always been grounded in wisdom, effort and caring. But as she would say, she didn't lick it off the stones. This book is about her own background, from whence came the foundations of her strength, where her joy in life was nurtured.

Dorothy tried for years to get us read her mother's writings, to have pride not only in our genetics but more importantly in our grandparents and their way of life. She also wanted us to share those writings with a larger audience.

When we finally found the time to read the crinkly newspaper clippings Mom saved for us, we were amazed at our witty and stylish grandma. And now, having answered one half of Dorothy's wish, we have now gotten around to the second half. We hope you enjoy *Chronicles of Ginger Farm* every bit as much as we have.

Jerry Patchell
Ed Patchell
David Patchell-Evans

Part I

WE'RE ALL RIGHT SO FAR

1929–1934

April 18, 1929

Partner and I decided aeons ago that should we ever own a farm we would call it 'Ginger Farm.' Why? Because whenever and wherever it was, it would surely take all the 'ginger' we possessed to run it.

After a few years wandering, we finally bought a farm in Old Ontario, and let me tell you right here and now, in case there are any who don't know it, that besides brain and brawn, it requires ginger of the highest quality and spiciest order to come anywhere near success, and the smaller the capital the more ginger required.

I must confess we have not yet summoned up sufficient courage to write the name 'Ginger Farm' on the gatepost. Situated as it is on a main road, it might attract too much attention. One hundred acres, more or less, is the extent of our property, which we have managed to farm with the occasional assistance of the most nondescript hired help imaginable. About them I might say more, only they deserve an article entirely to themselves.

Besides our horses, we have a dairy herd consisting of eight cows and two yearling heifers, Peggy and Betty. In theory, we are strong supporters of a fine herd of pure-bred Ayrshires, up-to-date stables and equipment, resulting in a fat monthly cheque of $100 or more. In reality, we have a herd of mongrel stock, good cows for what they are, but nothing to write home about.

They each have their characteristics. Janet, for instance, has always refused to walk the plank bridge over the creek. Instead, she wades through the water. In the summer twice, after heavy rain, the current being so strong she was in danger of getting washed away.

Another cow we christened 'Buffalo' on account of her malignant appearance, and she has since lived up to her name. No other bossy is allowed near the trough until her thirst is quenched; no other cow may enter the yard before her. I don't believe she is intentionally malicious or unladylike, but she apparently means to impress them with her dignity and they respect her accordingly.

Then we have 'Roberta,' the brood sow. Roberta roams at will. She is a lady of the greatest intelligence and has an unfailing instinct for finding out when the hook has been left undone on the kitchen-garden gate. One can almost imagine her grunt of satisfaction at the discovery.

Last summer en route for the garden she would raid the hen-house, disturb the broody hens, upset the feed-bin, chew bits out of the shell and grit hopper and scare all the laying hens but fortunately could not reach the eggs.

She would next visit the ditch close handy and there wallow

in the mud, afterwards proceeding towards the garden. Fortunately for the garden, as she reached her goal she was usually discovered, and persuaded — not necessarily in endearing terms — to return from whence she came.

We have a small flock of Barred Rocks. They are not the only inhabitants of the hen-house; however, by continually chasing the others (e.g., red mites) with a mixture of machine oil and kerosene, we do manage to keep the hens healthy and productive.

Then we have, of course, a dog and cats. 'Stump' was one of a litter of six collie pups. He was the dearest little round ball of brown fluff with a decidedly abbreviated tail — hence his name. Stump is by instinct a 'heeler' but he is so zealous that we have, perforce, to curtail his activities in that direction. To get even with us, or as an outlet for his energy, he has acquired the annoying habit of running to the road and barking at every car that passes.

To complete the list of animals, there still remain the cats. Besides two nameless felines at the barn, we have 'Jinnie,' who is a great-grandmother, and 'Lady Jane Grey,' both, as nine-year-old Daughter says, as 'keeping-inside cats.'

Such is our farm and its quadruped family. Between them they provide board for Partner and myself, two children, occasional hired help and an uncertain quantity of visitors.

We have to do a deal of stretching to make both ends meet. It is so at any time but recent years have made a wider breach. However, we don't sit down and brood over our troubles. We are up and doing most of the time. A sense of humour and an extra dose of 'ginger' are of great assistance.

It is also surprising how it helps to see the funny side of things. At times, of course, one is apt to overlook the humour of the situation. For instance, there was the occasion last fall when Partner was sitting on the beam at the top of the mow fixing the hay fork-track. "Look out!" he cried suddenly. I, of course, looked up, only to receive the butt end of the hammer right on my front teeth. Yes, indeed, it was quite fifteen minutes before I saw the funny side of that episode. But I felt it, oh yes, I felt it in my front teeth for at least two weeks afterwards.

APRIL 25, 1929

Friends, neighbours, countrywomen, lend me your ears: I come to enlist your sympathy, for here before you is the most sorely tried woman in the district. Why? Well, sure, isn't it wet, green wood I'm after burning, and not a cake, pie or even a cookie have I been able to bake for at least ten days. 'Tis lucky our house is made of brick, for dear knows to what lengths I might go in search of good dry wood. Half the wood is in the shed and half outside, but for dampness there is little to choose between them. So now if you detect a note of irritation between the ensuing lines you will know what it is all about, and if any of you have a pie or a cake going begging it would be an act of charity to send it along.

Life after all has its compensations — what we lose on the swings we make up on the roundabouts — and so, when I get tired of coaxing the fire, I take a look at my garden and there I find the perennials coming along splendidly and how I look forward to the time when all the new plants I set out last fall will, in the glory of their full bloom, repay me for my time and labour.

There was once a good garden here, but it has been left to run wild. Narcissi and daffodils spring up in the most unexpected places, and lily of the valley and snowdrops appear along the front fence. It is now my ambition that there shall be a good garden once again, so last fall I set to work and dug with a spade and the sweat of my brow a perennial border twenty feet by eight. Therein I set any plants I could beg, borrow or steal, as well as the waifs and strays scattered around the house.

The children and I also brought trilliums home from the bush and used as a border, but since they have bloomed we find the 'trilliums' are really hepaticas.

I also dug two strips for flowering shrubs, and so far I have collected mauve lilac, white and pink honeysuckle, wild rose, bridal wreath, forsythia, snowball and a lovely big bush of spirea. I suppose for the two latter I should say Hydrangea Arborescens Grandiflora and Van Houttei Spirea, but you'll notice I'm not strong on technical terms as I feel more sure of my ground when I stick to the common or garden names.

There were two lilac trees and I built a rustic arch at the corner of the house. Now I am wondering what I can plant to grow quickly to make a good show. Can't some of you experienced gardeners give me a few suggestions and thereby help a novice over this difficulty? I still have beds to dig for annuals, so you see whatever the outcome I have the best intentions of being a very busy woman.

In the meantime, there are broody hens to fuss with and, in due time, I hopefully presume there will be chickens. Thank goodness the setting hens have consented to set. For small hatches I must say I prefer to have the chickens with their natural mother in the good old-fashioned way. We once bought a hundred baby chicks and raised them with a brooder but never again for this child. They were so abominably tame they were continually under my feet and it would take me about ten minutes to cross the yard as I couldn't put my foot down without nearly killing a few at every step — the 'light fantastic toe' not being one of my outstanding qualities.

Speaking of hens brings me back to the time when we first started farming ten long years ago. I was tremendously enthusiastic but had not the least idea of my duties as a farmer's wife and in this case ignorance was far from bliss — neither did enthusiasm make up for lack of knowledge.

Of course we had some hens, and Partner set out to instruct me in the art of setting broody hens. All went well until I was left to take them off the nests by myself and so fearful was I of getting pecked — very thoroughly! However, I was never one to let anything beat me so I overcame the difficulty by wearing leather gloves. Now of course I am quite an old hand at the game and since pecking hens hold no terrors for me, I go unmolested.

We are debating the advisability of hiring help for the season. Last year we did without and as the overalls I bought are still perfectly good it seems a pity not to repeat the experiment so I can wear them out. I confessed to ignorance of the farm life when we started, but now I can build a load of hay or sheaves and do it right.

Last year I even built a hay stack, but oh ye gods, I got such a high peak on it to finish, I was afraid to come down. Partner had the rack with half a load of hay on it beside the stack. On it he stood the ladder, but as I sat on the peak of the stack my feet wouldn't reach the top rung. I had a bad five minutes and how I ever slid down until my feet reached the ladder I don't know, but reach it I did, and here I am, still alive to tell the tale.

I don't pretend to work as hard or have the strength of a man, but I do love to help in the field during haying and harvest and I see nothing derogatory in a woman working outside if she can do so without neglecting her family. This, I know, is a matter upon which there is a great divergence of opinion, but every one to his own mind.

The nearer we are to nature the closer we are to God, and where else can we come closer to nature than on our own farm? Within doors one sometimes gets a perverted perspective — a cramped vision as it were, but outside one cannot help but realize, in spite of the vagaries of weather and crops, that:

God's in his heaven
All's right with the world.

MAY 2, 1929

Had anyone asked me a month ago if I could run the farm single-handed, I should have answered most emphatically "No!" Yet that is exactly what I was doing last week. Partner had the misfortune to hurt his foot, and as the wound had to be kept open by poulticing it was impossible for him to get around at all, so it was me for the overalls. I suppose some women think nothing of taking charge during their husband's temporary absence, but — must I confess it? — I'm really not much of a hand when it comes to milking and barn chores and I never turned the separator in my life, so you will understand it was somewhat of an ordeal for me and we certainly had plenty of adventures to relieve the monotony.

Partner had arranged to ship pigs on the Tuesday, so I had to call one of the neighbours in to my assistance. There had been a heavy rain the night before, so we had to hitch up the team and pull the truck around the yard to where it was supposed to go.

The next day, Roberta, the brood sow, excelled herself. I went to visit her in the morning with her daily ration of milk, and she very obligingly met me at the pig-pen door! Upon inspection I found she had torn the front of her pen clean out — not a board remained — so I barricaded the doors and again called in the assistance of our good neighbour.

I got along surprisingly well with the milking and separating until Wednesday — Daughter helped by milking her own heifer, Peggy. Wednesday night I started to separate quite gaily as usual, and I turned and turned but not a drop of cream did I get! "Well," I thought, "there must be something wrong with the speed — I'll try again." I did and after that I tried again but the result was still the same, so I gave it up.

I came to the house a rather crestfallen woman as I did not like to admit defeat. Partner asked me did I do this and did I do that, and then he said, "I suppose you tightened the ring on the bowl?" That, of course, was exactly what I had not done so they certainly had a good joke on me. Partner says he thinks he will write an article himself entitled "When Mother Does the Chores"! I'll see that he doesn't, though; it might be too illuminating!

Oh, all's well that ends well. Partner is able to get out again so my barnyard activities are a little more limited. Now I am going to give my attention to the house and garden once more.

Yesterday we got five hundred spruce and cedar trees from the Government, and if I know anything it is going to take quite a little while to put them in.

Who would be without conifers and trees when for less than a dollar express it is possible to get such a splendid quantity? What a much more interesting appearance they give to any home. To my thinking, a house minus trees is like a picture without a frame, but yet one can have too many.

Just as a frame can mar or accentuate a good picture, so trees, shrubs and evergreens can produce the same effect upon a house. I passed a house the other day with a beautiful, unbroken sweep of lawn in front of it and spruce trees on either side, but alas the new owners were busy making a bed for shrubs about twelve by four, right in the very centre of this beautiful lawn, completely spoiling its perfect symmetry.

Our wood at last consents to burn, so I feel a little more amiable on that score than last week. Of course it sizzles and smokes occasionally, but between times I manage to get enough cooking done to ward off starvation for the family.

My big worry now is whether we shall get chickens or not. I am realizing the wisdom of the proverb 'don't count your chickens before they are hatched.' Yesterday I sent Daughter to let the 'broodies' off. I thought she was gone a long time and upon inquiring the reason, learnt, to my horror, that she had been busily shaking the eggs to see if any of them were addled!

For a few seconds I felt like shaking her, but realized in time that it was not mischief but misplaced interest that prompted her. I feel quite sure she will not do it again. Next week I will tell you the result of my hatch, and then you will know just how much an unborn chicken can stand rough handling.

MAY 30, 1929

Partner and I have been reviewing the situation — no, that is not the right expression — contemplating the future would be more correct, and we foresee the need for rigid economy, but the problem is *how* to economise. I am tempted to wish we had been guilty of some extravagance, then it would be easy to know where to begin, but the situation just at present is like a piece of elastic that has lost its stretch — it just won't go any farther!

We can't save on gas for we have not a car, or on shows and dances for they have never appealed to us and a permit we have never desired. It does not worry me if I am not up-to-the-minute in the latest fashion fads, and I have not heard Partner say he is actually hankering after one of the new Whoop-ee hats.

Really, there seem very few avenues open to us. To work we must have food — incidentally to have food we must work, and decency demands that we be adequately clothed, that is, adequately according to present standards. Of course I think it might be possible to save on tobacco; Partner retaliates by suggesting postage stamps, but as I tell him, every stamp bought increases the revenue, increased revenue is good for the country and what is good for the country on the whole is good for each one of us individually. Perfectly logical isn't it — at any rate sufficiently so to justify my supply of stamps when slightly more than normal?

There is just one thing we feel perfectly sure we shall be able to save on and that is binder twine. At that I leave it. No doubt other ways and means will come to light and we will deal with them as they come along.

Our feathered family has increased by thirty-seven — that is from our four hens. Not so many as I had hoped for, but one broody hen claimed the privilege of her sex and changed her mind. It was most unfortunate for the chicks to be, who required another week to bring them to a state of hatchability.

Was there ever such a gamble as raising chickens? I am beginning to wonder why there isn't a law in force to stop it. One of my friends bought 115 baby chicks, lost about 20 and was so pleased with the progress of the others that she bought another 100 but from a different place. To-day she has about 20 left from the second 100.

A near neighbour paid $40 for 200; she has 15 left. Another neighbour set her own incubator and had a hatch of

122 chicks from 160 eggs. At a week old they started to die, and now there isn't one left.

Even supposing one is lucky in raising them, there are always the crows and hawks to consider, to say nothing of rats, skunks and weasels. Yet each year we go on raising chickens — or trying to raise them. It must be that each of us is possessed of an innate gambling spirit.

The cattle have been quite a study this week. The young stock were turning out to grass, and the milch cows when they came out to drink would rend the air in protest at being left behind. To-day they, too, were turned out to grass and when I went to get them before supper the mothers and grandmothers were as frisky as their daughters and grandchildren. Janet is being fattened for the butcher and from an avoirdupois standpoint one would have thought her life to be a burden to her, yet there she was with her heels in the air like the youngest calf in the herd.

In the stable they are the essence of contentment; one can hardly imagine them to be anything but placid, yet we who have to deal with them know from experience they can be anything but! My right knee is still black and blue as a result of milking last Sunday. Peggy suddenly decided to move up in her stall, but the pail was in her road so she put her foot in it, took it out again and then rested it on my knee. Possibly she was still 'placid,' but believe me, I wasn't!

No, I can't say I think of milking as one of the pleasures of farm life. Some people seem to like it, but I can't see much fun in having ones neck brushed with the end of a cow's tail or slapped across the mouth as one is rising from the stool.

Possibly they (the cows) mean well; it may be just a friendly way of imparting a final salutation.

Well they are out to grass — contented, pro tem, but it won't be long before they start poking their heads through rail fences, catching their horns in wire fences, and stretching all the wires in their endeavour to get loose again, and then the fun begins.

How we enjoy it, when, on returning from church we find either our own herd or the neighbour's making the most of their time in the crop. 'Tis well if we are fortified with words of wisdom from the minister. And how pleased we are, when after inviting friends to tea, we have to stop in the middle of our visit and chase the marauding creatures. 'Pigs is pigs' I agree, but might we not add 'and cows is cows'?

However, I suppose all these trials are sent for our good. If we did not have something to disturb our equilibrium, with so much beauty around us we might all turn artists and poets. Artists and poets have their place in the scheme of things, but a redundancy of them would, you'll agree, be rather drastic. Of course, after all, I am rather anticipating trouble: perhaps this year our cows, likewise the neighbours', will keep within bounds — perhaps — yes perhaps!

AUGUST 1, 1929

Last Saturday all farming operations took a back seat; getting alsike in before the next rain was of no importance, and the problematic outcome of the alfalfa seed crop was a mere detail. The children were on the tip-toe of expectancy. Why? It was the annual Sunday School picnic and the first time they had been allowed to go. Such excited voices, such eager faces, and about every ten minutes they were inquiring if it were not yet time to start. Time hung heavy for them, but it went quick enough for me.

Finally we were ready: lunches, bathing suits and towels were packed, and money boxes rifled for spending money 'of their very own.' After a short train journey we arrived at the public park which was so admirably adapted for the needs of the children. There were about a dozen swings, three slides, seesaws, shallow water for paddling, deep water for swimming and oh boy, a merry-go-round where one could get a splendid long ride for five cents.

There was absolutely nothing in the way of amusements for grown-ups, yet as I looked around from time to time I could not find one bored-looking face among the motley collection of mothers and fathers, big sisters and brothers. The spontaneous gaiety of the children seemed infectious, and from beginning to end there was very little to be heard of petulant voices; each child took his or her turn at every amusement, and little friends and little strangers played happily together as one big family.

The end of the day found them all tired with the natural physical tiredness of a normal child, but their nervous systems had not been over-taxed; a good night's rest was all they needed to prepare them again for every-day conditions.

It seemed impossible to me not to make comparisons. Imagine those same children and parents taken to a show by way of a treat. They would enjoy it at the time no doubt, but childish nerves would be over-wrought, little limbs by enforced idleness be deprived of natural activity, and instead of taking home a happily tired crowd of children we should have perverse, cantankerous, unreasonable boys and girls of every age.

There would be repeated cries of 'Mummy, I want this' and 'Daddy, buy me that,' and sounds of scoldings and slappings and tired parents, themselves with nerves on edge, impatiently wondering how on earth they were to deal with a bunch of children apparently hard to please.

As we were preparing to leave the picnic grounds on Saturday, a neighbour very kindly offered us a ride home in their car instead of going by train, so we very willingly climbed into their good-natured Ford which almost seemed to expand, as Fords will to accommodate an ever increasing number of people and parcels.

The ride home, in the cool of the evening, was surely an end to a perfect day. The scenic beauty for description needs the pen of a poet or the brush of an artist to do it justice. Small wonder, I thought, as we passed along, that the greatest poets of every age have found in Nature a theme for their very best work. Shelley discovered a poem in a cloud, Tennyson in the wash of the waves, Pope saw happiness for the man 'whose wish and care a few paternal acres bound.' But Wordsworth explains to our dormant sensibilities why we do not better appreciate the beauty that is ours.

The world is too much with us; late and soon,
Getting and spending, we lay waste our powers
Little we see in Nature that is ours

How often one hears farm people say that the country is very beautiful and all that, but they have not the time to appreciate it.

Why, oh why, will they persist in thinking such a thing? It is not time we need; it is vision! How much time does it take a man to lift his eyes from the ploughing and see for a few seconds the subtle movement of the leaves varying with every shade of green in the early spring? When his wife pegs her washing out on the line, does it interfere with her work to any great extent to notice the rhythmic sway of the ripening grain in the breeze? There are all kinds of things that we may see if we will as we shake our duster from the bedroom window.

All these little beauty pictures we can imprint upon our memory as accurately as upon the film of a camera. We can carry them around with us and some time when we are employed in a more or less mundane task we can take our pictures out and look at them, as it were. To look at them cannot possibly interfere with our work; in fact it may speed things up, for if we can keep our minds off the monotony of an irksome job it is liable to get done that much quicker.

I have such a wonderful collection of pictures, but it takes longer to write about them than to look at them, and as these are busy days they must be left until I have more leisure. I am trying to get in a little sewing before we start drawing in the wheat. Yesterday I made a washing suit for Son and to-day a dress for Daughter.

Last night we had a storm and how glad we were to hear the rain. The flowers have made very little progress just lately and the pea-pods were drying up instead of filling out but we hope for great things now and the paper says showers again for to-day. The wheat is practically ready to cut. Some farmers have theirs cut and stooked, but ours is in a somewhat exposed position and so, I suppose, takes longer to ripen. However, in due course of time, ours, too, will be cut, stooked, and we hope stacked in the mow in good condition to wait the thresher.

August 29, 1929

It is quite a change to pick up a pen instead of a pitch-fork and certainly a little easier on the hands. By which remark you will understand I have recently been working in the mow. True, and for the benefit of those who wonder how a farm-woman puts in her time, I will give you an outline of yesterday's work.

It was about 5:30 a.m. when Partner and I realized that here was dawning another blue day. In a very little while we were indulging in the cup that cheers; that is to say *tea* in case any should misunderstand my meaning, and then I went off to the bush for the cows.

While Partner was milking — stripping would be nearer the mark — I was away to the house — gave the floors, etc., the once-over, made the porridge and got the breakfast, fussed with the chickens a bit and took them their supply of water and sour milk. Breakfast over, I attacked the separator and pails, washed, scrubbed and scalded them and put them out to air with a heart-felt sigh of relief. Ask any farm-woman to tell you her greatest cross in life and the chances are she will say the separator.

Next came the breakfast dishes and then a hurried round of the bedrooms. Downstairs again and out to the garden. Dug potatoes, picked beans and pulled carrots, inspected citron and corn, and picked a few ripe tomatoes. Back to the house, prepared the beans and carrots but left Daughter to scrape potatoes. Made a chocolate pudding, slipped down for the mail and just had time to look at the weather forecast and the 'Funnies,' when in came Partner and his brother with the first load of oats.

Away I went to the barn quite ready and anxious to help stow the sheaves away, safe from wind and weather. Partner was using the slings and in about ten minutes the rack was empty and all the sheaves dumped into the mow.

Sounds quite nice and easy, doesn't it, but if you could see the tangled mass of sheaves jammed in so tight and then realize how it takes all one's strength to pull them out from one another, you would understand it was no light job I had undertaken. But still, I was working alone and could take my time, and if I wanted to stop and get my breath I could, so I didn't feel I had any cause to feel sorry for myself.

Anyway I set to work with a will, and by pulling and struggling, lifting and falling I managed to get the mow looking fairly presentable. And let me tell you, I didn't throw the sheaves around just anyhow; each sheaf was put exactly where it was meant to go.

When I was about three parts done I suddenly remembered my vegetables, so I clambered down from the mow with my feet full of thistles and my throat full of dust and went off to see to my house-keeping duties. I got the dinner ready, left my vegetables cooking on the oil-stove and then went back to the barn, but when I picked up the pitch-fork it was all I could do to hold it, the palms of my hands being full of blisters. Of course I should have worn gloves, but I don't like gloves and never did. I always think my hands will get used to it, but I suppose the dish-pan and wash-tub keep them from getting hard.

Just as I was placing the last sheaf, in came the men with the next load and by the time it was off it was dinner-time. Partner told me not to come out after dinner, that he would straighten the last load, but I wanted to see the oats in and I thought the more I did the quicker he would get done, so I went.

The afternoon was just a repetition of the morning and at five o'clock the field was cleared. There were just five loads, and last year there were ten, but this year the sheaves are all heads and last year all straw, which means to say we shall have as much grain, if not more, and half the work.

After we were through, I went off to hunt the eggs and pick some apples. A wash and change of clothes seemed to be next in order and then supper to get. I looked around and wondered what I would like to eat and wished there was someone here to get it for me but there wasn't, so I got busy and put up a respectable meal for the men, but by the time it was on the table my own appetite had vanished.

After supper, the children being away, I got the cows, fetched them home and then walked after the horses. Raided the barn and hen-house, found four clucking hens and shut them up in coops with advice and admonitions as to their future conduct.

By this time the children were home, and as I supervised their bedtime preparations I heard most graphic accounts of the fun they had had at Jean's birthday party. The children being settled down, I thought I might take a little time to do some writing as thoughts were running through my head which I was just longing to get onto paper.

Pulling a comfortable chair up to the table, I soon was busy with paper and pen and was just nicely into my theme when Partner came in from the barn, so I jumped up and washed the milk pails and then noticed my good man had put one knee through his trousers. He changed them and I proceeded to stitch away at a really gorgeous patch which, being of a different hue from the original garment, proclaimed its presence somewhat forcibly but was quite suitable for working in around the binder.

That done, I got a few more ideas down on paper, but by that time it was half-past nine and Partner was beginning to throw out tentative remarks about it being near bedtime and there being plenty of work ahead of us next day, so at ten minutes past ten, while Partner locked doors and put out lights, I regretfully put away my barely started article, set the mouse-trap, put out the pup 'and so to bed.'

NOVEMBER 28, 1929

Our chronicle this week is in memory of Judy O'Grady! Yes she is dead, defunct — deader than last year's jokes, and, what is more, she was guilty of *felo de se*. In a fit of pique, jealousy or what-not, she committed the awful act and none witnessed her going or guessed her intentions.

The circumstances which culminated in her tragic end were these: she had a rival. Some other person entered her literary field and took unto herself the pen-name of Judy O'Grady and has twice appeared in print expressing sentiments entirely different from those of the original Judy.

Now Judy, that is Judy of Ginger Farm, had been in undisputed possession of this particular name for several years and it came as somewhat of a shock that another should also desire to be known by this same name. Judy the 1st felt that nothing could be done about it. At any rate, being of a peace-loving disposition, she considered discretion, in this case, to be the better part of valour and took this opportunity of fading away lest the day might dawn which should see her usefulness outlived.

Let none mourn her passing — gladly she lived and gamely she died and the Chronicles of Ginger Farm still go on, continued by she who was to Judy as a twin soul: namely, Gwendoline P. Clarke.

In case any reader takes the fore-going remarks as serious, let me hasten to add that the above twin souls were incorporated in one body and G.P.C. for personal reasons preferred to be known by the fictitious name of Judy O'Grady. However, since two contemporary writers by the same name would only lead to confusion, Judy the 1st prefers to sink into oblivion. After all, 'what's in a name? A rose by any other name would smell as sweet,' and so I don't expect our troubles to be any less or our joys any greater because of this slight change in nominal authorship.

What I do regret is that Clarke doesn't sound nearly so Irish, and I love all things which hail from the Isle of the Shamrock. Sure, isn't it meself that was born of Irish parents, at least one of them was? And the only thing I regretted leaving behind me when I married was me good old Irish name: Fitz-Gerald.

Memory goes back years and years and I recall visiting my grandfather, a fine old man of ninety-four. He would take me into the room where he hung a reproduction of the picture which was meant to illustrate the family legend. According to my grandfather's story, centuries and centuries ago, a certain Earl of Leinster, who was head of the Fitz-Gerald family or clan, had as a pet an ape.

Soon after acquiring this pet, the earl married and his wife developed an intense hatred of the ape but she could not persuade her husband to get rid of it. In due course of time a son arrived and while he was yet a baby a terrible fire broke out in the old family castle. The baby was trapped in the burning building beyond all hope of rescue and the mother and father were almost frantic with grief, when to the joy and amazement of everyone the ape suddenly appeared, from where no one seemed to know, and slid down the drain pipe with the baby in his other arm which he had so bravely rescued.

That is the legend as I remember it but I was a very little girl when I last heard it so it may not be correct in detail.*

---

* The story refers to John Fitz-Thomas Fitz-Gerald, fifth Lord of Offaly and first Lord of Kildare, who died in 1316. Since his day, the family crest has featured an ape.

Very interesting, did you say, but nothing to do with Ginger Farm? Indeed but it has for it was just that about which I was thinking as I darned the family socks this afternoon, and those same socks, let me tell you, had every appearance of belonging most surely to the inmates of Ginger Farm. So much so that to avoid the discouragement which accompanies an almost hopeless task I let my mind wander a-down the avenues of pleasant thought. However, I was not allowed to enjoy my reminiscences undisturbed very long for, like the ogre at a feast, along came the tax-collector and left his bill.

Why, oh, why must taxes coincide with Christmas? And why, oh why, must they go up ten dollars every year? Last year I remember the tax man came just as the threshing machine moved out and this year he came on the very day we had shipped some fat stock. It just seemed as though he timed his arrival so we should not forget our financial obligations or take any satisfaction in our grain bins or the cheque from the stock yards.

From now until the 14th of December, if you see a group of farmers standing at the street corner you can be pretty sure that the one topic under discussion is taxes. They splutter and grumble and make an awful fuss, and then when the time comes they each one hand over their hard-earned money like a lamb.

Well I suppose these things have to be and quite possibly in a good year one would hear very little about taxes, but in lean years they certainly do seem to take the gilt off the gingerbread. Be that as it may, since there is no way out of it we might as well smile and look pleasant and think of taxes as a necessary evil.

Ugh, have we got winter at last? I hear a miniature blizzard raging outside and the wind is sweeping under the door at about sixty miles an hour. I keep piling wood on the fire, but the room still feels like a most efficient ice-house. Methinks a nice little city apartment wouldn't feel too bad on a night like this. There are times, once in a while, when farm life seems to lose its charm — it takes a lot to fire one's enthusiasm when the blood in one's veins is congealed.

FEBRUARY 26, 1931

"Bobby, you look at your hands. Why don't you go and wash them?"

"Oh, go on. You know Daddy told us not to waste the water!"

The above was a short conversation I overheard between Son and Daughter, and I am perfectly sure Son was filled with unholy joy when he thought he had a legitimate excuse for refraining from very necessary ablutions. Much to his sorrow, Mother came on the scene and decided that the water would hardly be wasted if it were used on the hands, which were reluctantly held out for her inspection.

The fact is, we have at last come to the stage when the well threatens to give out. Partner has never pumped it dry yet, because he always stops directly it starts to kick, but it is an awful feeling to know there actually is a bottom to the well. Never in the history of the farm has it been known to go dry, so we really were in hopes it was endowed with the same capacity as the widow's cruse of oil.

Fore warned is fore armed, so Partner has been drawing water from our own creek all the week, and was very thankful to find there was water to draw. Just at present I can't imagine any worse calamity than to be short of water — that is, really short, so that one has to think twice about drinking a glass of water.

If we stop to consider, it does seem as though we take all the bounties of nature very casually and only wake up to their real worth when we are afraid of losing them. And yet there are times when we do not welcome the gentle dew from heaven, even though it falls alike upon the just and unjust.

For instance, this afternoon I drove to town in the cutter. It had been thawing, the ruts in the roads were filled with water, and I endeavoured to give every car as wide a berth as possible. But there came a time where the road was narrow and I could not pull out without getting into a snow bank. Along came a truck and went swish, swishing through the water.

Prince, as it happens, has no love for trucks, so I had my hands tight on the lines, and my eyes on Prince, but after the truck had gone by I could not see Prince at all. Of course, he was still there, but my glasses were smothered with mud and water, and when I took them off I found the cutter, robe and my own coat literally plastered with mud.

Everyone knows what wet mud is like — it can't be brushed off, so you can imagine I looked a sorry looking object to be going into town. As it happened, besides doing some shopping I intended to make a call. The call did not get made! But that's what comes of living the simple life. There are times when I am driven to exclaim, "Oh for a car, a car, a car!" And yet I have an idea there are occasions when the fellow with the car has been known to sigh, "Oh for a horse, a horse, a horse!"

I wonder how many appreciated the two wonderful days of sunshine we had this week. I simply gloried in the brightness and warmth of Old King Sol, and went about my work treading on air. I think I did more work in those two days than in the two weeks previous.

One day the telephone rang and I was so surprised to hear my friend say, "Well, how do you like this cold day?" I was really taken aback — I suppose I did know it was cold, but somehow it did not seem to matter because it was so bright. Sunshine to me is better than a tonic, and I love to get as much of it in the house as I can. I hope I never possess carpets, curtains and walls so precious that I shall be afraid to let the light in on them. I have no use for shutters and blinds except in extremely hot weather, and I count it among my many blessings that we have nothing on Ginger Farm that is good enough to spoil!

When I was in England a friend and I shared an attic room — for preference, because it was large and airy. The house was of Gothic architecture, so the front window in our bedroom was high up and narrow, but at the side was a good-sized square window, which looked out on to a small flat roof, over the bathroom.

We used to pull our mattresses through the window and make our beds up on the roof. It was lovely to go to sleep by starlight, and then to wake up and see the sun rising over the meadows.

It was also quite an adventure, because we had to get up early in the morning and have our beds inside like respectable people before the maid came up in the morning with our early tea and hot water. We thought it would not do for a school ma'am and the matron to be caught in such undignified sleeping quarters, and so we sacrificed good sense to convention. But oh, it was the grandest bedroom I ever had until one night a bat flopped into my face, and I never slept on the roof any more.

I composed poetry, or rather what I hoped was poetry, out on the roof, but even my love of beautiful scenery and fresh air and sunshine was not proof against a bat.

Thus do we descend from the sublime to the ridiculous.

April 23, 1931

We have been just glorying in work these last few days. Perhaps you think that a slight exaggeration, but it is not. This business of living is far more satisfactory when one has definite work to do. Partner has been busy on the land, and he, I and the children have all accomplished about three times as much work this week as we did in any one week all winter.

Monday Partner broke the news to me very gently that I was expected to do some of the morning chores. "Water the cows about nine-thirty," says Partner. "Leave them out for about an hour, then put them in and feed them. After that you can let the heifers out. There isn't much to do, so it won't take up much of your time."

It sounds quite simple, of course, and it does not take Partner long when he is on the job, but when one's education as chore boy begins late in life, then troubles loom on an erstwhile cloudless horizon.

Partner explains to me that this cow has one measure of chop, that one two, the Ayrshire heifers half a dish a-piece and Tiny just enough to keep her quiet. Off I start with the chop and I am all right until I start to think, then I wonder if I have given two measures to the cows whose ration is one and whether it is Bessie or Tiny that is supposed to have enough to keep her quiet.

Meanwhile the cows have come back to the barnyard and moo pathetically at the stable doors. Six of them have quarters in the front stable and four in the back. Thus am I in a quandary — or perhaps as it is cows I am dealing with, on the horns of a dilemma would be a more apt expression. If I open the front stable, those from the back also try to crowd in; open the back and it is the other way round, although they never try these stunts when Partner does the chores.

However, necessity is the mother of invention, so now I stand at the stable door, valiantly waving the stable broom at all marauding trespassers. Once in a while I make a slight mistake, of course, and chase away cows that have perfect right of entry, and sometimes I let in others who should not be there.

Stella is my worst trouble. She is a very nervous little heifer, and starts to do a cakewalk every time I go to let her out. The other day she was unusually obstreperous, lowering her head and trying to bunt me as I fumbled with her chain. She has a pair of the most unhealthy-looking horns with which one would hardly want to come in contact more than once.

Yesterday I was not quite quick enough — as I undid the chain she sharply raised her lowered head and caught my arm with one of her horns, the impact causing me to subside unexpectedly, ungracefully and without ceremony into the manger where I was quite content to stay for a while, nursing my powerless arm and wondering whether it was sprained, broken or lacerated. However, upon investigation, I found it was only bruised and not very badly at that. Then I remembered I was in a terrible rush, because it was my duty to catch the noon bus down to Hamilton.

Some time ago, at a misguided moment, I consented to go as delegate for the Daughters of the Empire to our annual Provincial Meeting, thinking it would work in just nicely before seeding, but with this early spring I was somewhat out in my reckoning. It would have been just as much work and not half so much pleasure to hunt up someone else to take my place, so there was nothing else for it but to put my best foot forward, and go.

On Wednesday I attended the afternoon session, and on Thursday the afternoon and evening sessions. It was an awful scramble to get away, but the pleasure and enlightenment which was the inevitable result of attending these meetings was well worth the time and effort spent upon them.

Bishop Owen, from the Niagara Diocese, gave a most inspiring address on the qualities necessary to successful leadership, and on Thursday night, Miss Charlotte Whitton gave us one of the finest addresses I ever heard from a woman in my life. Her subject was supposed to be 'Immigration,' but she covered far more ground than the title would lead one to expect. Everything she said was so clear and to the point and obviously so well thought out.

Certainly one does reap some benefit through going out and after all participation in public affairs is surely a social obligation. There is nothing that can broaden our outlook to the same extent, but it requires time and interest. How much time can be given depends upon individual circumstances, but circumstances need not control our interest.

Life is so crowded these days that we may unconsciously set up a scale of values relegating our work and other activities in relation to our personality. What one may deem of importance, another may consider of little moment. It may be difficult to find time for outside affairs, but we never shall find time if the will is lacking. Great men have been born and raised on farms, but they did not attain greatness by confining their interest and energy to purely agricultural interests.

Attention to crops, cattle, pigs and chickens is necessary to our existence; interest in the world at large is vital to our mentality. We consider that the ultimate outcome of the League of Nations, the legislation of our country, provincial and municipal politics have as great an influence in the Chronicles of Ginger Farm as do the cream, chicken and egg returns.

JUNE 25, 1931

Last Monday Partner and I went to Toronto. It was meant to be a purely business trip, but we got a lot of pleasure mixed up with it. We went by bus, and were only away a few hours, but we saw some lovely little bits of scenery and some very beautiful gardens. But the loveliest thing we saw was a living picture of Darby and Joan.

Somewhere along the road at the entrance to a farm, a couple stood waiting for the bus. They both looked around seventy; the man appeared well and strong, but the old lady was almost bent double like a person subject to chronic rheumatism. Yet it was she who boarded the bus; Darby was just there to see her off. And how tenderly and carefully he did it. In his hand he carried a box which he placed by the bus to lessen the height of the step for wife Joan to mount. Such a dear old lady. She got off right in the heart of the city and said as she stepped off, "I'll just wait here until my young man comes."

I hated to see her left alone and wondered whether she would be all right and if someone would soon come along to take care of her. But I need not have wondered. On our return trip there was our old lady at the street corner waiting to go back to her Darby. Away we sped along the road, presently we came to her home and there was Darby, box in hand and a smile of welcome on his rugged old face, waiting gladly and patiently to do this little service for his Joan. Slowly and painfully, with her husband's help the old lady got off the bus and step by step they crossed the road together.

One could imagine them in just that way, travelling step by step along Life's Road, sharing one another's burdens — the weaker helping the stronger. It brought to my mind this very beautiful piece of poetry:

> *More lovely grows the earth as we grow old*
> *More tenderness is in the dawning's spring,*
> *More bronze upon the blackbird's burnished wing,*
> *And richer is the autumn cloth of gold;*
> *A deeper meaning too the years unfold*
> *Until to waiting hearts each living thing*
> *For very love its bounty seems to bring*
> *Entreating us with beauty to behold.*
> *Or is it that with years we grow more wise*
> *And reverent to the mystic profound*
> *Withheld from careless or indifferent eyes —*
> *That broods in simple things the world around*
> *More conscious of the love that glorifies*
> *The common ways and makes them holy ground.*
> — Helena Coleman

Sometimes it takes us a long time to be "more conscious of the love that glorifies the common ways and makes them holy ground."

Of course we saw other things not so beautiful as this little picture of Darby and Joan. I wanted a typewriter ribbon, but the saleslady in the store with her reddened lips, penciled eyebrows and enormous ear-rings got me so excited I hardly knew what I was at. I answered her questions at random, "Yes, yes plain blue — oh — er — no. Five Standard." Now why do you do it, I wondered. You have nice regular features, pretty hair — ought to be quite attractive to any nice boy.

"Two spools — oh no, I'm sorry, just one please." But now whatever kind of boy would you possibly attract? The make-up would be all right on the stage but at close quarters it's — why — it's just appalling. Finally I began to feel sorry for the girl. It must be, I thought, that she lives in rooms, and probably all she has for a looking glass is one of those green-hued mirrors specially designed to make one appear a female Caliban. Of course this girl was not the only one; we found her species in every store.

Fortunately we had not very much shopping to do, and do you know the more we see of the cities the better we like our home town. At home you soon get to know where you can get the best service, the best quality and the cheapest price. In the city you make a purchase from one store, walk down the street and possibly see the same thing in another store fifty cents cheaper.

As for the fifteen-cent stores, they are a snare and a delusion! Granted, things are very cheap — naturally — but just take them up and look them over. Made in Germany, made in Austria, made in Japan, and you can't get away from it in any of the cheaper stores. And then as to saving money, I question how much we economise. You know how it is, neighbours —

you walk through the stores and you see this thing and that and you are quite convinced you cannot live another hour without them. Then something also catches your eye and before you know where you are at, a five-dollar bill has gone west — that is presuming you have one to start with!

There may not be as great a variety in your home town, and because of the small demand there are possibly some things impossible to get, but generally speaking you know what you want before you set out, you are reasonably sure whether you can get it or not, and since you know you may be down town to-morrow or the next day you don't go out and buy stuff on the 'now or never' principle.

It is hard these days to be patriotic when it comes to shopping; we have more or less reached the stage when it is each man for himself, but still if we reason things out we shall find we are just as far ahead, and perhaps a little farther, by giving our home town a boost. If we have to economise — and who doesn't — that is among ordinary every-day people — we might as well begin at home and make a virtue out of necessity.

July 16, 1931

This last week at Ginger Farm will hardly go down in family history as the most fortunate ever experienced. Eventful, yes, but not fortunate.

It started on Sunday. The morning and afternoon passed as

usual, but after supper things began to happen. While Partner was milking, I went up to the bush — to the far end — to bring home Daisy and her new born calf. The calf was strong and frisky, Daisy anxious and obstreperous. For every yard she went forward, round she went three times in a circle.

If Partner had been on the job, he would have picked up the calf in his arms and Daisy would have followed. Not having the strength for this, the best thing I could do was forcibly propel the calf from the rear. Progress was terribly slow, and I was terribly heated. Overhead the sky was black and threatening, and it was no surprise when the first ominous roll of thunder struck my ears.

I began to get worried; Daisy didn't — not one jot did she care about rain, wind or thunder and lightning. All she cared about was getting her calf home as slowly as possible, and all the calf cared about was getting a meal on the way.

After much tribulation I did at last get cow and calf into the lane and was rejoiced to see Partner coming to my rescue. Progress after that was quick enough, which was fortunate as we had just got into the house and settled down when the storm broke. Down came the rain, down, down, down — howl and flash after flash lit up the room. It was past the children's bedtime but we would not send them to bed during the storm so we all sat in the dining-room talking and wondering whether the crops and the garden would stand up against the heavy rain.

And then — crash, crash, crash! Oh the horror of that ear-splitting sound that tells you something has been struck. At the same instant I saw the sun-room filled with red sparks.

Petrified, for a split second I stood watching and waiting for the explosion I thought was bound to follow. Both children stood crying helplessly — what I was ready to do I don't know, but Partner brought me to my senses with a few words, "Take care, the kiddies are here!" It was enough.

After that we sat down together and talked of all kinds of re-assuring things: that lightning never strikes in the same place twice, that a house is always safe among trees, etc., etc. I forgot my own fright in comforting the children, and then Partner, who had been prowling around looking for damage startled us by saying, "Good heavens, the tree has been struck!"

As we looked through the door, lightning flashes revealed to us our poor wounded tree, great pieces of bark stripped off. Our beautiful tree, only a few yards from the house, that has always been such delight to us. Bricks lying on the ground bore evidence to the chimney having been struck. We thought that was all, but later on we found the sink trap on the floor, and in the morning we discovered several holes in the eaves-trough and the pipe going through the sink was disconnected at the elbow. We felt we had had a pretty close call, but for some reason had been mercifully spared.

Monday we could hardly think or talk of anything else but our near tragedy. Tuesday we got down to work again — at least Partner did, but what with shock and an aching head I found it impossible to concentrate on anything at all; my wits would persist in wool gathering.

As if the storm and its consequences were not enough, the children had to give us a little more excitement. Wednesday morning they were playing around in the stable. "Mummy, Mummy, come quick!" With my heart in my mouth I ran and found that Son, by accident, had run the stable fork into Daughter's leg. Dear, oh dear, such a nasty looking wound. Out came the first aid box and every means of precaution taken against infection. Since then she has been through her paces with bathing, poulticing, iodine, etc., and now she is beginning to hobble around without much trouble.

Trouble came from another direction. The children had four pet ducklings — the first we have ever had on the place. They loved to be let loose to go fly catching, paddle in mud puddles, get after the hen feed and their quick moving antics were a delight to the children. But alas, one morning Black Feet was missing and was never found. Next morning I heard a fuss going on among the hens and ran out to find them pecking and chasing the other little ducks.

I rescued them, but it was too late; their poor wee necks were so badly pecked two of them died. Now, the one remaining little fellow is kept in a wire netting run all the time and he does not like it one bit.

As Daughter says, "It has been a dreadful week," and I agree with her, but life after all is much like a book. Each week is a chapter: we turn over the pages and turn another — one life, one book, but many chapters.

AUGUST 13, 1931

Jig-saw puzzles are rather out of date — that is, the kind that come in boxes and are bought from the store. But there is another kind of jig-saw that is never out of date, and that is the jig-saw of Life.

When you go out to visit your friends, or perhaps to attend a meeting or a church service, have you tried picking up a piece from one place and trying to fit into a piece picked up from somewhere else? Perhaps I had better give you an instance to explain what I mean.

Piece No. 1. I was invited to a meeting a few miles from home. There was a gap in the program, and to fill in one member read a poem from a magazine, entitled 'The Woman Trustee.' Now that's an idea. I thought: Why should there not be a woman Trustee on every School Board, and who is better qualified to know what is best for children's welfare than a woman? Then I began to wonder how many communities were sufficiently progressive to appoint a woman Trustee and how many women there were brave enough to sit in on the School Board. Lo and behold, I afterwards discovered I was at that minute visiting in just such a community and was even talking to a woman who had had the courage to take office as a woman Trustee.

Piece No. 2. I was writing to the editor of the magazine from which the Trustee poem was taken. She was so glad to hear a poem from her magazine had been read at this meeting. And I am quite sure she was glad, because editors very often have to do a lot of guessing in regard to whether what they publish is pleasing to the readers of their paper or magazine.

Piece No. 3. A preacher I heard just recently said in his sermon, "We all have forces within us — forces waiting to be used in so many ways and all we need is the power to release them." The power to release: what grand words and how pregnant with meaning! Think of the unused talent in this world, think of the wasted opportunities, all because so many people have not yet discovered the power which releases dormant talent or unexplored traits of character.

Piece No. 4. I was speaking to the wife of a retired minister and she told me that for many years she had cut out and saved the scripture column in a certain magazine, because she thought it so well written and the ideas so well expressed. I happened to know the person who wrote this column and told her what the minister's wife had said, but of course without mentioning any names. And was the writer pleased! There you have two perfectly fitting pieces in the jig-saw picture of life — the writer and the reader.

To go on with the puzzle. Piece No. 3 can be fitted to Piece No. 1: the community with the woman Trustee. There you have a live-wire community who decided they wanted a woman on the School Board. And what did they do? They discovered that, to "release their power" as ratepayers, all they had to do was to attend the Board meeting and use their voice. They did — and it worked. The woman Trustee was appointed. Thus two more jig-saw pieces were fitted together.

Of course, carrying out my illustration — Piece No. 2 fits the other side of Piece No. 1.

Do you get my idea? If you stop to think about it, doesn't it also strike you that life isn't just a disconnected affair? We can, if we will, discover an almost uncanny continuity of thought in widely separated situations. We can see people and go places that have absolutely nothing to do with other people we see or other places where we go, and yet we ourselves may be the connecting piece that makes it possible for us to use them — to put the rest of the puzzle together.

Occasionally something happens and we call it a co-incidence, but I believe a co-incidence would be a very rare thing if it were not for this spontaneous continuity of thought.

For instance, in our morning paper an expert on handwriting said that handwriting in which the lines sloped downwards betokened that the writer was very far from being well or else led an unhappy life. By that same mail I received a letter from a relative with a terrible downward slope. But I don't really consider that a co-incidence. I would say that was a typical instance resulting from continuity of thought — two more pieces of a jig-saw puzzle, with myself connecting them.

There now, I think I'll go and put some ice on my head. Jig-saw puzzles always did give me a head ache!

FEBRUARY 10, 1932

Really, the daily news is getting quite exciting these days — that is, if one gets past the war news without getting cold shivers down one's spine.

What I really refer to is news which is much nearer home — that is the discussion of farm problems: the cut in milk prices, the probable outcome of the Farm Council, with representatives from every county, and last, but not least, the heated letters which have been written as a natural outcome of the Honourable T. L. Kennedy's expressed opinion re the farmer.

The Honourable Mr. Thomas has a habit of hitting straight from the shoulder, but there are times when he aims a little wide of the mark. Hardly any farmer will welcome the suggestion that he has been "babied," or that he has been "given" education, good roads and Hydro. The general impression among farmers seems to be that the farmer pays and pays pretty highly for any advantages that come his way.

And then you know this 'prosperity' yarn is getting to be rather a myth. Of course it may be true that prosperity is just around the corner, but the corner must be an unconscionable long way off, for to look for it seems rather like hunting for the foot of the rainbow. We may do our best to get to the corner, but no matter how persistently we travel nor how fast we go, the corner recedes as we advance.

As far as newspaper reports go, one might almost say the conflicting reports are rather like a jig-saw puzzle, with some of the pieces left out. Compare the large optimistic headlines on the front page with the market quotations at the back, and you realize you are up against a puzzle. A puzzle, yes — but the parts don't fit together; where, then, are the missing pieces?

Prosperity — and yet eggs, eighteen cents a dozen; churning cream, down three cents; cattle market draggy; drop in potatoes; fifty-six cents top price for wheat; small seeds unchanged; and alfalfa apparently not worth quoting at all.

Sounds like prosperity, doesn't it? We are beginning to think it is quite a joke — but a grim, desperate joke. Every day we are sure farm prices must have reached rock bottom, but the next day they seem to have gathered momentum, kicked the rock clean out of the way and gone hurtling down again. Either that or they go right through the rock like a diamond drill. Partner remarked to-day that we had better hurry up and get the egg crate away, otherwise the returns might not cover the shipping charges.

But there is just one consolation — it is no disgrace these days to admit one is hard up. Without a comfortable bank balance, no farm, however well managed, can possibly be self-supporting under the existing conditions. What can we do? There is only one thing we can do, and that is economise in every way possible. Not so easy, perhaps, when we consider we have already economised up to the uttermost limit. Economy has a different meaning to different people. Some think the only way to economise is to go without things they want, others still get a few of the things they need but by dint of much scheming make every dollar give them in return one hundred per cent value.

And then there is false economy — penny wise and pound foolish. We have had a wonderfully good instance of that this week. Partner has an old root pulper — it is dear knows how many years old, and was second-hand when Partner bought it. Its usefulness was outlived several years ago, but to economise Partner made it do. It has only two cutting knives left and they are in one corner, so that the roots have to be pushed, shoved or in some way persuaded to pass through the knives.

Every time Partner is late in for dinner I have visions of him mangled up in the root pulper. Last week he left part of his thumb behind; yesterday I heard his step in the wood shed too early for dinner and there he was with a terrible looking finger. The doctors were away, so there was nothing for it but to fix Partner with a tourniquet on his finger until such time as the doctor could arrive. When he finally arrived it required four stitches to close the wound.

Now we do the chores between us under difficulties — Partner hindered by his awkward bandaged finger and I hampered by inexperience. Daughter does her share when she is here to do it, but how much time does a school girl have to help at home?

So that is the predicament we are in through practising economy and I have not the least doubt but what Partner will still use the pulper and go on using it until such times as farm prices take a lift.

Of course we are not down-hearted — not a bit of it. Somehow, some time, things will change and the farmer come once more into his own, but in the meantime the best we can do is keep scratching. As I read in the paper the other day — a hen does not quit scratching when the worms are scarce! Indeed no, if I know anything, she scratches all the harder and so I guess we will take a lesson from the hens and go on scratching, too.

I started to write this week's Chronicle with every intention of telling about a few odd adventures incidental to seeding, and about the night we were up in the bush until one a.m., rescuing Patch, our little fox-terrier, from the inside of a huge elm tree; in fact, I had a page and a half written, but oh dear, it read like a school-girl's composition, and the reason was that, although I was thinking about what I was writing, I was not writing about what I was thinking. You see, when you have never in this life owned a car, and suddenly acquire one, why it is a little apt to upset one's equilibrium.

Now the cat is out of the bag, I might as well go on with my confession, or explanation, whichever you like to call it, because a car in times of depression does need a little explaining. One person expressed pleasure that the wave of prosperity had struck us, but it hadn't — at least, not so that we notice it — but the wave of necessity has, in fact it has given us a knock-out blow.

To give the whole story — away back in the beginning of time — or so it seems — we bought a beautiful second-hand top buggy, and considered it quite a smart turn-out. We did not need it much for business then, but it was necessary as a means of personal transportation. Then our farming expanded; we had more cows year after year, more poultry and incidentally more business as we tried to build up a reputation for quality.

Now hardly a day goes by without a phone order for eggs, cream or chickens, and besides that, we have our eggs and cream to ship. Partner cannot spare time for running stuff into town, and so the job falls to me. Lately I have almost taken my life in my hands with every trip I made. The buggy wheels would rattle, three spokes were loose and the tires are as thin as paper. The whole buggy needed fixing, and then if we spent twenty or thirty dollars on it, we should still only have a buggy.

So we bought the car entirely on business principles, but it isn't a new Ford '8' — it isn't even a new '4.' It is — must I confess it? — a used Ford coach. The children like to give everything a name and asked what we should call it. I suggested that it might be christened the 'Last Hope.' However, it isn't really so bad as that — the car is really in splendid condition, and we expect it to save us a lot of time.

Apropos of time — I have hardly had time for anything this week; it has all been taken up with learning to drive the car. Partner absolutely refused to learn until I had done so, as he said he was quite sure if he learnt first I should not bother to learn at all. Personally I am not so sure of that — if a woman sits at home and waits for a man to take her out she sometimes has to wait an awful long time.

Now Partner says he does not care whether he learns at all, but I can tell already he will make a champion back-seat driver, so he will just have to learn, then when he starts telling me what I ought to do, I can just vacate the driver's seat in his favour, and give him a chance to show what he can do.

Yesterday I was backing the car out of the buggy shed — I mean the garage — and Partner got quite annoyed because I tried to take the driving shed wall along with me. Such a little thing to get annoyed about — after all, a person has to learn.

Then there is a small bridge in the lane to navigate. I can take it beautifully now, but once or twice I came over on three wheels — the fourth one coming along on its own in the ditch and then Partner started talking about breaking springs and axles and a few unpleasant things like that. Really, I began to feel quite hurt, but I was far too busy with the wheel and those other mysterious contraptions to think out any adequate retort. The best I could do was to say, "All right, you wait until you start."

And then to tease me Partner is forever whistling the military 'Short Reveille' — veterans will probably see the connection between our car and the short reveille. So long as he doesn't have to whistle the 'Last Post,' I guess we will be all right.

So that's that. We have got a car, and, oh boy, it's a grand and glorious feeling not to have to worry about a horse in town, and to step out to church with shoes free from dust and a coat that isn't covered with horse-hair! Why, it lifts a load of depression from one's shoulders that has nothing to do with eggs at twelve cents a dozen!

Perhaps the 'Last Hope' is a misnomer after all; perhaps it would be better to think of it as symbolic of the Dawn of a New Era and call it 'The Optimist' instead. Optimism and ginger surely go together, and one is the natural outcome of the other.

FEBRUARY 24, 1932

This has been an eventful week. Last Sunday we got up with every intention of going to church, but as the thermometer registered a little below zero, and a cold wind blowing, our good intentions got so badly frost-bitten there was nothing left of them at all.

To make assurance doubly sure, soon after eight o'clock there was a knock at the door, and a man asked admittance to warm his hands. I invited him in, sat him behind the heater until he was thawed out and then asked where he came from and where he was going.

"I've just come away from the gaol," he said, "and I'm going on to the next town, but my hands and face got so cold I could not stick it."

I confess for a few minutes I felt a little uneasy. What had we got here, I wondered: a gaol bird? However, the man was clean, decently dressed and not at all alarming in appearance, so I decided not to get unduly perturbed. After a while Partner came in and we had breakfast.

Our visitor said he had been given porridge and tea at the gaol, but evidently it only acted as an appetizer because he managed to clear the decks at our table without much trouble. Before he dispatched his eggs, his glance wandered over the table, finally he looked at me and said, "Salt and pepper, please!"

I had forgotten to put them on and the idea of a man being given a free meal and so coolly voicing his requests was almost too much for my sense of humour; however, I meekly produced the condiments. It was a pity I had not given the matter a little more forethought, then I might have provided our friend with a menu card.

After he had fed sufficiently he talked and talked and talked. I kept looking at Partner to see if his hair happened to be standing on end as mine seemed almost to have left the roots. He seemed very well acquainted with gaols in England, Canada and the States, and was apparently quite familiar with the way of the underworld in general.

'Riding the rods' and being caught as a stow-a-way on board ship were not the least of his experiences. He could hardly be called a desirable acquaintance, yet his varied life made him an interesting conversationalist and he did not make any attempt to enlist our sympathy with a hard luck story. One of his remarks struck me as very apt.

"Yes," he said, "I'm telling you these things and you can hardly believe me, because you don't know. You have never had to beat your way or run against people who are little more than the vermin of the earth. But some men, just as well brought up as you, have to share their lodging house with all kinds and conditions of men if they haven't the price to go anywhere better."

The man was intelligent but hard and bitter, yet often his words rang true. After all, what do we know of conditions outside our own environment? We read the papers but how much interest do we take in people we have never met, or places we have never seen? If we hear of conditions that are repulsive we don't want to know about them, yet human beings are born, live and die under conditions from even the hearing of which we turn away, in disgust.

It was nearly eleven o'clock before our visitor took his leave and I was able to finish my work. Of course I might have got on with it before, but I did not want to miss anything worth hearing — a natural desire for 'copy,' I suppose. Fifteen minutes afterwards, another stranger, whose car had run out of gas, came in to use the telephone. Then Patch, the pup, nearly got run over by a second car. He had to run all the way under the car until it stopped because he could not get out, while I stood helplessly watching, with my heart in my mouth.

Wednesday it was bitterly cold again, and because I get almost solidified when I drive I walked into town to attend the

Women's Auxiliary meeting, but oh how glad I was coming home when a nice, kind neighbour gave me a ride in her car!

May 11, 1932

This week we had a letter which might quite easily have been written thirty years ago as far as the news in it was concerned. It told of the death of Partner's grandmother, who in another month would have seen her one hundred and fourth birthday. There were two columns about her in the paper, and a photograph showing her busy making pillow lace, at which she was an adept. In her young days she used to live near Mr. and Mrs. Isaac Disraeli, whom she knew very well, and Miss Disraeli, sister to the famous Benjamin, afterwards Lord Beaconsfield, was at one time her Sunday School teacher.

Littler great-grandma, as we used to call her — she was no bigger than a minute — had lived in five reigns and at the time we last saw her, she still had a remarkable memory and would tell us many interesting things belonging to a bygone age. She had eight children, twenty grandchildren and fourteen great-grandchildren, and was interested in the welfare of them all. Her husband, who died fifty-seven years ago, was a stone mason, and it says in the paper that he was responsible for much of the work at Windsor Castle, notably the facing with stone of two of the large towers.

Grandma's recipe for long life was, "Work and plenty of it. Don't eat too much and refrain from intoxicants. Live plainly."

Family history has always had an intriguing interest for me, and only this week a strange co-incidence came my way in connection with it. A little while ago I had a short story published and for want of a name I made use of my grand-mother's maiden name. It had not struck me as being in any way uncommon, so I was quite surprised when I got a letter asking if the name was fictitious, as the writer did not know of any family bearing that name except those related to them. A few letters went back and forth, and as far as we could judge we were both branches from the same family tree.

After that I let the matter drop, and practically forgot all about it, when lo and behold! One afternoon this week a strange car drove in the lane and unloaded a whole crowd of newly found forty-fifth cousins. What I shall do if I unearth any more relations, I don't know, as my last count of relations, known and unknown, ran well over a hundred, scattered all over the world, and the half of them I have never seen.

My grandmother had ten children. All of them grew up and married and they each had about ten children each. They in turn grew up and married and simmered down to families with two, three or five, so on the face of it I suppose I am liable to find relations popping up in all kinds of unexpected places.

Now my interest is revived, I must write to a cousin in England and find out a little more about the family tree. Tracing ancestors is quite fascinating — there is always the chance one may dig up a belted earl! — On the other hand there is an equal chance one may find some grim skeleton locked away in the family cupboard. So far nothing like that has happened.

I showed these people who came to see us my mother's photograph, and the old gentleman declared she was exactly like his sister Annie! After this I shall have to keep an eye on the agony column and run through the list of unclaimed money every once in a while.

OCTOBER 19, 1932

I have been extravagant, most frightfully extravagant, and thus it is, that after worrying away for fourteen years with no other convenience for laundry work than a wash board and a zinc tub, I have actually treated myself to a washing machine. Not a new one of course, just a 'has been,' and it hasn't got any electric power attached or gasoline motor or anything like that — just a handle to push backwards and forwards to work magic on the clothes being swished around in the tub.

Plenty of women with electric machines would turn up their noses at my bargain, but I can tell you it looks pretty good to me. Why, I can hardly wait for Monday to come and I wouldn't wait, either, if it were not that I am absolutely hemmed in on every side by work, other than washing, that really needs to be done. But just wait until Monday comes. Hail, rain, snow or shine, I'm going to *wash*! Oh yes, absolutely, and every swish of the clothes in the water will sound like sweet music in my ears.

What a lot of fun people miss who get nearly everything they need without much trouble. Why, I wouldn't have got half the kick out of acquiring a washing machine if I had had it when we were first married. I am beginning to think we should be awfully thankful of the things we haven't got. Maybe that sounds a bit Irish, but I can't think of any other way to express what I mean.

I am not sure that Partner looks upon my recent innovation with unalloyed approval because I believe he has heard rumours from other men of some few occasions when they were called upon to perform a certain menial duty in connection with a washing machine.

Partner knows very well that nothing short of sickness or sudden death would ever make me suggest that he should ever try dabbling out washing with a wash board and tub, but I rather fancy he has a sneaking fancy that, from now on, if he should happen to drop into the kitchen at an auspicious moment he might possibly be called upon to convert my machine into a man-power washer. In fact, he has even forestalled any possible suggestions on my part by announcing that Monday morning is always a busy time with him and not to be expecting any help.

So be it — I'm not grumbling; in fact I would say perish the thought that I should want a man around when I am busy working. Not only that, but I shall be so busy counting my many blessings that I shall not have time to think of anything else. Just imagine — I have a sink with two pumps attached, the rain from heaven in a cistern, a tub, a wringer and now a washing machine. Why, I am positively up to my eyes in clover!

Of course, as I implied before, I know there are some women, with nothing left to wish for, who are blessed with electric washers, electric irons and hot water on tap, but there are also other women who haven't even the convenience of a sink and who have to carry every drop of water from the pump outside or dip it out of a barrel under the eavestrough, so it really seems to be that I have struck that delightful state — the happy medium.

To-day we have been to our local fair and found it greatly improved from other days. In fact, it was quite the nicest fair I have been to for a long time.

It was late before we got away, as in the morning Partner was away to a corn cutting and I had to go to town with our weekly orders, so what with one thing and another I wasn't awfully anxious to take in the fair at all, but Partner and I always look upon it as something that ought to be done. After all, it is no use growling about your local fair unless you give it your support to help make improvements possible.

Sometimes we enjoy ourselves and sometimes we don't, but we certainly thought to-day's fair exceptionally good and were pleased to see the many improvements that had been made. We sent the children off early and later on, when Partner and I approached the fair grounds, we saw a 'joy wheel.'

"Oh, my goodness," I exclaimed, "I hope the children have not been in that thing!" But they had — at least Daughter had, as I might have guessed — that child would take a trip to the moon, given the opportunity. Ten cents worth of joy, she called it — to me it would have been a hundred dollars worth of misery. Another attraction for the children was a miniature train on a track: six rounds for a nickel, and I am quite sure every child who had a ride was conscious of a thrill that will last for days.

There were a lot of splendid horses in the show ring and the dearest little pony turn-out. The races were good and the exhibits just splendid.

There was only one thing to which I took any exception, and that was the monkey race in the midway. Three poor little monkeys were chained into three little cars and were supposed to race on a triple track. Children naturally thought the monkeys were really racing, but of course the little cars were mechanically controlled and the poor little monkeys were sent tearing around the miniature track, at a terrible speed, each one gripping the side of his little car and blinking his pathetic little eyes.

Why are such things allowed? Whenever I think of the fair it will be to remember those poor little monkeys and the look of misery on their expressive wee faces.

NOVEMBER 30, 1932

"Soon the middle class people will be worse off than those on the Dole." In Canada there is no class distinction — that is theoretically — actually — well, "I ha'e me doots!" At any rate, we have business men and farmers, men who want work and men who don't want it, those who ask for relief and get it and those who need it and won't ask for it.

We had a married man in here last week — a splendid worker but only able to get odd jobs. Partner asked him why he didn't put in for relief. "Me — me, put in for relief? Not while I have a pair of hands and breath in me body! No sir-ree."

And there are many like that man.

We hear a lot of stories about the unemployed — kindnesses abused, relief wrongly taken — but we should also remember that these cases are exceptions. It is the unusual that attracts attention. We hear little of the heroism of daily life — with or without relief, the sacrifice and continual effort to simulate a recognized standard of living. Pride makes so many hide their desperate need, and they are often the ones who most deserve to be helped.

One time I knew a family in the city. The father had a very poorly paid job, and there were two children going to school. Each morning their mother would sew up holes in their hoses; each night they would have burst open again. This woman was a splendid needle woman and would help her neighbours with their sewing, but pride would not let her take in sewing as a paying proposition — 'She had seen better days' — yet she would walk miles to save a car fare and be among the first to get in the basement of department stores on bargain days.

Relief for that woman — not while she had a pair of hands and breath in her body!

There seems to be a tendency these days to hark back to the pioneer age. Any time during the last two years that I have heard Bishop Owen speak or preach, he has drifted, unconsciously, I think, back to the days of the early settlers.

To-day I was at a meeting and listened to an address on 'Pioneer Days in Old Ontario.' Last week I read a book on the same subject. This morning I saw pictures in the newspaper of a Women's Institute Fashion Parade, featuring beautiful old shawls, most of them treasured family heirlooms.

It seems to me, intelligent people are trying to reason things cut from a new angle — comparing the past with the present, pigeon-holding this, that and the other, figuring out whether we are as badly off as we think we are or whether being sorry for ourselves is dimming our vision. The survival of the fittest is nature's law. Might it not just as reasonably have a moral and mental application as well as a physical one?

After the depression — what? Shall we realize that it hasn't been a depression at all, but a very necessary course of adjustment? Will false standards and personal greed go into the melting pot, along with high wages and inflated prices? We hear much about the low prices for farm produce, but farmers would not worry about the prices if they could get dollar value for every dollar earned and spent.

DECEMBER 7, 1932

We have all been tearing out hair and writing frenziedly to get our English mail away by Monday, and, oh dear, it is no joke. I think one of the hardest things to do is to write Christmas letters a long time before Christmas. It doesn't seem possible to propel one's enthusiasm into the spirit of things and yet it has to be done.

There have been very few parcels to tie up this year, so we had to do the best we could with letters. I had been wondering so much what to send to a very dear friend of mine, and then one day, as I was passing a shop window in town, I saw a number of pictures — most of them reproductions of famous paintings — and among them was a landscape by John Constable.

Before you could wink an eye I was in and out of that store with the picture in my possession. Constable's Country — what memories! Had we not spent a most delightful weekend — my friend and I — tramping each day through this land of dear delight; had we not seen sheep peacefully grazing along its moss-grown lanes and the sun, sinking rosily to rest, tinting every leaf and flower with restful light?

Had we not risen in the dewy light of early dawn, breakfasted meagerly and early and gone on our way rejoicing? Had we not knocked hopefully upon the door of one country inn after another as the day advanced and been refused such services as we needed to allay the pangs of hunger?

On the day of rest, had we not tramped twenty-one miles along highways and byways and worn holes in our stockings and blisters on our heels, so that each step forward meant excruciating torture? And when at the long last we limped painfully across our own threshold, eaten heartily and thankfully of good plain food, changed our shoes and our clothes and our spirits and were wondering what to do next, did not this very dear Amazonian friend of mine brightly suggest that we go for a walk! And walk we did — we walked up Waldingfield road and back again — a matter of two and a half miles — neither of us admitting that we were the least bit tired!

So I think it is very appropriate that I should send this small picture of Constable's Country to my friend, and I have written on the back — "To memorialize a week-end when two crazy Janes set out for a week-end tramp." Whenever I see a picture of Constable's Country I shall always think of it as a country of rare beauty but scanty hospitality.

Of course writing letters to England has set us thinking about Christmas an awful lot, and we have just been talking about it — Partner, the children and I. As I write, it is three weeks and two days away and we haven't been able to make any plans for it at all. Of recent years after paying the tax bill it has kept us pretty busy to find money for Christmas festivities, and sometimes it has left us feeling rather blue. We don't mind for ourselves, but of course we do like to give the children a happy Christmas — and I think we always have.

This year we have just as much to sell but no chance of selling it, and yet the tax bill comes in just the same and as I said before, in three weeks and two days it will be Christmas. I realize it all — the shortage of cash, the heavy expenses every farmer has to meet at this time of the year and the utter futility of trying to sell anything to advantage — and yet I don't feel the least bit blue.

I have been sitting here thinking and wondering about it and asking myself, "Why?" until now I think I have the answer. Other years it has almost seemed that we have been tightening up our belt while other people were letting theirs out — that we were doing more getting than giving, which is never a very happy state of affairs. But this year, if at any time we are inclined to feel sorry for ourselves, we have only to stop and think for a minute, to realize how very, very fortunate we are to be on a farm at all. And although we have little to give, it is easy enough these days to find a home where that little will be appreciated.

For weeks past the children have been eagerly scanning the pages of the mail order catalogue, picking out this thing and that which they hope they may get for Christmas. But to-night we told them — tried to explain to them — just why this Christmas was different from any other and how it would be wrong to spend money wastefully when there are so many people in want.

And like the good little scouts they are, there wasn't one word of complaint although Son suggested that we buy them school books and scribblers, which we would have to get any-way, and put them in their stockings so that they might have something to unwrap and look at on Christmas morning. Children are so good at pretending — I often think we spoil it all with lavish generosity. All they really ask is someone to pretend with them and a little something to pretend with.

Hard times notwithstanding, I don't believe there need be one unhappy child at Christmas if only the parents and grown-ups would have as much intelligence as the children.

JANUARY 5, 1933

To be ready for this week's publication, I should have started this chronicle several days ago, but I didn't because I wanted to wait for the New Year. There is something so alluring about doing things in an unsullied year — like the time-honoured idea of writing on a clean slate. And yet you know I never think the clear slate notion is very logical as a simile because it isn't possible to wipe out last year's problems as though they had never been, as one can do on a slate. Life isn't so simple as that — there is always a carry-over from one year to another. Even so one welcomes a new year — there is something about it that is cheery and hopeful and clean.

Sunday morning I wondered whether this pert little infant '33 had been born with rose-coloured glasses and, if he had, what difference it would make to our world. I was out to give the hens their breakfast on New Year's Day, and looking towards the west I was surprised to see, in the distance, trees, houses, barns and fields, all enveloped in a soft red light. It was very beautiful and I wondered at the cause until looking behind me, I saw the sun peeking, rosy red, from behind a bank of clouds. The warmth of colour only lasted a few minutes and then the trees and buildings could be seen again in their own prosaic hue.

Shortly afterwards I was back in the house, where the light was dim and the lamps still burning. I was in the dining room, my back to the window, when suddenly the room was flooded with light — not just ordinary every day light but so bright and so sudden that its brilliance was startling. It may be foolish but I like to think that such a roseate dawn on New Year's Day was symbolic of better days to come.

I have forgotten — if I ever knew — what kind of sunrise we had last New Year's Day, but I do remember — and I expect everyone else does, too — how stormily 1932 was ushered in, screaming and protesting like a badly spoiled child.

This year it was clear, cold and reasonable, by comparison a far better beginning than last year, if one cares to look upon it as an omen.

And now, of course, it is time to trot out the New Year resolutions. It certainly won't hurt to look them over. A lot of them are probably coated with dust through being laid away so long. It will do them good to see the light of day once again.

I wonder if there is anyone living who ever made New Year resolutions and kept them? If there is such a person, I don't think I would ever want to meet him — or her — so much perfection would be unbearable. I often think we love our friends quite as much for their weaknesses as their virtues — at any rate we accept them as they are.

What fun it would be if, instead of making good resolutions for ourselves, we compiled a list of the good resolutions we think our friends should make. They, in turn, would make a list for us, and when they were ready they could then be exchanged. Wouldn't they be illuminating? We might then see ourselves as others see us. And should we like it? Well, that's the question.

We might even extend the idea and send, say, six resolutions to tradesmen suggesting, among other things, that less personal conversation be carried on across the counter when people are waiting to be served. Another six to customers, suggesting that they make up their mind what they want to buy before entering a store and carrying away such parcels as they can manage.

We might send about a dozen to the local paper, telling the editor how it ought to be run. A score to the Township

Council, two dozen or more to the Country Council, fifty to the Provincial Parliament and reams and reams to the powers that be in Ottawa. Oh yes, and we could, of course, think of quite a few to send to our debtors but towards our creditors it might be as well to observe a discreet silence.

And oh, how much I should love to send a few resolutions to our manufacturers, asking for better quality in the goods they make — tin pails a little thicker than paper, children's stockings that will last more than three days without going into holes, shoes that will stand the abuse of stone roads and stoned playgrounds, lamp chimneys that will not break for no apparent reason, cotton goods that will neither fade nor shrink, enamel ware that will not chip. In fact I would like to see 'Quality Goods' the slogan for manufacturers, rather than 'the cheapest goods on the market.'

I would even like to make resolution for the barnyard family. For instance cows should resolve not to switch their tails more than once when being milked, calves that are weaned should not kick the pail and drown the feeder with milk, calves being taught to drink should turn their noses down and not up, horses should not roll in wet weather and come back to the stable plastered with mud, hens should decide to be useful at all times and not ornamental, roosters should resolve not to crow in the middle of the night, dogs should not chase cats or pull clothes off the line, tom cats should decline to start howling and howling underneath one' s bedroom window, and feminine felines should make a point of having only one family per year, and that be restricted to two in number.

Yes, I can think of all kinds of good resolutions for other folks and the entire barnyard family, but heaven help me if they ever start sending New Year resolutions to me!

Mercy — here's a carload of visitors! Here I am, caught in the act ... good-bye ... Happy New Year everybody!

January 26, 1933

It is very nice at times to be just sitting and thinking and sometimes to be just sitting, but now I guess I've got to start thinking, and that's not so good. At least the thinking part is all right, but when you happen to be in a lazy mood and have to use a typewriter to get your thinking down on paper why, you don't quite see the fun of it! Dear knows there is plenty to think about these days — the trouble is to pigeon hole your ideas — trot out to the light of day those thoughts that are worthy, and relegate to the background those which lack general interest.

And you know a person can get awfully tired of thinking — but how to stop it: that's the question. The trouble is if you want to stop thinking about one thing about the only way you can do it is to start thinking of something else and when you are tired of that — well, there you are — it's a vicious circle.

The funny part of it is, after all is said and done, it doesn't amount to a row of beans what the average person thinks of the weather, price of produce, trade conditions or the general economic situation. Everyone has their own pet theory for shattering the world to bits and remoulding it nearer to the heart's desire. World conditions to-day seem to me rather like a bunch of tangled yarn, with everyone holding a different strand of wool and none letting go — making it impossible for the tangle to ever be straightened out.

This month sees the inaugural meetings of Councils — municipal, township and county — and it will be interesting to watch results. With — I should imagine — half the taxes in the country unpaid, how are the Councils going to meet expenses, and how form their estimates?

In one respect, the Great War has its parallel in our present depression — neither was realized by the great mass of people until it touched them individually. In 1914-18 it took British people an unaccountable age to realize there was a war on at all, or to grasp the immensity of its far-reaching results. Without doubt, we ordinary every-day people find it hard to think in the aggregate, but as soon as conditions touch us personally then we begin to sit up and take notice.

During the war, the Reaper brought realization to many homes, but where his hand was withheld his ally was found in Fear — the almost hourly dread of air raids — by night and by day — in industrial problems and in the intense inconvenience of having one's food rationed out. Yes, it was finally brought personally home to everyone that there really was a War.

The depression, which began — who can say when? — at first affected only a few, like ripples caused by a pebble thrown into the sea — the inner circles so small, yet gradually widening and widening. One wonders that such a seemingly small pebble could be the cause of such huge circles. The circles caused by the pebble of depression have also widened — widened tremendously — and there is hardly anyone now that is not within either one circle or another; consequently we are all beginning to realize at last that there is something wrong somewhere. That is all to the good; the sooner people shake themselves out of their apathy to a realization of what is going on around, surely that much sooner can we expect better times.

I have heard some good ideas expounded just lately, which may or may not be practical.

1. That everyone go bankrupt and start again with a clean slate. (Did I hear a chorus of "Hear, hear," "Suits me," "Now you're talking," etc., etc.?)
2. That instead of unemployed insurance and curtailing of a man's working hours, the number of years a man shall work be restricted instead and a government pension be given at the end of that time. The man who aired this idea pointed out it would do away with old age pensions as well as unemployment insurance and taking older men and women from competitive service would thereby give greater opportunities for young people leaving school to procure suitable work and by thus utilizing their abilities help them to develop into honourable self-respecting citizens, which they cannot do under present conditions.

Well, after that I had better get on with my knitting — I mean literally, not theoretically, because I have really got plenty on the go: a sweater for a friend, one for Son and a pair of stockings for the missionary bale.

I can hear Partner swinging the axe in the woodshed in his endeavour to keep the home fires burning. I don't often see him sitting and thinking or even just sitting. As for thinking — I suppose he must do that when he is on the business end of the axe handle or perhaps when he is taking his recreation milking cows.

JUNE 29, 1933

And now the Government speaks of wheat control or rather the reduction of wheat acreage. It may turn out to be a good move — it may — but, I don't know — I'm just afraid ...

To limit the supply of anything so vital to human life as wheat is certainly taking drastic measures. I have heard several Ontario farmers with hundred-acre farms speak quite enthusiastically of the idea — "That's right, limit the acreage, that's the idea. Less wheat, less work but more money in proportion." It does sound all right, doesn't it, and that's what the Ontario farmer thinks — the man with a hundred acres, including his ten or fifteen acres of wheat. Of course they don't all think that way; generally it's the ones who have no conception of what reduction in wheat acreage would mean to the West.

When we were out on the prairie, Partner had a half section, that is three hundred and twenty acres, as we were only farming in a small way, but our next door neighbour had a whole section and would put in about four or five hundred of wheat every year. We have seen that man's granaries so full of wheat, that in one instance, a granary full to the limit actually burst — the side walls, which had previously been braced, broke away and the wheat was strewn on to the ground. This crop took four weeks to thresh, and cost, on an average, about $100 per day to thresh.

The following winter this same man would go by our place twice a day. Day after day and week after week and always a grain wagon loaded with possibly a hundred bushel each trip. It was seven miles to the elevator and many of the trips were made when the temperature was twenty below zero, so certainly whatever a Western farmer gets he works for.

Perhaps you will think that it is high time such men had their acreage cut down, but wait a minute — there's another story.

After this bumper crop, for three years in succession, we saw this man's fields — the same acreage, the same amount of wheat sown — but the production, well, that was another matter. The acreage was not another matter. The acreage was not reduced, but the production certainly was. It was not the Government who did it — it was grasshoppers! Grasshoppers that rose in a cloud as one walked through the fields. Little winged insects that by their methods, so deadly and sure, can, in a short while, make a field appear as if it had never been sown. If a person has not seen the destruction a plague of grasshoppers can leave in their wake, then they must do some very hard thinking before their imagination can supply them with a picture anything like the actual scene of destruction.

While we were in the West, grasshopper poison was supplied by the Government, was sent out in sacks and came by the car load. Farmers used to make a round of the fields about three o'clock in the morning, scattering poison as they went, but it seemed, though many might be killed, there were always reinforcements waiting to carry on the attack. They were non-political, they were no respecters of persons and they had never heard a whisper of wheat-acreage reduction, but certainly they were the most effectual curtailers of production that could possibly be found.

As far as we know, there has been very little talk of recent years about grasshoppers, but now, in the same paper in which we read of the proposed cut in wheat acreage, we also read that a grasshopper plague has descended upon the West once more. If the plague is anything like it was as we knew it, then reduction in acreage will hardly be necessary, because the farmers will need every acre they can sow to make up for the loss by grasshoppers. More acres, more work, but alas, less wheat!

According to what we have read, the West has had several fair years in succession, but they don't always have good years, as we know to our sorrow. Supposing for the next few years acreage is reduced, and grasshoppers and weather conditions join forces with the Government — what then?

What Ontario farms produce is only a drop in the bucket, but when we think of restriction in the West it is a different story, and if the Government steps in with the hope of improving things, at best it can only be a gamble. But still, they ought to know. With so many experts putting their heads together, possibly they have something up their sleeve to meet any unexpected situation that may arise; perhaps they have grasshopper delegates at the wheat conference.

NOVEMBER 23, 1933

It seems the fashion nowadays to have special weeks for every-thing — apple week, insurance week, potato week, book week, onion week and almost every other kind of week you can think of. If taken in their proper sequence, I think we should really have insurance week first and then onion week — after that it wouldn't matter in what order they came because you would know by then you could stand anything.

But that is all beside the point; what I really set out to tell you is that we have just had economy week at Ginger Farm. As far as that goes, every week is economy week, but this week we have made a special drive as it were. Partner needed a hair cut but decided he could wait a little longer. He also wanted a new tin of tobacco but, unfortunately, just as the old can gave out he suffered from a temporary loss of memory!

Then Son economised on education by staying at home with bronchitis and croup and a few other things. Daughter economised in foot wear by forgetting her rubbers when roads were wet and slushy, and I have been economising from daylight to dark.

What I have been making over is mostly night attire for the family. It was a situation that had to be faced. Either something had to be bought or made or else we would have to wrap ourselves around in winding sheets.

I raided the cupboards and trunks and boxes, collected all the 'has-beens' and set to work.

For Son I managed to make two pairs of pyjamas — the pants were made from old khaki flannel shirts and the coats from new mauve-striped pyjama cloth. Partner's were made from new goods I had by me, but no two garments had the same kind of stripes. But what's in a colour — pyjamas in any other shade would be warm! Son thinks his are wonderful. Last night he wanted to go to bed earlier, so that he might put them on.

For Daughter I made a dress. It was all one colour, but there were dozens of joins hidden under pleats and gathers, etc. My biggest job was Son's windbreaker. Last year we half promised him a leather one for this winter, but as the year advanced the leather windbreaker receded further into the distance and yet he had to have something.

So I hunted the house over — there were coats I might have made use of. but I didn't want to cut them up. At last I unearthed a relic of the Great War — Partner's khaki tunic. It was practically new and the goods almost as wind proof as leather. So I picked it to pieces, put bits in here and took bits out there, cut up an old brown velvet dress to line it and — hey, presto, Son had a windbreaker after all. It took all my odd time for three days to do it and another day to make a pair of serge pants out of an old navy skirt, so perhaps the one thing in which I did not economise was time.

Oh, yes, and there was also a small matter of underwear, which had ceased to be ankle length. These I cut off at the knee, let in a piece of patching about four inches wide, and our son was once more equipped with ankle length underwear with strongly reinforced knees.

Now I have serious intentions in regard to Partner's old work sweater. It also is an army relic and has most decidedly seen active service, both during the war and since, until it has now reached the stage when both arms stand in danger of amputation. In this case I intend to be the surgeon, and I shall replace the original members with the tops of old knitted socks to which I shall knit a cuff to draw the sleeve in snug and warm to the wrist.

Now I could fill up a few columns by telling you other ways in which I mean to economise, but I would rather wait until my intentions have materialized, because, you know how it is — things don't always work out the way you expect them to. But you know this economy stunt is really all kinds of fun, and if you can turn out something presentable by utilizing what you already have you naturally feel you have accomplished something to write home about.

Farm people are practically sure of a roof over their heads — even though it be a leaky one — and of course three square meals a day, but apart from that it is undeniably true there is very little else that we can be sure of. Moaning about it won't get us anywhere, and we don't want to degenerate into a slipshod way of living, so to spare our pocket and save our sanity, I would suggest that we start an economy campaign of our own.

We women might go through the house from attic to cellar and what we can't use give away. Anything rather than harbour goods and clothing to feed the moth when little children all over the country are so badly in need of clothing. Missions are all right, but little children right at home in Canada need warm clothing as well as the 'little Indian, Sioux or Crow.' If we have the money to spare we should boost trade by spending it, but if we are in the position of having to make every dollar take the place of two, then I should say, economise — *and take pride in doing it!*

JANUARY 11, 1934

Once upon a time there was an old gentleman and his small nephew on board ship. One day the little boy said, "Uncle, is a thing lost if you know where it is?"

"Why, of course not, my boy, of course not — how could it be?"

"Well, I'm very glad of that," said the boy, with a sigh of relief, "because, you see, Uncle, I just dropped your gold watch overboard!"

Which goes to show, it is poor policy to answer a small boy's question without knowing the thought that prompted it. But that's not really what I am getting at. What I really want to point out is that we — and when I say we, I mean you and me and everybody in the country — we are in danger of losing something already. It can't be lost all at once, like the old gentleman's watch, but we lose it rather as we might lose a pocketful of money through a small hole in our pocket. Of course, that is a ridiculous simile because no one could lose a pocketful of money as no one these days has a pocketful of money to lose. But you get the idea.

And this something that we are gradually losing is — what do you think? I suppose I had better tell you. It is History. We know where some of it is: buried in God's Acre with those early pioneers 'who blazed the trail for Canada's future greatness.' Yes, we know where it has gone and it is lost as irrevocably as the old gentleman's watch.

Some of it has been saved as we know from the very interesting records in various archives, but I don't suppose all the records in the country constitute more than a tenth of Canada's early history. The pity of it! And to think the loss is still going on.

Many persons who read this article say or have said, "Yes, it is a shame we are losing so much first hand knowledge of early Canada. The old people are passing away one by one. Soon there will be none to tell us what our country was like before it became so well populated!"

Yes, you think it a shame, don't you, but are you doing anything about it? Do you keep a family record? Do you know the history of your own family, your own farm and the district in which you live? Have you got it all down in black and white, or are you just trusting to anecdote by word of mouth? Memory is a fickle jade. You may think you may never forget this and that, but circumstances may arise which make everyday living require your utmost concentration. The present and the future are enough to worry about you think, without fussing about the past.

It may be that you tell your children stories of the early settlers just as your parents and grandparents told you, but a child's memory is short lived and the chances are, your children, when they are grown up, will have completely forgotten what little you have been able to tell them. They want to remember; in fact, they may wish intensely they had something authentic to aid elusive memory just as you and I do to-day.

Where is the person, past the colt age, who doesn't long to know something abut his ancestors — their home, their farm, their country and the conditions in which they lived?

Breathes there a man with a soul so dead
Who never to himself hath said,
This is my own, my native land.

— Sir Walter Scott

There's a thrill in the above words, but it can only be felt by those who love their country, who suffer and rejoice with their country. To every person who has a living soul comes, sooner or later, the urge to know all he can about his native land or the land of his adoption, and about his own people. Intensive search may reveal some things that are not pleasing, but why worry, there is a black sheep in every family, so they say.

Judging by press reports, there is a movement on foot to awaken interest in local history. People are beginning to wake up — may they wake to some purpose!

Preserving history for posterity depends upon you and me — we mustn't shirk by leaving it to the other fellow — and the time to start is NOW.

I would suggest that a member of every family be responsible for a family scrap book. Write in it your family history as far as you know it. Paste in any newspaper clippings pertaining to family affairs: weddings, births, deaths, re-unions, presentations, school reports, etc. Collect data as far back as possible, but don't neglect the present. Remember, what happens to-day is the history of to-morrow; things which may not seem very important now will be far more interesting in later years.

The fact that Johnny gets a medal for oratory may not be exactly startling, but in the years to come, when Johnny is able to write M.P. after his name, his boys and girls will be glad to know something of his early boyhood days.

A faithful record, if kept, should be handed down from one generation to another and preserved as a sacred trust. In time it would become a priceless personal possession and from its records much valuable information might be given to county historical societies. These societies are doing wonderful work but they might as well cease to exist unless they have the co-operation of the individual.

What about it, friends and readers? Are you game to start a family history?

February 15, 1934

What a week — it's a wonder we are all alive to tell the tale! Where is that fellow who predicted a mild winter? I shouldn't wonder if he were hiding down a rabbit hole — and well he might. Can't somebody think of some kind of refined torture specially suitable for false weather prophets?

I'll never believe in weather prophecies again — never — never! Of course I must admit there were two weather prophets last fall — one said we were likely to have a mild winter and the other said cold. But you know how it is — if there are two prophecies and one is something you like while the other is something you don't like, you naturally feel more inclined to believe in the one that you like.

Oh well, we are having a tough winter, but one man's meat is another man's poison, and vice versa. This weather may be hard on the coal bins, but it must mean a fine harvest for the coal dealer, and as for garage men and plumbers, they will surely be rolling in wealth — supposing they ever get all that's coming to them!

Our worst problem has been getting the children off to school. Twice they have started off on their mile and a half walk with the thermometer at twenty below. Sometimes we were in doubt as to whether it was wise to let them go, but they were warmly clad — under protest, I admit, which did not make any difference — and so they got through each day without being any the worse for their journey.

But not so all children. We have heard of many cases of frostbite this week and have seen children, and grown-ups, too, starting out in most unsuitable clothing for such bitter weather. It does seem ridiculous, but it must surely be that people have forgotten what real cold weather is like. Recent mild winters and closed-in cars have brought about a change in dress so that most people find themselves inadequately clothed when we get a spell of sub-zero weather. And the trouble is they don't realize it until they find themselves chilled to the bone or suffering from frostbite.

And then, in regard to cars. Because roads are good — no drifts to make driving difficult — people are tempted to take their cars out, however cold it is. The idea is the car has been going all winter, as well keep it going. May be a bit hard to start, of course, but oh, it'll go in the end — might as well take a chance on it, anyway. So the chance is taken, and the garage men, it they wanted to, could tell you the rest of the story.

Is it worth it? Cold weather driving is hard on the car, hard on the owner and harder still on the pocket. If we are going to get old-fashioned winters, it looks as if we shall have to get back to old-fashioned ways of facing them.

Perhaps this cold winter has just been a little trick of the elements to make us sit up and take notice; perhaps we were getting a little too sure of ourselves. Perhaps fashions will change. One or two winters like this and we shall see stores advertising ankle-length underwear and cashmere hose instead of chiffon silk hose and step-ins.

MARCH 1, 1934

Possibly next week we may have to use as our address, 'Ginger Igloos' — it begins to look rather like it anyway, and if we had snake fences along the front lane, we might be using it even now.

Such a lot of snow as there is in some places — the back lane is almost level with the fences, and the children are having a grand time making themselves a snow house. I haven't been to see it yet, but there will be a terrible hue and cry if I don't soon go.

There, I knew I wouldn't be left long in peace. Now Partner is calling, "The kids want you to go and see their snow house." Well, I guess there is nothing for it but to go.

Back once more, but what a walk! At first we were walking on the ground level, and then suddenly came up against a steep snow bank which had to be climbed before we could walk along the top of the drift which, in places, was even higher than the fence. I can't say I like drift-walking: there is too much uncertainty attached to it. One minute the snow is as firm as a hardwood floor, the next the crust gives and you lose sight of one foot altogether, while the other stays high and dry on top of the drift. It really isn't dignified, but it's very exhilarating, warming and mirth-provoking, only I shouldn't like to be going anywhere in a hurry!

Half way up the lane we came to the igloos — three of them with a tunnel behind connecting all three. They were really just splendid and of course nothing would do but I must go inside, which I did on my hands and knees. The children came in, too, and then the big dog, and after him the little dog, so by the time we were all in the igloo was a trifle crowded.

We crawled through the tunnel, still on our hands and knees, and out through the third igloo. My knees were getting colder and colder every minute, because the floor of the tunnel was solid ice! What astonished me most was the amazing energy which must have been used to shove and scrape away such a quantity of snow. And what a state the children were in! Simply plastered with frozen snow from head to foot, and now the kitchen has so many stockings, mitts, overalls and coats hanging about there simply isn't a peg or a nail for anything else at all.

Some people are saying this weather seems more like a western winter. To us it does and it doesn't. We certainly used to have this kind of weather on the prairie and we didn't mind it a bit — in fact we used to enjoy it and had a pretty good time on the whole. Winter time was the western farmer's holiday, but winter time isn't the Ontario farmer's holiday — far from it.

In the West we only had a team and three or four cows in the barn; the young cattle and the rest of the horses roamed the prairie at will and we didn't see them for weeks at a time. They used to paw through the snow on the stubble fields for feed, and in normal times come home in the spring as fat as butter; so we had no worry in connection with them, excepting for rounding them up occasionally to make sure they were all there.

But here everything the farmer owns must be housed, fed and cared for, and only a farmer knows just how much work those three words imply.

In the West there were no trees, so we had to burn coal, and so naturally there was no wood to cut or draw home, and no sawing bees like we have down here. We never used to bother about getting up early, but here if we rise later than six o'clock we feel rushed for the rest of the day. We were often out to parties two or three times a week, but now one night out and we need a week to get over it. People attended church on Sundays whenever there was a service and it was no uncommon sight to see a crowded sleigh-load, which had driven miles to get there.

Altogether we had quite a good time in the West, unless we happened to want a doctor, and then it wasn't so good, if you lived a long way out and had to pay a dollar a mile to get him there, or there might be a blizzard and he wouldn't be able to come at all; so Ontario certainly has its advantages, after all.

Comparing the two Provinces, we have come to the conclusion that cold weather is easy enough to stand if you don't have to work too hard. But cold weather and hard work combined use up altogether too much energy and body heat. So many people complain of more than ordinary tiredness this winter and even children look as if they were doing just a little more than they can comfortably stand.

Another thing just lately has reminded me of the West, and that is the smell of fresh-baked bread. Out west, of course, I had to make my own bread all the time, and I did for a time down here, but of late years I have given it up. However, a few weeks ago, as an economy measure, I started making my own buns, and, oh dear, the smell of yeast and the crisply baked buns was my undoing. I simply couldn't resist until I had made a batch of bread, and 'though I say it as shouldn't,' it did taste good.

It was funny to wake in the morning in the same old way, wondering how far my dough had risen and then taking a peek the very first thing and finding it way up near the top of the pan. The other night, Daughter was setting the supper table, and said to me, "Why, mother, nearly everything I put on the table is home-made!" It was and I suppose that is how it should be, but I'm afraid it isn't always so.

Another reminder of the West is that I am now having to melt snow to do my washing in; the soft water pump is apparently frozen solid.

SEPTEMBER 6, 1934

Just once in a while I find it hard to write because there seems so little to write about, but to-day I find it even harder still because there is so much.

This last week we have been doing things! With the harvest finished, we thought we might take a little time off to celebrate, and so we have been to the Exhibition twice, Son went off visiting, I went on a trip to the Falls, but it seems that no power on earth could make Partner stay away from the farm over night, so one day at the Exhibition was the limit of his celebrating.

An invitation to the C.N.E. had me wondering whether vanity or curiosity would win out. Well, as you might suppose curiosity won the day, so about eight o'clock Wednesday morning the children and I started out in The Optimist. I had never driven through Exhibition crowds before and only once to Toronto, but one has to make a start sometime and I felt there is no time like the present, so away we went and reached our destination without any trouble at all.

Together, the children and I made a round of the buildings, with Son wanting all the time to look at tractors, farm machinery and motor cars, and Daughter equally anxious to look at anything historical and also to give individual attention to all the horses, cattle, goats, poultry, guinea pigs — in fact anything that happened to be alive. As for me, I just wanted to see whatever there was to see with no particular objective in view.

And so we wandered from place to place until four o'clock, and then I gave the children a little spending money and turned them loose, with instructions to be back at the car by six o'clock. This little scheme worked very well — we each saw what appealed to us most and spent as much time as we liked and where we liked. After supper we took in the show at the Grand Stand, had a good seat and thoroughly enjoyed the whole program, including the splendid show of fireworks at the finish.

We stayed to the very end — in fact it was eleven o'clock before we started making tracks for home, because the children wanted to wander around a bit to see what the grounds looked like when illuminated. And of course when we did move we did not get along very fast because the jam of cars coming away from the grounds was a fright. However, we did eventually get out of the tangle and on to a quieter road leading towards home, finally arriving home safe, satisfied and tired, about twelve-thirty, which of course was only eleven-thirty standard time.

On Friday Partner thought he could get away, but with the hundred and one things there are to do on a farm when the whole family takes a day off, it was nine-thirty before we got away.

The cows and heifers are in separate pastures, so of course they had to be watered separately. While the cows were being milked the children went to the back fields to bring the heifers down to drink. When they got there it was to find three of the heifers had broken out and were nowhere to be seen. Only once this summer have they got out of bounds before, and now, on this particular day, when we wanted to get things done up as quickly as possible, they chose this particular method to put the brake on our activities.

Eventually we found them — away over in one of our neighbours' fields. We had to do a lot of chasing and running around and then had to fix the fence, but that's the way things go on a farm sometimes. And then, of course, horses, poultry and geese all had to be fed and watered and the separator washed and a lunch fixed up to take with us.

However, it all got done and we finally reached the Exhibition once again. After lunch we turned the children loose again — they seem to have a much better time on their own — and Partner and I were able to sit and listen to the splendid band to our heart's content.

Of course we did make a round of the buildings and looked at most of the exhibits. We also watched the big swim for a while, but we failed to get much pleasure out of that. We liked better to watch the diving, which was really very good. In fact the water-front activities were quite an attraction. There is something very alluring about the blue water of the lake, perhaps it is because it is so quiet and refreshing after the crowded buildings.

One exhibit we specially enjoyed was the display of old-time implements and furniture and yet, when one looks into them, how like they are in principle to things we use at the present time. The binder of to-day is only an improved and refined model of the original idea. And so it is with many things. The credit for many of our modern advantages lies at the door of the pioneers. When we see the things they were able to do and to make with the crude tools at their disposal, we begin to realize the truth of those words we often read, 'they builded better than they knew.'

There now, my space is done, and I have hardly told you anything at all yet, so now the best I can do is to say: to be continued on our next.

DECEMBER 27, 1934

Well folks, how is everybody?

Of course it is after Christmas with you but it isn't with me: I am at the stage of having the last minute rush still ahead of me. For this is Saturday — Saturday before Christmas — and I am taking a few minutes before breakfast, while the house is quiet, to get started on this week's Chronicle. Partner is at the barn, milking, the children have not yet come to life, the kittens are still down the cellar, Patch is asleep on the couch, and the only sound of activity comes from Peter, who occasionally rattles the back-door latching asking for his breakfast.

It is a white world outside. It begins to look as if The Optimist may have to stay high and dry in the garage while we go to town in the sleigh. I do hope the weather doesn't get rough and stormy, because it makes it so much more difficult for visitors who are spending Christmas in the country — and what is Christmas without a family gathering? That, I think, is one thing Partner and I have missed more than anything else since coming to Canada. In England, members of one family do not often drift so far apart but what they can get home for Christmas — unless, of course, they happen to be abroad.

When Partner's mother and father were both living, there were four boys and one girl in the family, and an aunt, uncle and cousin also living in the village. Two of the boys were in London, two at boarding school and the girl at a nearby town, but at Christmas back they all came like homing pigeons and with the other relations the happiest possible Christmas was always spent by a united family.

With the passing of the years there were changes. One Christmas found one of the boys in Canada, one in Holland and one in Spain. Then came the war, with one boy still in Canada, one in Egypt and two 'somewhere in France' and the daughter at home.

And now the father has gone home, and this Christmas there is a married son in Toronto, one son and three children in Northern Ontario, one son and two children in Australia and one son and two children at Ginger Farm, while the widowed mother and her daughter are living in England, quite a distance from other relations in the Old Country.

With my family we did not spread our wings so soon nor travel so far. There were two girls and two boys in our family, and I was the youngest living child, but I can only remember one parent as my father died when I was three.

Except when one brother was away at a language school in Switzerland, I cannot remember any Christmas with any of us away from home. Later one brother was married but lived in the same town and so still spent Christmas with us. During the war this same brother, medically unfit, was still at home, and the other was with His Majesty's fleet somewhere on the high seas. My sister was here in Canada, while I, after taking my V.A.D. training (Voluntary Aid Detachment), was fuming in England because the doctors would not pass me for service abroad.

After the war, I can remember that one Christmas when we were all together again. After that, one brother went to Italy, my sister came back to England, my eldest brother was still at home and Partner and I were away out on the Western Prairie. And well do I remember my first Christmas in Canada. The weather was stormy, mail was delayed and we did not get even so much as a card from home on Christmas Day! But we did not have time to feel homesick, because during the morning a man with a broken leg and frozen hands and feet came to the back porch and fell at our door.

Only twice since coming to Canada have Partner and I had any of our own kith and kin to visit us at Christmas, but now my sister and her little boy are back in Ontario and are coming to spend Christmas with us. I managed to keep it a secret until yesterday but when I did break the news both children said, "Oh mother, it's going to be a real Christmas, with Auntie Kathleen coming to stay!" Since then they have been very busy collecting small presents for the little boy, who is just about half-past five and has implicit faith in Santa Claus.

Partner says, "What are you writing all that stuff for? Nobody wants to hear about our families."

"Well," I said, "if people are interested in any particular writer they often like to know something of their private life. They like the personal touch which makes them feel that the writer is just one of themselves, with the same problems, the same joys and sorrows common to all of us as we voyage along Life's road."

Perhaps I am wrong — perhaps you are not interested at all — in which case you have the privilege of not being obliged to read what I write.

A happy New Year to everyone.

Part II

WAR AND RUMOURS OF WAR

1935–1939

FEBRUARY 14, 1935

Ginger Farm is going modern! Last week Partner and I passed our seventeenth wedding anniversary, and to celebrate we treated ourselves to a radio — not a new one, of course, we couldn't be quite so modern as that — but yet quite a good one of its kind.

A radio is one of those things we have thought we could very well do without — at least we have always persuaded ourselves into thinking that — but the time has come when it is increasingly more difficult to determine the border line between luxury and necessity.

So often we are asked, "Were you listening to Bennett's speech last night?" or "What did you think of the hockey game?" or "Didn't we get lovely music over the radio yesterday?" and always we have had to answer, "We haven't got a radio." Just a few common place words in reply and yet they often acted like a conversational shutter. We had been excluded from so much that was worth while because music was played, games lost and won, speeches broadcast of which we had known nothing because, until now, we did not possess a radio.

When anything that has been a luxury becomes so commonplace and is used in so many ways as the radio is to-day, then it can almost be looked upon as a necessity — that is for anyone who wishes to keep abreast of the times.

Music, in some form or other, and political news are almost as necessary to Partner as the breath of life, yet he has neither the time nor the opportunity to get out to hear very much of either, but now with a radio installed, I am hoping he will get all he wants of both.

As for myself, I cannot begin to tell you what it will mean to me. Last week I put in an awful time. The radio was supposed to be here on Tuesday, but it did not come until Friday. We had done without a radio all these years but waiting those few extra days was the worst of all! I felt I could not settle to anything. I did manage to write this week's 'Chronicle,' but was so disgusted with it I put in the fire, so here I am doing it all over again.

Of course, as usual, this new venture had its funny side. It was about two o'clock on Friday when the radio was properly installed and all ready for action. It took us a little while to get used to the dialing, but by the time the children came home from school we knew enough about the stations to meet their demands for Skippy and Orphan Annie. Apparently the comics and Eddie Cantor are all our children have heard over the radio, but we hope to have them better radio-educated before very long. Some of the comics are not too bad, but deliver me from Eddie Cantor!

As the evening wore on, programs failed to come in so clearly, and after eight o'clock it was too painful to use it at all. When Partner came in from the barn he tried to see what he could do, but eventually gave it up and shut the thing off in disgust.

Early next morning Partner tried it again, turning from station to station at random. Result — silence! But suddenly across the air came a loud, derisive voice: Ah-ha! it said to Partner — just that, no more. I was still in bed and in the distance it sounded like diabolic laughter from a demon of the under-world, chortling at Partner for his futile efforts to get music from a wooden box!

Later in the day we called in the radio man, who after a few adjustments soon had the machine running again in good shape.

That night we all got properly thrilled following the hockey game. We also heard some splendid music, and learnt the very best pills to take for the relief of indigestion and con-stipation and the right kind of syrup to use to make children healthy and strong. We heard the official news broadcast by a man who talked so fast we lost the half of it, and then at twelve o'clock we went to bed.

After breakfast on Sunday I was exploring the stations to see what I could get and to my disgust tuned in on a comic strip program. Of course you people who have had radios for a long time know that this kind of thing goes on all the time, but to me it came as a distinct shock. It seemed almost sacrilege that such coarse programs should be allowed to come over the air and be transmitted by the same machine that could produce such inspiring music as that which I heard coming from St. Stephen's Church, Toronto, during their evensong service.

During the afternoon, while the children were at Sunday School, Partner and I listened in to the York Bible Class, and if it had been all we were able to get for one day, it alone would have been worth the installation of our radio.

We realize there may be drawbacks — crossed stations, static and perhaps when we most want to use it something will go wrong with the works — but in spite of all this, I believe our radio will prove a profitable and pleasurable asset to our home life, keeping us in closer touch with the outside world when circumstances compel us.

APRIL 11, 1935

This week is our fifth birthday — that is to say Ginger Farm is five years old as far as the press is concerned, and so this, I think, is an opportune time to size up our situation — past and present.

Five years ago, my first Chronicle appeared in this paper. The editor said he would give it a trial to see how people liked it. Maybe it is still on trial — I don't know — but I do know that for five years — for two hundred and sixty-two weeks — Ginger Farm has appeared week by week, month by month, and year by year, and not one week have I missed. With me, you have seen a good many ups and downs; we have come — thus far — through the worst depression our generation has ever known, but we have not, I can thankfully say, ever really lost heart or felt like quitting the game.

What have they brought to you, these ordinary every-day Chronicles of farm life? I wish I knew.

Have I been successful in creating a little amusement, of giving you perhaps a slightly different viewpoint in regard to the ordinary problems that we share in common? Have I at any time helped you to realize, as I have tried to realize myself, 'that the blue of heaven is greater than the cloud'? Have I done any of these things? I sometimes wonder.

About twelve years ago — before I started Ginger Farm — I sent my first article to the press — to 'The Farmers' Advocate,' and it was accepted. What do you suppose were my feelings when, for the first time, I saw my own writing in print? Do you suppose I was proud, conceited or excited? Far from it.

I was afraid, yes, literally afraid. It seemed to me that a power, even though it might be very small, but yet was still a power, and had been given to me in trust to use as I saw fit. By my pen I should be able to reach hundreds of people — people whom I did not know, people who by my writing might be influenced in a right or a wrong direction.

'The pen is mightier than the sword' — if authors would only bear that thought in mind and, realizing the influence of their own writing, would only commit to paper thoughts that are worthy, stories that are clean, thus write, not merely for personal gain but from a desire to benefit, inspire and entertain the reading public. Then we should have Canadian literature of which we might be proud — books and magazines that we might with comfort place in the hands of our 'teen age boys and girls. I believe that the moral standard of a country is no higher than the class of literature which it allows to circulate among the common people.

But I am getting away from Ginger Farm.

For the benefit of those who were not reading these Chronicles from the beginning, let me tell you how they came into being.

Of course it all started with the urge to write and what better subject could I choose than our every-day life?

In my introductory article I skipped lightly over the years from the time we started farming on the prairie to the time we settled down in Ontario. I said, "Partner and I decided aeons ago that should we ever own a farm we would call it 'Ginger Farm.' Why? because it would take all the 'ginger' we possessed to run it." So there you have the origin of the title, although this place isn't really called Ginger Farm. At that time I wrote under the pen name of 'Judy O'Grady,' but someone else started using the same name, so I decided to come out in the open and rise or fall by my own name.

Our children at that time were ten and seven years old; we had been farming here for six years, and were just beginning to feel our feet when — presto — along came the depression. The usual joys and sorrows that are the lot of everyone have come our way. We have lost dear ones; sisters and brothers have found husbands and wives; and a new generation has been started on its way.

Sickness in the home, stock losses and crop failures have occasionally come to us, but for every failure there has generally been something to balance the scales. Sometimes when the way ahead seemed full of uncertainty and worry, the fog has lifted and we have found, as I have said before, 'the blue of heaven is greater than the cloud.'

In these five years of writing, we have added to the comforts of our home in small ways; we have kept pace with the times by using a car and a radio. We have watched our children grow and develop until to-day our daughter stands, a little uncertainly, upon the brink of young womanhood.

Partner, the children and I have had many good times together in a quiet way. We have lost none of our old friends, but we have gained many who are new.

And so on this, our fifth birthday in the press, I want to thank you who have followed me so kindly from week to week and also those who have favoured me by their comments, either through the press or by mail, and whose opinion I have always valued.

So here's to the start of another year, and may you and I and Ginger Farm together see the dawn of a new era, a time of peace and the beginning of an average prosperity.

And if you would like to know it, writing this week's and last week's Chronicles have been the hardest in five years because I've got neuritis or some kind of itis in my shoulders, both arms and all my fingers! Isn't that a good way to celebrate a birthday in the press?

May 9, 1935

Well, it has certainly been no hardship to stay in the house this week — the hardship has been for those who have had to be out, rain or shine. And what bitter east winds we have had! One day, when it was fine but cold, Partner was out riding the disc all the afternoon, and came in just about chilled to the bone. The next day I was glad he had to work with the harrows and walk behind the team instead of ride.

But in spite of cold weather and its incidental unpleasant accompaniments, this week has gone by with amazing swiftness and, for me, it has been helped out tremendously by welcome visitors, cheery letters, flowers, plants and fruit to say nothing of the kindly offers of help, some of which have come from quite unexpected quarters.

Then again I had a letter from a lady editor which gave me rather a new interest. Up to the present, with the exception of 'Ginger Farm,' any stories or articles I have written have been entirely a speculation, but this week along came a letter, with a small picture enclosed, requesting that I write a short story to fit the picture and send at my earliest convenience.

"With the greatest pleasure," said I to myself, and set to work that very afternoon with the result that the story was in the mail the next morning. Of course, the doctor had to come along that same day and take the gilt off the gingerbread by scolding me for doing the things I shouldn't do and not doing the things I ought to do.

I need hardly say how much we have appreciated the radio this week, and I have purposely put off finishing this week's 'Chronicle' so that I might include a few impressions of the Jubilee celebrations — by next week it would seem such a long way back.

Of course I know a lot of you people have radios and many of you will have heard most of the Jubilee programs. At the same time, there are some who have not, and even those with radios may not have heard all the programs as I did. Lying in bed, I could listen in all the time.

We started in on Sunday afternoon and listened to the preparation service attended by the Royal Family and at which the Archbishop of Canterbury gave an inspiring address. Sunday night we made sure the alarm clock was accurately set and at 5:00 a.m. Partner, Daughter and I listened in to what I believe is one of the most memorable programs we are ever likely to hear over the radio, and I don't believe there was anyone more thrilled than the announcer himself, who, from his vantage point of sixty feet above the ground level of St. Paul's Cathedral in London, described to us each detail of the Royal procession as it moved slowly from Temple Bar across London to the Cathedral.

His description was perfect — just a few words at a time — so that listeners might miss nothing of the wild cheering, the tramp of horses' feet, the ringing of the church bells — how I loved the sound — and the word of command, "Slope arms," and then again, "Present Arms," which gave Partner a bigger thrill than anything.

Surely it must have been an impressive broadcast to anyone in Canada sufficiently interested to listen in, but can you realize what it meant to Partner and me — or to any other Old Country person — knowing London as we do, recognizing, as it were, each step of the procession, visualizing the crowded streets with a line up of soldiers on either side of the street making a roadway for several miles for the procession to pass through. And the decorations — there would be bunting, literally miles and miles of it, flags from every window and gateway. Fairy lights strung across the street, little children laughing and shouting and waving miniature flags.

And then the Royal carriage appears! Of course, only about one out of every hundred is able to catch a glimpse of the King and Queen, but enthusiasm is infectious, and when one shouts, they all shout and cheers and applause are deafening.

London — Cockney London — is hard to beat for enthusiasm, and in a crowd you would hear many examples of Cockney wit and humour — the most unconscious humour in the world. Something like this would be heard on every side:

"'Ere comes 'is Royal 'ighness! Come on boys — give 'im a cheer — long live the King — Gawd bless 'im!"

"Old George ain't 'alf a bad sort, that's wot I say!"

"'Ere, move over a bit and give us a chawnce to use me blinkers — 'o d'yer think yer are — 'e's not your blooming uncle, is 'e?"

Coarse — yes — but do you doubt their loyalty? Listen to their cheers — that's your answer.

Realizing by the broadcast the denseness of the crowds, we were not surprised to hear the announcer say, "Many people have been standing here all night, there have been many casualties, and people are still being carried into the Law courts," presumably being used as a casualty station.

We enjoyed this service in St. Paul's, and even over the radio we recognized that queer reverberation which is peculiar to any service — or, in fact, any voice — spoken within St. Paul's Cathedral.

This afternoon we listened breathlessly to the King's reply to his people, his voice husky with emotion as he responded to the tremendous ovation given him from all parts of the world. Partner even stayed in from the field to hear the broadcast — something quite unheard of for him — and if at any time he spoke, it was only to tell our young son to be quiet.

And what can we glean for our comfort from these Jubilee celebrations? Surely, even though we may possibly be on the brink of an international crisis, surely there is some comfort in the thought, that, hard times notwithstanding, the loyalty of His Majesty's subjects is still, as ever, undeniably beyond question.

By the way, I have started a new hobby — I am making a scrap-book with pictures of the Royal family. It occurred to me there was no better time than the present.

August 20, 1935

Here follows a play in one act. Enter Son, after answering the telephone.

"Whoopee-e-e … hurrah … three cheers …!"

"Good gracious, boy, why all the excitement — what's the matter?"

"There's nothing the matter — it's just that the threshers will be here about Tuesday!"

Collapse of mother . . . curtain.

Yes, it's a fact — the threshers really are coming, but we are not quite sure about the day. Of course there is nothing so very wonderful in the fact of their coming, but when the woman of the house is still supposed (supposed, please note) to be in bed, it makes rather a difference, doesn't it? Partner had not even mentioned to me the possibility of their coming. I suppose he thought what I didn't know I couldn't worry about. But apparently the neighbours knew, as feeding the men has been practically arranged and most of the load been taken off my shoulders.

Partner is obliged to thresh because he couldn't possibly get all the stuff in the barn. Why, the sweet clover alone would need a whole barn to house it. Oh yes — that sweet clover . . . It really is cut, and I don't believe Partner had half as much trouble as he expected to. But I don't really know, because, to tell you the truth, I didn't ask!

You know there is sometimes that in a man's face which keeps one from asking questions, and when Partner was cutting the clover I found it to be just one of those times. I used to watch him from the window, sometimes, as he drove the horses on the binder. Generally he would go up the field very well, but coming down his speed was slow and his stops were frequent and lengthy. And so when he came in at noon it really seemed wise to talk brightly about the weather or about the latest news of the day and discreetly ignore the very existence of any such thing as sweet clover.

And now it is going to be threshed and we shall soon know if the game was worth the candle.

There has been some high financing going on here this week — it was just too funny for words. A dealer in scrap-iron came in, ready to buy any old iron. Partner told him he had not any collected, but if he came back in the afternoon there would be some ready for him. Then Partner turned to our young hopeful and said, "If you collect up all the old iron, you can have what you get for it. This man here says he will give you twenty cents a hundred pounds for it."

Oh my — I don't believe I ever saw a boy work harder or faster before! From every corner of the farm, east, west, north and south, scrap-iron appeared as if by magic. Trip after trip our young lad made with the perspiration running in little rivulets through the red iron rust, covering his hands and face. By three o'clock there was quite a large pile of iron collected outside the driving shed, all of which had been carefully weighed as each load was brought in.

While all this was going on outside, Daughter was in the house collecting rags, for which the man had promised to pay one cent a pound — and I am thanking fortune that I was around when the rags were collected, so that we still have something to wear!

Altogether there were forty pounds of rags and six hundred pounds of iron, When the junkman came along he handed over forty cents to Daughter without a murmur, but began to pick a quarrel about the scrap iron, which he said only weighed five hundred and eighty pounds. From what I gather, something like the following conversation took place.

Junkman: "I'll give you $1.10 for the lot, and dat pays you well, eh?"

Our Boy: "Nothing doing. You give me $1.20 or you don't get my scrap iron."

Man: "Well, I don't know as I really want it."

Boy: "All right, then — you don't have to take it. There's another man coming in to-morrow. He'll give me just as good a price as you will."

Man: "Oh, well, here you are then — but it's too mooch — too mooch!"

So saying, our worsted friend of the road reluctantly handed over $1.20 to our young bargain driver, who was obviously gloating over the deal.

This little episode was quite a revelation to me, as I had no idea our boy was capable of standing his own ground so well. I thought the man would put it all over him when it came to making a deal, and I was amused that he could not quite manage it. We don't want a niggardly boy, but we certainly prefer that our boy should be able to stick up for himself when the occasion demands it.

SEPTEMBER 17, 1935

Yesterday we had some neighbours drop in — two boys who are quite good mechanics — so after they had been fed, I asked them to look over the car and see if they could get her started. I knew there was nothing really wrong with her but since she had been sitting in the garage since last Easter, it was only reasonable to suppose she might be a little difficult to get stated.

The car was pushed out, and then one of the boys tried to crank it, but oh — was she tight. Not one inch would the crank move. The boys kept trying it in turn, and Partner tried until he was breathless and red in the face. One boy even stood on the crank and jumped up and down, and I certainly expected something would give or break. But nothing happened.

Then they did things to the engine, cleaned this and oiled that, scraped dirt and oil out of the carburetor, cleaned the spark-plugs and oiled everything in sight and out of sight, as the motor was absolutely bone dry. After that they managed to get things moving a bit, but to make a good job of it Partner hitched the team to the car and towed her up and down the field. One of the boys was at the wheel and, oh, joy, when they came down the field I could hear the engine running.

Good old Optimist; you and I together will never say 'die' until we have to, will we?

Really, when I heard the purr of her engine, I felt as proud as if I were Sir Malcolm Campbell and owned the Bluebird. When the boys were working with the car they said, "Gosh, I never knew a car like this before!" and that is what I often think, but I guess what we mean is not quite the same.

After she was running properly, the boys drove down town and got The Optimist fixed up with gas, oil and another battery, and then I told them to leave her in the lane and I would put her in.

When I was quite alone, I got into the car. She was dirty, dusty and her windows were all spotty and smeary, but I sat in the driver's seat, with my hands on the steering wheel, and I thrilled with the thought that the time had come when The Optimist and I could be on the road again — two optimists together!

Of course we shall have to go slow and not any great distance from home — which, perhaps, will be just as well for both of us — but even if we do no more than run into town, it will just be one grand adventure after weeks and weeks of enforced inactivity. I badly wanted to laugh when the doctor gave me permission to drive — just to his office and back again, so he said, because I thought if he had ever driven a Model T he would not have given his consent quite so willingly. Anyway, when I do go to town I shall be very careful not to park within sight of the doctor's office, in case The Optimist may need a little friendly help from the crank.

NOVEMBER 5, 1935

Now, to be absolutely up to the minute, one really must talk about the earthquake. And why not? It seems everyone has a different story to tell. One of our neighbours said she felt as if she were being rocked in a hammock, while another one knew nothing about the earthquake at all!

Our experience was this. Everyone in the house wakened as the house rocked and found his or her bed also shaking, windows were rattling and dishes clattering. Geese were squawking and hens cackling. Son called out from his room — "Whatever is happening? I was pretty near thrown out of bed!" Daughter thought someone had got into the house and was playing a Halloween trick on her!

Partner donned his boots and outer garments in double quick time and was away to the hen-house before I could say 'Jack Robinson.' Not that I thought of saying Jack Robinson, but you know what I mean.

I don't know what Partner expected to find at the hen-house, or what he thought he could do — he says his first thought was chicken thieves. Anyway, when he got there he found the 'quake had shaken open the hen-house door and half the birds had flown, walked or been otherwise removed to the outside of the hen-house, and were walking around in the starlight, telling the world about it. Since there was very little Partner could do to help the poor biddies, he was soon back to the house, and after a while we all settled down again and went to sleep.

I have since heard of people who were so frightened they got up and would not go to bed again, but after all, what good could anyone possibly do by staying up? Personally, I felt much the same during the earthquake as I used to feel during an air-raid in England. One was just as safe in bed as anywhere else. Of course, if we were in Montana it would be a different matter, but here in Ontario where it is not expected that earthquakes will seriously endanger life, doesn't it seem rather foolish to get worked up to a state of high nervous tension?

I have heard some people say they thought the end of the world was coming. Supposing it were, we couldn't stop it, could we, and after all, isn't it showing rather a lack of faith to get so scared about it?

Perhaps I am a bit of a fatalist over things like this, because I do feel that one cannot run to cover with any certainty of safety, as one has no means of knowing at what spot safety may be found, and so wherever one happens to be is just as good a place as any other. I knew people in England who left their own homes during an air-raid to run a house where there was a cellar, and they were killed as they ran through the street. The same thing might happen in an earthquake, so why not just stay where we are and keep cool about it?

Friday morning the children were quite anxious to get off to school — to swap stories, I suppose. In the driving shed they found the 'quake had knocked down their bicycles. One man near here had his straw stack toppled over, and in his brother's house the wallpaper cracked on the freshly-papered walls. On the radio that morning I heard some wise wag assert that in New York one had even had his hand shaken!

An earthquake is hardly a thing to joke about, and yet slight tremors such as we felt in Ontario certainly produce some ludicrous situations, so that when the worst is over and no one seriously hurt, may we be forgiven if we see the humour of it as well as its more serious aspect?

Speaking of 'seeing,' I am up against a problem right now. My oculist, instead of giving me bi-focal glasses, thought fit to give me special glasses for reading and close work. Until now, one pair of glasses has served every purpose and so now I am trying to get accustomed to this awful business of changing my 'specs' about forty-seven times a day.

The trouble is, I never seem to be where the other glasses are when I want to change them, and yet if I go where the glasses were, they are always somewhere else. Now, that may sound like Irish or Double-Dutch to some people, but anyone who has had the same experience will know exactly what I mean.

Then again, the difference in the two sights is a nuisance. For instance, I stop to look at the morning paper with my reading glasses — that is, supposing I can find them — and then the telephone rings, or I smell my cake burning in the oven — and I run to attend to whichever it is — with the same glasses on, of course, and after that I get on with my ordinary work, and after awhile I begin to wonder why my head aches. I have still another pair of glasses — clip-on sun glasses for driving — which I usually carry in my purse. The other day I sat on my purse, and it did not agree with the glasses.

These personal appendages are altogether a terrible nuisance. The dentures, for instance, which have to be removed when taking an iron tonic. Yesterday I got kind of mixed up when taking my medicine and instead of the dentures, I removed my glasses! And then the whole family came running to the kitchen to find the reason for my mild attack of hysterics!

DECEMBER 3, 1935

If you were to walk into our house now, you would probably be quite surprised to see wires strung across the room and perhaps you might wonder if anyone was attempting exercises on the flying trapeze. Closer inspection would reveal that these wires are far too fine for any such act — in fact, they would hardly be strong enough for a bird to perch upon, but they are strong enough to carry sound, and that is just exactly what they are there for.

You, see, our son is sometimes of an inventive turn of mind, and it occurred to him that, although the radio couldn't be moved — at least not without considerable trouble — the loud speaker might be. So he went to his treasure chest and brought out yards and yards of cotton-covered wire — where he got it or when, I don't know — but he was able to produce it, anyway. Then he disconnected the loud speaker cord from the radio horn, joined a strand of wire on to each point, covered it with electric tape, attached the other end to the horn again and walked triumphantly away with it through the dining-room, through my bedroom and into the living-room.

Back he came again turned on the radio key, paused a breathless second and then, "She works — she works!" he shouted in delight, and after he had finished making a noise about it, we could hear sweet strains of music emanating from the living-room.

So now we are able to enjoy the radio wherever we happen to be. Not only can we carry it into the living room with us, but I can have it right in the kitchen and do my washing to the accompaniment of a Gilbert and Sullivan opera, straight from Buffalo.

I am not sure that it speeds up the work at all though because, last week for instance, I just had to hear 'Patience' out to the end before I went to hang the last lot of washing out. Maybe you will think I don't take my work seriously enough, but 'what is life if full of care, we have not time to stand and stare' — or listen!

Of course, not knowing anything about electric contraptions, I told our young son to call on our local electrician, tell him what he had done, and ask if it were perfectly safe. He came back with the report that it was all right as long as two naked wires were not touching.

While we are on the subject of inventions, let me tell you this one. Since by doctor's orders I am not allowed up very early in the morning, Partner has taken to making the morning porridge, and, until he became experienced in the art, it was sometimes too thick and at other times too thin. When it was too thick — well that was easily dealt with — but when it was too thin, and I did not know it until breakfast time — well, it was quite a problem to know how to thicken it and have it ready in a few minutes.

But one morning I hit on the right idea, at least it seemed so to me. All I did was mix up a tablespoonful of corn-starch with a little cold milk, stir it into the porridge and — hey presto, the trick was done and at breakfast time I was able to compliment Partner on the splendid porridge he was able to make — and he was none the wiser!

But there is still one thing I wish someone would invent — it is quite beyond me — and that is some device guaranteed to wake one up at a given time when necessary. An alarm clock is worse than useless — so we have found. The circumstances leading up to this desire are as follows.

Partner and our young son were offered a ride to the Winter Fair. Neither of them had ever been, so they were only too glad to accept the offer, and I was just delighted to see Partner get a break for a change. Of course it meant an early start and early rising to get the milking and chores done. Partner carefully set the alarm overnight. I don't know what his feelings were about it, but I went to bed absolutely scared in case that alarm should go off and we not hear it.

Well, when I had been asleep hours and hours — or thought I had — I wakened and my first thought was the time. "Wh-what is the time?" I asked waking Partner. "Oh, go to sleep," he answered, after looking at the clock. "It's only half past one!"

So I went to sleep and next time I wakened, of course I knew it was morning. Partner was sleeping peacefully. "The time — look at the time," I said, waking him again. Partner groped for the clock hurriedly. "Say, what's got into you?" he exclaimed in disgust. "It's only five past three!" Repentantly I turned over and went to sleep again.

Next time I wakened I knew I had only been asleep a little while, so I lay there not daring to ask Partner the time again. But after a while I became a little uneasy and at last I said, not much louder than a whisper, "Is it nearly morning yet?" Partner was awake in an instant, "Holy Moses," he exclaimed, "the alarm must have gone off an hour ago! Now why the dickens did you worry me about the time in the night, and then let me oversleep in the morning?"

But all's well that ends well. By dint of hurrying and helping, the two of them managed to make the grade and only kept our friends waiting five minutes at the most.

JANUARY 30, 1936

Sometimes one is almost stunned with the thought of the possibilities that lie in the unknown future. Last week as I wrote, news had just come through of the death of Rudyard Kipling, and before my article was actually in print, every corner of the

British Empire was shocked at the sudden death of the late King George V.

The very suddenness of his passing makes one realize the significance of the fact that not even the King, when the time comes for a Higher Calling, can be held back, either by the skill of his physicians or the prayers of his sorrowing people. We may truly say of our late King — greatly he lived and peacefully he died. A King loved and respected wherever his name was known and, in his own words, "A friend to all, an enemy to none."

Before the almost unbelievable announcement came of his death, we heard on the radio the latest bulletin of his condition, following which a band played, with heart-breaking solemnity, "God Save the King!"

How often we hear the National Anthem and how little attention we sometimes give it, but last Monday, as we listened, we were struck with the significant simplicity of every word. Our King was dying, and in our hearts was the thought, 'God save our gracious King, long live our noble King.' It was the prayer of every loyal subject, that even yet, he might be spared 'long to reign over us.'

But even while the anxious thoughts of so many millions of people were with him, our beloved King, his life swiftly drawing to its close, waited — even as kings must wait — for the loving summons of a King, even greater than he, calling him home.

Following the death of the King, it was so very obvious how greatly he was loved and respected that I could not help thinking how remote was the possibility that Great Britain could ever become a Republic. We hear rumours now and again that the British Empire is splitting — rumours like that will, no doubt, be heard to the end of time. Every age has its agitators and its soap-box orators.

I remember, as a child, being terribly upset because I heard someone say there wouldn't be a King in England much longer. That Royalty had had its day and that we were fast approaching the eve of a democratic era. It worried me then, but it doesn't worry me now, because I do not think there is any fear of Great Britain becoming a republic, when the passing of a Sovereign is such a real grief to the common people and when the ascent to the throne of a new monarch is the occasion of nation-wide rejoicing.

Looking back over the years, one of my earliest recollections is that of playing in the drawing-room at my home in England. My brother and sister came in, dressed for going out. They had booked seats for a theatre that night. Someone ran in with the news that the Queen was dead. My mother cried, my brother and sister, to whom a theatre was a great treat, took off their things without a word. Everyone was stunned into silence.

Strangely enough, King Edward's death I do not remember so clearly, except that, at the time, I was serving in a millinery shop and the shop was almost besieged with women wanting to buy black hats. I was serving one lady, for whom I could not find a suitable hat. She followed me wherever I went.

"Look," she cried suddenly, "there's one you haven't shown me," pointing to a wide-brimmed hat in the corner of a glass case.

"I'm sorry, madam, but that is my own hat."

"Never mind — let me try it on. I will pay you for it. I simply must have a black hat."

And so, rather against my will, I gave in and sold the customer my own hat! After all, her need was greater than mine, since I was only a young girl. But still, it was with rather a guilty feeling that I attended, with my mother, a memorial service for King Edward VII, and wore a white hat with a broad black band.

That was twenty-seven years ago, but the heart of the British people is the same now as it was then. There may not be the same rush for black hats in this day and age, but the sense of loyalty remains unchanged.

And what of the new King? Partner has been asked that question a good many times, because, while serving in France during the Great War, he was fortunate enough to see the then Prince of Wales, upon several occasions. And Partner says that although enthusiasm ran high among the soldiers and villagers wherever the Prince happened to be, yet the Prince himself was happy to serve as an officer with his fellow officers. It can certainly be said of him, that through travelling and through association with people all over the Empire, in every phase of life, our new King, through personal contact, has come closer to the people of his great Empire than has been possible for any of his predecessors.

FEBRUARY 20, 1936

Partner is very tired and very busy. The continued cold weather makes a lot of extra work and hard work in cold weather uses up twice as much energy as hard work in any other kind of weather. The spring calves have also started to arrive, which means warm water to be carried to the stable and little calves to be taught to drink.

However, whoever else is tired of this weather, the children certainly are not. Sometimes I look at the weather rather dubiously as they prepare for school, but not so the children — I don't believe they could be bribed to stay at home these days. Generally there is an outcry when I insist on extra sweaters and scarves and our young son usually arrives home with his wind-breaker flying open and his scarf in his pocket. Cold? — oh no, that's just a rumour!

Sometimes I am glad I don't have to go out, and other times I envy their young vigorous spirits. Oh well, maybe I'll be young myself next year. 'May I grow "young" growing old' — why not? I am a firm believer in age being a state of mind rather than of years.

Speaking of age reminds me of a few things that came to light yesterday when I was looking through a box of long-forgotten oddments for something which I thought was there. Among the treasures brought to light was a pair of radio ear-phones, which Son promptly seized upon with a shout of delight. I did not quite share in his excitement at first, but since they have been attached to the radio, I am beginning to realize they were quite a find. Now we shall not be required to listen to Orphan Annie, Dick Tracy, Buck Rogers, Popeye and other radio classics as has been our habit in the past. Son can now enjoy them to his heart's content in solitary bliss.

To-day when I walked into the dining-room Partner was trying the ear-phones on himself. He did not see me come in, so I slipped quietly over to the radio and turned on the volume full blast, or nearly so. Anyone who has ever tried ear-phones will know what it sounded like!

Another treasure the box produced was a piece of black spotted net.

"Whatever is that?" asked Daughter.

I laughed. "Wait a minute and I will show you," I answered, going off to my bedroom and taking the net with me. Presently I returned, dressed up as a 1906 model with my black hat and a black net veil over my face, neatly twisted under my chin to keep it tight and shapely, just as I remember my mother wearing her veil all those long years ago.

Oh those veils! My mother would have thought it almost indecent to have walked out down the street without one. Now they are a curiosity and an occasion for hilarious laughter when produced. Now, it would seem that veils, bonnets and widow's weeds have passed into the limbo of forgotten things.

Well, well — so this poor old world has once more passed over the critical day on which it was supposed to end. But strangely enough, the man who prophesied its demise did not omit to place his milk bottle out on the doorstep just the same as usual!

Which reminds me that, when we were out West, some of our neighbours, who had adopted the faith of an unorthodox religion, prophesied the end of the world would come on a certain day in 1922 or 1923, I forget which. They were farmers like ourselves, so after Partner had listened to them discoursing along these lines for quite a while, he turned to the speaker and said, quite quietly, "Well, if the end of the world is coming next fall, why are you going ahead with your spring seeding?" There was silence. Strange, isn't it, how illogical these so-called prophets are in their own actions?

To change to a lighter topic. Last week I had the offer of a trip to the city, and fifteen minutes to get ready in! Did I go? Did I? After having only been out of the house three times since Christmas, I certainly did, and I was also ready at the appointed time.

Added to the pleasure of the trip was a visit to a picture show to see 'Magnificent Obsession.' Having read the book some time ago, I was more than anxious to see the picture. It was just splendid and surprisingly humorous in places. The screen production was also very different from the book. Now I am hoping that somehow, somewhere, I shall be equally fortunate in seeing 'A Tale of Two Cities,' which I predicted long ago would appear on the screen some time or other. Isn't it splendid that we are now able to see such worth while pictures in our theatres?

APRIL 9, 1936

Well, we breathe again! The music festival is over for another year, so there will be no more need for Partner to come the heavy father with our son when, instead of going to choir practice, he wants to go to the bush and watch the tractor-man saw lumber. Or go to the dentist — have a tooth out or one filled — anything rather than practise. Is such an attitude typical of boys in general, I wonder, or just our son in particular? It seems like a very lazy attitude — to want results without the trouble of working for them.

Generally speaking I think it is a great thing for children to learn music, either vocal or instrumental, but at times I have been tempted to wonder and wonder seriously, whether, in regard to musical festivals, the game is worth the candle. It means a tremendous amount of work for the teachers, a lot of coercion from the parents and a marked degree of nervous tension in the children.

And so I get these spasms every so often, right up to the time of each festival, and I ask myself, "Is it all worth while?" And then comes the festival. I go, generally as often as I can. I listen to the children singing and playing with varying degrees of proficiency. I watch the easy grace with which some of them face the audience and I remember from year to year, the individual performance of a good many of the children and note also their yearly improvement. By the time the festival is over I am absolutely in favour of its continuance.

A feature that has pleased me so much the last few years is the inclusion of high school entries in the festival. Until music was encouraged in our high schools I could not see the sense of spending much time or money on it in public schools because, just as children were getting some benefit from music being taught, it was dropped — rather like kindling a fire and after it was going lively, putting it out again.

But now things are much better. In public school children are able to obtain at least a rudimentary knowledge of music. They are encouraged in solo work. They learn to overcome natural timidity and stage fright, and by the time they reach high school, their interest in music helps them over that difficult period in which a growing boy or girl is so urgently in need of self expression.

If I may be permitted a personal allusion, I would like to tell you something about myself. When I was a child — say from five to eight — I was desperately fond of music; so fond of it that I could hardly bear to hear it. That may sound like an exaggeration until one takes into consideration that I was also unusually reserved. Not for worlds would I have anyone see me cry so when my mother sat at the piano and my brothers and sisters and their friends would crowd round her, singing hymns or the old favourite songs, it was generally too much for me and I would run from the room and hide and oh, how I would cry! But no one ever knew it.

Then came the time when the piano was taken away — it really belonged to my aunt. I don't remember how she came to leave it with us but I well remember it going away and my mother crying and saying it was like a coffin going out of the house. It was an apt description, for music, which within our home had become a living thing, was dead.

Now supposing music, as it is taught in our schools to-day, had been taught in the school that I attended. (It was taught but only as chorus work.) Supposing I, as a child, had been encouraged to sing or play as I longed to do, but dare not show it through nervousness. Perhaps through music I might have

been taught to overcome that dreadful unnatural childish reserve and might not now look back with an ache that almost
hurts because of the opportunities that I never had.

Because of the musical facilities in our schools to-day
and because of the platform training made possible through
musical festivals throughout the Province, the children of
to-day, when they are grown to men and women, will not
have to look back and regret not having taken better advantage of it.

However, I do think if music is included in the regular
school curriculum it should also be included as one of the necessary qualifications for teachers applying for general school
work. And if music is recognized as having an educational
value then why should not time be allowed for extra practice
during the school hours in preparation for the annual festival?
After all, children are only children once and they do not have
any particular fondness for anything which robs them of their
playtime. I believe most of them have a natural love for music
but care should be taken by music teachers not to defeat their
own ends by driving the children too hard.

April 23, 1936

I foreswore house-cleaning a few weeks ago, intending only to
work in the garden — in the nice warm sunshine, of course —
but now, in despair, I have foresworn the garden and taken to
the house-cleaning! At least I have got so far as house-clearing

— and considering none of the rooms were spring-cleaned last year I have a nice little job on my hands.

I am not quite sure that the children appreciate my new-found energy, because I am continually finding jobs with which I need some help.

House-clearing may be hard work, but it's lots of fun, too, and full of surprises. Every now and then I turn up something about which I had completely forgotten. Here is a paper, there a magazine. I look them through — wondering all the time what there was in them that I particularly wanted to save.

How strange it is that what attracts one's attention at one time ceases to interest at another. This clearing job really shouldn't be hurried. One should have time to sit back occasionally and enjoy reminiscences which seem inseparable from this job. There are things which we know it is foolish to keep. Perhaps they are no earthly use and never will be, but there is a happy memory connected with them, and so if we can get up courage to throw them out, we should be allowed a little time to be foolish and sentimental before we turn them over to the discard of unwanted things.

This is supposed to be a common sense age in regard to keeping house. We know, to be modern, everything in the house should be of some definite use. It is an age for space and freedom. No cluttering up of cupboards with odds and ends that have only a sentimental value. If we don't want a thing ourselves then we should give it away to someone who can make use of it.

Yes, of course we should — it is an excellent theory and I quite agree, but still, show me the mother, who when opening up an almost forgotten box and finding a pair of baby's shoes, can, willingly, give the wee things away for another baby to wear. Perhaps she remembers it was these very shoes that her first baby was wearing when she took her first steps alone. Well, yes, I must confess it; I have a little pair of shoes tucked away. I have never yet come to the point where I can bear parting with them. Any other baby things — yes — but not those shoes and my reason goes back a long, long way.

When I was about six there came a woman begging to my mother's door. I can see the woman now. She was pitifully ill-clad, and she had in her arms a baby about a year old, very thin and whimpering with the cold. My mother took them into her cosy, warm kitchen, and while they were having a meal, I followed my mother upstairs while she hunted up clothes for the child.

There was a chest of drawers in the hall, and from the bottom drawer mother took out little garments, one by one. She managed very well until she came to a little pair of red slippers, and then, with the wee slippers in her hand, she knelt on the floor and cried — and I wondered what it was all about! All the other garments were given to the poor woman, but not the slippers. You see, it was only six months since my baby brother had worn them for the last time, and he had always been so proud of them — I suppose the bright colour attracted him.

So perhaps it is on account of the little red slippers that my baby's shoes assume special significance for me. One should avoid sentimentality, I know, but I rather think there is a thin spot in everyone's armour, don't you? With me it's baby slippers. With you — well, you know better than I do, don't you?

One thing is certain — the rising generation will not have the same incentive to hoard as our mothers had, because what we buy to-day, or even make — isn't worth saving. I still have the long, hand-made, hand-embroidered gown my father was christened in, but little dresses do well these days if they last from one baby to another.

And now I have a very appropriate little poem to pass on to you, which I found in one of those magazines I was telling you I rooted out. I wish I could say I wrote it, but I didn't. However, when you are beginning to feel — well, shall we say a little on edge —after house-cleaning activities, just read this little poem and you will know what to do. And by the way — it might apply to the men, too!

HOUSE-WEARY

I am going out! I'm tired of tables, chairs;
I'm tired of walls that hedge me all about;
I'm tired of rooms and ceilings, carpets, chairs,
And so — I'm going out!

Somehow or other what I need to-day
Are skies and birds that carol, winds that shout!
I want Dame Nature's friendship. This I say,
"Good-bye — I'm going out!"

It's just house-tiredness. Trivial hum-drum-strain!
Monotony! But when I've climbed the hill,

My heart refreshed will laugh and sing again,
Dear home! I love it still!

SEPTEMBER 3, 1936

This week has been a period of 'ohs' and 'ahs' accompanied by long-drawn-out sighs and soulful expressions. For isn't it the last week of holidays and isn't it true that in just a few days our poor, defenceless children will be once more enduring the martyrdom of scholastic life? Poor dears — fancy only ten weeks' vacation — it is too bad, isn't it?

Of course there are very few children who will admit they like returning to school but my private opinion is that they are all quite glad to go back — not for the school work, perhaps, but because they enjoy the companionship of their school-mates. Undoubtedly all work and no play makes Jack a dull boy, but all play and no work makes Jack irritable, listless and just not so well as he might be.

Regular habits mean everything to a child's health and that is something that very few of them get during holidays. And I rather fancy ten weeks' holiday for the children is quite long enough for the average mother. She loves the precious darlings — of course she does — every last inch of them, but she can love them just as well when they are out of her sight for a few hours every day. Perhaps she may even love them more because they are away just long enough for her to realize how dreary life would be without them — without their fun and naughtiness and their hundred and one calls for assistance — from the very biggest son to the very littlest girl.

And so parents, children and teachers, say good-bye once more to a long happy summer holiday and find themselves ready and eager to begin again their appointed tasks.

And now to change the subject. I want to tell you about the fun the children and I had last week. All this summer, I would have you know, I have been kind of rooting things out in this house. Poking into boxes and things which have been undisturbed for years. Looking over the white elephants, making use of anything that was useable and discarding elephants that could never be anything but white. In this way I came across a box which my sister-in-law had left in my care.

Generally I am free to make use of anything that is left behind, but for some unknown reason I had never looked in this box. But this time I opened it and what a find! Here was an old, old tea chest, which has been in the Clarke family for several generations. And here were some curios from Switzerland — the Clarke family were fond of spending their holidays in Switzerland. There was a little hand-painted cow or sheep bell; a Swiss scene, painted in oils on a thin slice of wood, presumably cut from a tree grown in Switzerland.

There was also a resurrection plant, which looked like a ball of dry seaweed. This we put into a dish of water, and in a little while it opened up like a brown fern. There were also odd pieces of silver flat ware, some old-fashioned silver bracelets, necklaces and brooches and also two silver watches — and dear knows how old they are. One perhaps is fairly modern, because it is of the keyless variety, but the other is so old that the only way to move the hands is to open the face of the watch and turn the hands with a key made for just that purpose.

A day or two after my 'find,' my brother-in-law happened to drop in for a visit, and he, being the head of the family, was able to tell us what should be done with the various contents of the box. I asked him to take care of the things that were really valuable — that is from a family point of view. The other things he disposed of by giving the silvery jewelry to Daughter, the flat ware and curios to me, and the two watches to our son, with the advice that they were not worth spending any money on.

However, I thought differently, so I took both watches to the jeweller. The jeweller found a key to fit the oldest watch, wound it up and away she went, and my brother-in-law said it had not been used for at least twenty years! The other watch only needed a small spring on the winder. I could not see what use two watches would be to our young son, so I made a bargain with him that he allow me the use of the older watch if I paid for the repair work on the other one. "That's okey-dokey with me," he agreed.

So now he is satisfied, and so am I. I have a watch at last — which is something I have been wanting for years. Oh no, it isn't a wrist watch of course — in fact it isn't even a lady's watch — but it is a novelty and it goes, so what more could one want?

I did have a wrist watch once — Partner bought it for me — but I wore it when I went swimming, and the watch didn't like it!

Daughter has just been reading what I wrote about children being glad to return to school and she waxed most indignant. "That may apply to Public School but not to High School children," she asserted. I wonder if she is right and, if so, why is it? I could understand her saying it is she had failed in her examinations, but she got through, so there must be some other reason. I have also heard a good many other girls say they wish they could quit school. It is quite a problem — does anyone know the answer?

OCTOBER 22, 1936

Yes, we have threshed. Daughter was away in Toronto last week-end, so I spent my Thanksgiving Day all on my own, baking and getting ready for the threshing meals. Tuesday morning, more cooking, and, of course, dinner to set for twelve hungry men, and then what it took me a day and a half to prepare, the men sat down and ate in fifteen minutes!

When we first heard the threshers were on their way, I thought I would not need any help — surely to goodness I could manage one, perhaps two meals by myself. But when the day arrived, I got panicky and was glad to accept the help of one of my neighbour friends. That last minute rush — and really so unnecessary! It is almost impossible for one woman, working alone, to get everything on the table at once — that is, if she wishes to keep the food hot and appetizing. Anyway,

I was glad I had help, especially as the men were through early and we had four o'clock supper.

As for the threshing — it was the smallest we ever had. Even so, it had its compensations. The crop was harvested with far less work; less binder twine was used; the threshing bill was exactly half what it was last year but because of the increase in grain prices, the cash value of the granary contents is as much, if not more, than it was last year when we had such a heavy crop.

Then again, we were able to get all our crop into the barn this year without any trouble at all, which meant the threshing machine only had to come in once, instead of twice — meaning fewer meals, less fuel oil and certainly much less work and worry for everybody.

So you see, there is really something to be said in favour of drought-year crops, after all.

And now we are nearly into Winter again. Isn't it queer how the same old jobs pop up, time after time, like flowers in a perennial border? The jobs lie dormant, just as the flowers do, but with the beginning of each season we find the jobs waiting for us every time.

At this season we start thinking about storm windows, and stove pipes, and turning sheets 'sides-to-middle' and hunting up winter underwear with the hope that it will all last out another season. But somehow it never does — at least not all of it. And oh, those sheets! Does anyone else have experiences like I do? Take Daughter's bed, for example. I change the bed linen and put on sheets, which look as if they are good for several washings yet, but in a day or two, what do I find?

Nothing, but a disreputable rag, torn every which way, and no more like a sheet than I am.

"What on earth did you do with this sheet?" I ask Daughter.

"Oh, I don't know — I guess there was a little hole and I got kind of tangled up in it last night, and it ripped!"

"It ripped did it? Well now, I'm glad you told me, because I might not have known it," I answer, looking in despair at the remnant of a sheet in my hand.

It simply can't be mended, is generally my first thought, and after that I go to work and fix it somehow — perhaps I cut out what good parts are left and put them to the good parts of another sheet equally hopeless, and then the rejuvenated sheet ends its life on Son's bed, who hasn't the same propensity for getting tangled up in things the way Daughter has.

Just lately I have been trying to think out new ways for using old silk stockings. Here is one way, and I think it will make a good, hard-wearing, every-day cushion cover.

Collect your stockings, dye them any colour or colours you wish. Cut into one-inch strips, going round and round the stocking, making one long strip. With two coarse knitting needles, cast on two stitches. Knit one row plain. At the beginning of each successive row increase one stitch until work measures the same as your cushion from corner to corner diagonally. Then knit one row plain. For each successive row slip one, knit one, pass slip stitch over, until stitches are reduced to one. Fasten off. Make other side the same and join the two together.

This makes a square cushion cover with diagonal stripes and would be nice done in two shades of blue, green or whatever colour would go with your furnishings. The silk stockings are easy to work with and as soft as wool.

NOVEMBER 26, 1936

Are we frozen up, I wonder, for the duration of the winter? If we are, I suppose we cannot reasonably expect anything else, but oh, if we could only have cold days without so much wind! However, it is not of weather conditions I write this week, but of my visit to the Book Fair in Toronto. So back we go to Wednesday afternoon in Book Fair week.

Ralph Connor was the second speaker that afternoon. Now I know there are many people who like Ralph Connor's books, and they would probably have enjoyed his address, as he was speaking quite a bit about his own writing and how many of his books came to be written. But as I am not particularly keen on his books, I naturally did not altogether appreciate his address.

Wednesday I enjoyed myself immensely. The first speaker was Marius Barbeau, a French Canadian, and his subject was the folk-lore of old Quebec. Mr. Barbeau felt that Canada is in danger of losing something, which if lost, can scarcely be recovered, and that is the folk songs of the Quebec habitant. (Mr. Barbeau himself has been instrumental in saving folk-lore from extinction in many instances.)

Mr. Barbeau, quite unconsciously I suppose, appeared quite in keeping with his subject. How shall I describe him?

He was not old-fashioned, and yet there was a decided old-world charm about him which appealed to his audience at once — perhaps it was his mutton-chop whiskers!

Mr. Barbeau brought with him a delightful 'old-timer' — a French habitant in native dress, who hailed from Quebec and who sang for us many quaint action songs in a French dialect. The old man was seventy-two, but what a splendid voice he had! Although it was impossible to follow his words, yet through his gestures it was easy enough to understand his songs.

Next on the program, and by special request, was 'Grey Owl.' When Grey Owl began to speak, the microphones were removed, and, as he spoke, the tall native Indian walked backwards and forwards, the full length of the platform. Clearly, unhurriedly, he told us the story of his life. How he had been adopted by the Ojibway tribe and taught hunting and trapping by a very old Indian, well versed in the ways of the wild woods.

Grey Owl, as he became older, lived by the proceeds from the trap-lines just the same as the other Indians, until at last he became intensely interested in the beaver family and formed the determination to protect and preserve wild life rather than destroy it. As his love for the beavers grew, so did his desire to preserve them, and he did for the beavers what he might not have done for himself.

He made tremendous strides towards a better education. He mixed with the white people as much as possible, trying to stir up enthusiasm for his scheme to protect the little beavers.

Grey Owl asks nothing for himself. His only petition is that the natural wild life of our Canadian forests be handed over to the only ones whom, he claims know how to deal with it — the native Indians.

Grey Owl contends that large sums are spent annually by the Federal Government to keep the Indians in idleness — money which might be put to better advantage and the Indians be made happier and more useful citizens, by being allowed to revert to their own natural way of living.

There was no doubting Grey Owl's sincerity and enthusiasm, which appeared to completely captivate his audience, and I rather fancy the time may yet come which will bring success to his appeal for his fellow countrymen and also his beloved beaver.

Grey Owl has a remarkable personality. He has a natural, easy grace, an alert manner, an expression which betokens hidden humour and a physique which bears testimony to the hard outdoor life he has led.

After the meeting that night, hundreds of people gathered round the platform for a chance to speak to Grey Owl, to shake hands with him, and autograph hunters were there to get his signature. I sat back and watched the crowd, and I wondered — is their interest genuine or is it the outcome of curiosity?

To me the Indian is a pathetic figure — a man deprived of his birthright; demoralized by our so-called civilization, with his vitality and physical ability degenerated through an unnatural way of living.

The next day, I was unable to spend much time at the Book Fair, and Friday morning I came home, feeling that my short stay in Toronto had been the most satisfactory holiday I had spent in years.

I have heard 'The Bookmen's Association' spoken of as being no more than a publicity stunt for the benefit of the publishing houses. Perhaps it is — there are tricks to every trade — but even if that be so, it is a publicity stunt that also benefits the public, so why worry?

DECEMBER 16, 1936

What have we been doing at Ginger Farm this week? What has anyone been doing anywhere, on every farm and in every home? What, but wait from day to day for the latest news from England. Some people we know waited with greater anxiety than others, but I think there were very few who were really indifferent as to the outcome of this tremendous Empire crisis.

Not for anything would we have been without our radio during this last week, and there were very few hours during the day when it was not working. Partner would tune in first thing in the morning while he was lighting fires and several times was lucky enough to hear a commentator straight from England.

Of course work had to go on as usual. Even though a King abdicates the nation must be fed, but here's one who did not miss much in the process of feeding or the preparation of food. Thursday morning I peeled potatoes sitting by the radio. From the same position I also cut up meat for stew and skinned onions while Prime Minister Stanley Baldwin delivered his momentous speech to the House of Commons. And of course every night Partner and I had to wait up until the eleven o'clock news broadcast. No, not every night. One night Partner had a bad cold and went to bed early. But I sat up and the news broadcast found me asleep with my head down on the radio — but I came to my senses in time to hear the news, so I did not miss anything after all.

And now it is all over — 'the tumult and the shouting dies' — the British people have 'muddled through' again — and what comes next? What do we feel about our late King? I raise the question because of one or two criticisms which have been very harsh and condemnatory towards our late King. Is such criticism — after the event — really necessary?

In whatever way King Edward offended our principles, whatever he did that caused suffering and industrial chaos among his people, has he not now done his very utmost to restore the Empire to its former status? Most of us felt that his demands in regard to his marriage were incompatible with British principle, but since he has made reparation in the only way possible, surely we should now be able to accept the present situation without further censuring he who brought it about. In any case, to blame the Duke of Windsor for his shortcomings is the same attitude responsible for kicking a man when he is down.

It is hard to imagine who won out in this long and trying ordeal. It is up to us now to do our part — to show that British principle is big enough to include charitable thoughts towards one who we know must have suffered greatly. We approach the season of goodwill towards men — surely our goodwill may extend towards that lonely and pathetic figure — a King in voluntary exile.

FEBRUARY 11, 1937

Will you pardon me if I become a trifle reminiscent in this week's chronicle, because you see, this is our wedding anniversary! We have been married nineteen years. Yes, nineteen years ago this very day Partner and I were quietly married in the Anglican Church in our home town. There were only six people in the church. No one outside of the family knew we getting married — in fact, we did not know it ourselves until the day before. Things like that happen in war time.

The only arrangement we made in advance was that we would get married during Partner's next leave from the Front, but of course we had no idea when that would be. Then, after a year's absence Partner came home — on February 5th — and we were married the next day. There was no fuss and no frills — the only new thing we bought was a Prayer-book.

Of course people in England were on wartime rations, so a celebration spread was impossible. We could only get our quota of food according to the coupon value in our ration book. Our two ounces of butter, quarter pound of tea and one pound of meat per week — and everything else in proportion.

Trades people could not be bribed to give anyone an ounce over their allowance, and ration books had to be presented and stamped before one could buy food and of course the necessary coupon detached by the grocer or butcher. And so, our wedding feast was a mid-day dinner of cold sliced ham, vegetables and deep apple pie.

As I had previously obtained a few days' leave of absence from the school where I was matron, and the ceremony was now over, we felt free to go away on a short holiday — one could hardly call it a honeymoon. Our baggage consisted of a week-end case and our ration books!

When Partner asked me where I wanted to go, I remember saying, "Oh I don't know — let's go to London first, and decide where we want to go when we get there."

So that is exactly what we did, and then, because it didn't really matter where we went, we walked through the city and said we would take the first bus that came along and go wherever the bus went.

And we did, and the bus took us to Dorking, in Surrey about twenty miles from London. Our luck was in. If we had taken weeks to decide, we could not possibly have chosen a more beautiful spot than Dorking. Perhaps someone who reads this will remember Surrey in the days of long ago, and they will remember how peaceful and surpassingly lovely were the walks in and around the market town of Dorking.

After a few days I had to get back to my job, but Partner's leave was not up for over a week, so he visited among his friends and my own.

Then back to the Front again: to the mud, and stench, and thunder of guns and all the stark realities of war.

So there we were, two weeks married and then — goodbye — neither of us knowing whether we were seeing each other for the last time or not.

It was a common enough story in those days and one never knew what the morrow might bring. There was always the dread that some day a telegraph boy would come along on his bicycle, an orange envelope in hand, and in that envelope perhaps a telegram whose message might ring down the curtain on all one's hopes for the future.

Nineteen years ago, and to-day I still feel thankful that the ominous orange envelope was never brought to my door. But in my thankfulness I do not forget others who were less fortunate, and my heart goes out to those who knew the terror of that fatal message contained in the orange envelope. Of course a telegram did not always bring bad news — sometimes it was quite the opposite — but there was always that dread until one had read the message.

It was twelve months before I saw Partner again. The war was over, but Partner's battalion was sent on to Cologne with the Army of Occupation. When he finally returned to England it was February again and another five months passed before we set sail for Canada. But we got here at last. We are still here, and far as I can see, it is here we are likely to remain — so I hope everybody likes us!

Looking back, one wonders, was there ever a period of twenty years so crammed full of world events — such devastating, far reaching events? And looking forward — is it possible to imagine another twenty years equally eventful? One can only conjecture and hope that the British nation will never again know the wholesale sorrow and tragedy of those other years.

And now, in lighter vein. Partner, after the manner of men, completely forgot that to-day is our wedding anniversary!

APRIL 22, 1937

Last Monday I was shopping, and in one of the stores I met our Hen-Rag-and-Feather Man. Said he:

"Meeses Clarke, has you any ole hens at tome that you want to sell? I give you a good price. You let me pick out the hens and I give you one cent a pound extra!"

"Sorry," I replied, "but our hens are having a contest to see which pen can produce the most eggs. We couldn't possibly sell any just now."

"Then you have old rags — yes? And maybe feathers and horsehair?"

"Yes, we have all three."

"Then I come to-morrow, Meeses Clarke. You look out all you got — I take anything at all."

So next day I had a great time! I collected three old bran sacks and into them I stuffed everything that was no longer of any use to myself or anyone else. And I really mean they were of no use, because two or three weeks ago I had gone over all our discarded things and from them had made quite a nice little pile of children's clothing, which had gone into a relief bale to send up North. There were also some feathers which had become moth-eaten and some good clean horsehair.

Along came the H. R. and F. Man. He offered one cent a pound for the rags and feathers.

"And how much for the horsehair?" asked Partner.

"Twenty-five cents."

We were ready for some fun.

"Twenty-five cents — that's not enough. It is worth thirty cents, anyway," said Partner.

"Meester Clarke, at twenty-five cents you getting good money. Me — I make hardly anything. You have five pounds — then I give you $1.25."

"No — $1.50," argued Partner.

The man looked worried. It was evidently a life and death matter to him. We weighed all the stuff and then he said, "The rags, 50 cents; the feathers, 7 cents; and the horsehair, $1.25."

"$1.50," repeated Partner.

"Meester Clarke — I shouldn't do it, but I give you $1.30. That makes $1.87 I give you for ze lot."

"$1.90" I suggested.

"All right, Meeses Clarke, I give you $1.90 and you getting good money. Me — I make nothing at all."

And then having made his bargain, this hard-hit merchant of the road proceeded to tell us some of his business. From his own account he was a benefactor of the human race, paying out exorbitant sums for rags, hens, horsehair and feathers, out of which he made "nothing at all."

It would be interesting to know just how much is made by these men. Not that we worry about their profits — by selling to them we are at least helping them to make a living and ridding ourselves of moth-harbouring space-takers. To say nothing of the fun we get in trying to drive a bargain, being quite sure that whatever we get won't be the value of the stuff we sell.

Yesterday, a man came to the door who had a great line of sales talk. Directly I answered the door he started, "Lady, we have just been on a real big job laying linoleum, and we have a big piece left over, and rather than take it back to the store, we thought maybe someone might be glad to take it off our hands. We'll let you have it at a real bargain price, lady."

"Is it inlaid?" I inquired.

"It's better than inlaid," the man asserted.

I became curious. I wanted to see this linoleum that was better than 'inlaid.' So I went to the car with him.

There was another man in the back of the car, and on the floor was a roll of cheap printed oilcloth! I would imagine these two gentlemen of fortune had bought this roll of oil-cloth cheap and were travelling the country, trying to trade on the gullibility of country people.

We have no quarrel with the rag-man. He is getting an honest living in his own way, but we are incensed with these men who try to pawn off worthless goods.

The most exciting event at Ginger Farm this week has been the arrival of a huge heifer calf — so big that it had great difficulty in finding its way into this world. After the ordeal, neither the cow nor the calf could stand on their own feet, but now the cow is practically back to normal strength and the calf, with assistance, has been on its feet once, for just a few minutes.

I want Partner to weigh the calf as soon as he can. It looks now as big as a calf six weeks old, but of course it hasn't got much flesh on it yet. We are glad it arrived in the daytime, otherwise we should most certainly have lost both cow and calf, too.

We have had small calves and twin calves, but we have never had a giant calf before — and Partner says he hopes we never have one again!

OCTOBER 14, 1937

Daughter just reminded me that I promised to tell you of the latest antics of The Optimist, and that I haven't done it. Well, here goes, because it's worth telling. I don't believe any other car could ever do the things my car does.

The better the day, the better the deed, so it was on a Sunday that The Optimist decided to cut loose.

A friend of mine had a new baby not so long ago, and when Daughter and I set out to see her on this particular Sunday afternoon, the car started without the least sign of trouble and purred nicely along the road, past one farm, two farms and almost three. The sun was shining with unusual brilliance, but yet I noticed the windshield was suddenly covered with rainspots.

"There should be a lovely rainbow before long," I observed. But Daughter was not looking at the sky, her eyes were on the car. "Mother — your radiator is boiling!" she exclaimed.

I stopped and sure enough there was the old 'rad' steaming like a tea-kettle — the raindrops on the windshield were really from the radiator.

I knew there was a small leak, and thought possibly the water had got lower than I realized and that if we filled her up she would be all right. So Daughter borrowed some water and we went on our way rejoicing. Three lots further and the same thing happened again. I rubbed my eyes and thought I was seeing things. However, we only had three more lots to go so we borrowed more water and went on.

We reached our destination, and left the car for the house. Daughter exclaimed — "Just look at that!" I looked, and water was running away from the car in a steady stream. "It must be the tap," I thought, as I lifted the hood. But no, it wasn't the tap.

By this time I began to think it might be as well to visit a garage, but how to get there was the problem, as the garage where I like to get my repair work done is five miles from home. But get there I must, and this is how we arranged it.

We phoned a place about half way along the road, and asked if two pails of water could be brought to the road gate. Before we started, I borrowed a watering can, filled it and took it along with me, and then, after filling the radiator, I got on to the road and drove, as Daughter said, like nobody's business.

Being a light car, The Optimist fairly bounced along the road. The back seat jumped out of position and the jack pump and wrenches rattled together like a truck load of scrap iron. In due time I reached my first stopping place, filled the 'rad' again and replenished the watering can. A mile or so from the garage I stopped again, used the last of the water and went on.

Could I make it or couldn't I? My eyes were fairly glued to the radiator cap. The car was going as fast as I dare drive and only a merciful Providence kept us on the road. But I might say here and now, that I was risking no one's safety but my own. I had dropped Daughter off at the crossroads to go home and get supper. I slowed down at every sideroad and I kept most religiously to my own side of the road.

I reached the garage at last, with the 'rad' bubbling and steaming and water running out as before. I dreaded hearing the mechanic's verdict, because I was quite sure he would say, "You need a new radiator." But he didn't — glad I am to repeat it — he didn't say anything of the kind. He said there were three little plugs connected with the radiator and one of them had rusted, leaving a quarter-inch hole. It wouldn't cost much to fix nor take very much time, but he would have to get plugs from the city, and that would not be until next day.

So Mr. Mechanic took me home again, and I had one grand head ache and did not want any supper, but every time I remember I did not have to buy a new radiator, I began to feel better.

On Tuesday The Optimist was home again, with new plugs and a fresh supply of optimism. Since then she has behaved very well, except that one day she was hard to start — just a fore-runner of days to come when the cold weather will congeal the oil in her works, and Partner will get hotter than a summer day trying to get her started.

And now, what else is there — oh yes, there's Joanna to tell you about.

Our cows were tired of their pasture and giving less and less milk. Something had to be done about it, so Partner bought a fresh cow. As he walked up the lane with her, the children said, "I wonder what her name is?"

"Joanna," I answered, without giving it a moment's thought.

"Joanna?" queried Son.

"Yes," I answered, "the man who owned her was called John, so his cow must be called Joanna."

So Joanna she is, and Joanna is doing very nicely, thank you. She is buying our bread and butter and enough left over to pay for leaking radiators.

October 28, 1937

Are any of you people interested in the stock market, or do you consider it as something that has nothing to do with farming finance?

I believe a good many folk have the idea that, unless you hold shares in some of these big companies — mining or otherwise — then whether they go up or down doesn't make a difference to you. Doesn't it? Listen to this:

We don't hold a nickel's worth of shares in any company that featured in last week's crash, but we do, or rather we did, have four pigs that were being fattened for market. Two weeks ago the trucker came in and said he thought the pigs were a little on the light side and would be better to be kept another week. By the time the week was up, wet weather had set in and it would have been bad business to have a heavy truck came through the mud in the yard. So the pigs stayed with us, eating up more feed and not worrying a bit because the price was dropping twenty-five and fifty cents every day.

By the time we were able to ship them out we got about fifteen dollars less than if they had been sold two weeks previously — although they all graded select. And the live stock drop in price was the direct result of the slump on the stock market. Don't ask me how; I am not well versed in the ways of high finance, but I do know that what I have just been telling you is right.

How and when to market his produce is the farmer's biggest problem. Partner and I often talk this matter over, and we think that if a man is short of money the time to market his stuff is when he needs the cash. Any farmer who has a comfortable bank account can afford to gamble on what he has. And by gamble I mean to sell or hold back as he sees fit — but not the man without capital.

Then again, one often needs money to make money. Lack of funds cripples many an enterprising farmer, who may have the ability to forge ahead, given the opportunity.

DECEMBER 23, 1937

We are having a breathing spell! Most of the extra jobs that come along at Christmas time are behind us, and next week all we have to do is get ready for Christmas — 'all we have to do' — as if that were not enough.

This week has been an extra busy week. Something to do or somewhere to go every day. Monday I was out to a neighbour's helping pack a bale for the West. Tuesday Daughter visited the O.A.C. with the Short Course young people. Wednesday we picked chickens all day and Daughter and I seemed to be washing chicken feet all night. Thursday Partner was away to a wood-bee. Friday I was away on business. Saturday we were all chasing around at home or in town 'redding up' the jobs that had been left during the week.

One of these jobs was packing up and sending off a Christmas parcel to our little niece, aged two and a half. I'm going to tell you about the present, because it was not quite the same as what you might buy in a store and maybe some mother or doting aunt might like to use the idea for some other little girl — birthdays have a way of coming around even when Christmas is past.

When I was in Toronto, I discovered that Anna — my little niece — was just crazy over the Quintuplets, and at one time she had been given a set of Quints and had played with them more than any of her other toys. But, well, you know what would happen with a two-year-old mother of Quints. One by one the Quints got lost, broken or in some way came to grief, but Anne never forgot them or stopped asking for them.

Anne is a little girl who gets plenty of lovely presents, and for such a young fortunate it is difficult to think of something that will please and be a little different.

To give a set of Quints such as one might buy seemed a little too ordinary, so I bought five little composition dolls, all alike, and only four inches high. For each doll I knitted a little dress, wee panties and a crocheted cap with a white tassel on top. Each suit was knit in a different colour, but all of them were edged with white and were made to come off to be washed when necessary. Annette was in pink, Yvonne in blue, Cecille in mauve, Emilie in orange and Marie in yellow.

What to put them in was the next problem. Quints in woolly suits would hardly look well in a crib or cradle! Then I remembered having seen pictures of the Quints, one behind another in a sleigh. So I hunted up a cigar box, made it narrower, and then Son and I, between us, fixed it like a natty little sleigh with the dolls one behind the other, just as I had seen them in the picture, except that our sleigh had wheels on it so that Anne could pull it around in the house. Son made the wheels, complete with tongue and steering gear.

The dolls cost five cents each and the wool was odds and ends I had by me, yet I venture to think our twenty-five-cent present will bring one little girl a lot of pleasure. Don't ask me how I made the suits — I seemed to be casting on and casting off almost at the same time. Imagine the size of the panties for a doll four inches high!

CBL is on the air. That, of course, is no news, but how do you like it?

We have noticed a little difference, but nothing very startling. Some folk say they cannot get other stations near CBL. We get some of them. What we notice most is that the radio squeals if we dial in between stations. The broadcast from CBL is frightfully loud, but for nearly all the other stations we have to turn up the volume just as if the battery were running down. I suppose we shall have to get one of the gadgets they are giving out if we want to hear ourselves speak when CBL is broadcasting. However, we are not complaining — we haven't much use for the United States programs anyway.

Some of them are very fine, we admit, but we prefer advertising in small doses.

As I said before, the Short Course students were given a trip to Guelph and were not home until 6:30 p.m. Daughter is more enthused than ever with the Short Course and quite fell in love with Macdonald Hall. Partner and I are also very well satisfied with the practical common-sense knowledge that she is gaining. Naturally, the course for each subject is very limited — how could it be otherwise with so much ground to cover in such a little while! The girls have just finished the dress making course, and Daughter is the proud possessor of a blouse she made herself, which really looks nice.

Perhaps I should add that I am quite capable of teaching Daughter how to sew, but either she is one of those girls who will not learn at home, or I am one of those mothers who cannot teach her own children.

By the time I get through this 'Chronicle' and sundry letters I shall have writer's cramp. My typewriter is away to the hospital for its annual overhauling and do I miss it! What I should do without it I don't know, but one thing is certain, my handwriting, never anything to blow about, is getting worse all the time through lack of practice. But that's life, isn't it — what we gain on the swings we lose on the roundabouts, or vice versa.

Bye-bye — Merry Christmas once again — and may it be the happiest Christmas you ever spent, leaving in its wake no disappointments and no regrets.

FEBRUARY 3, 1938

We breathe again! I drove to town yesterday to get my car licence without getting run into court. And all the time I was on the road I felt about as conspicuous as if I were wearing a Hallowe'en false face. I imagine everyone I passed was saying — "Look at that woman, driving with old markers — what does she think she's doing?"

You can be quite sure I didn't stay conspicuous any longer than I could help — indeed no! I had our Son put little bits of fine wire on the car before I went to town, so I could wire the new markers on top of the old ones until I got home.

So now we are all set and I can come and go as I please — weather and roads permitting. Right now everything is just about flooded around here — and if it should freeze — oh ... oh!

I suppose everyone is just about on their toes these days to hear the latest news about the Queenston power house.

Doesn't it almost take your breath away to think of the tremendous force of an ice-jam? Anyone who has been through the power house can hardly imagine anything having sufficient strength to cripple the huge machinery that harnesses the water from the falls.

And then, think of the Falls View Bridge — a work of man costing millions of dollars — twisted into a mass of scrap iron by the relentless forces of nature.

It is when such things occur as the Niagara bridge disaster that we realize that man is, and always will be, subservient to a Higher Power.

And while we are on the subject of Hydro power, perhaps I should tell you that Hydro is being hooked up along this line, starting from the cross-roads just above us — so it looks as if I am doomed to go on filling lamps and cleaning glasses for a few more years yet.

This week has been a busy one for our Institute. Monday night there was a social evening — which we were not able to get to. Tuesday, some of the ladies were putting a quilt together that has been made under the direction of our Local Leader, who attended classes for the Home Utilization of Wool project. The work has been most interesting.

Wednesday, Thursday and Friday we were at the quilting. Many of our members were sick and some could not get out, so those of us who were near at hand got together and finished the quilt. Wednesday there was also a committee meeting to arrange for a banquet, for which we are catering, but when I heard Jim Hunter forecast 'zero or lower' for that night, and when I thought of having to walk against the wind from the house to the road, my courage failed me. I tried it one day last week, and it took me at least five minutes before I could get my breath back again after getting to the house. Yes, of course, it is a great thing to be tough and stand all weathers, but anyone who wants my share of the winter can have it.

Daughter is very busy these days with her Short Course work — getting ready for Achievement Day, which, I believe, is to be held very shortly. She has enjoyed all the work so much, and neither she nor I regret that she dropped high school to attend the Short Course.

And, speaking of high school — they are having their own fun at Milton these days. Monday afternoon Son came home in jubilant spirits — the high school furnace had completely 'busted,' and there might not be any school for two weeks.

But the Trustees decreed otherwise. True, it was absolutely necessary that a new furnace be installed, but while the work was in progress classes were to be held in the Town Hall. So, instead of two weeks' holidays, the students had only two days.

"Gee, but we have fun," says our Son. "Yesterday, when we assembled for prayers, first one seat was knocked over, then another and after that another. Then one of the boys saw the blackboard starting to fall — he took a dive to save it and kicked over a chair on the way. Gee — you never heard such a racket — all the kids were laughing to beat the band, and the teachers were laughing, too."

Sounds like a nice quiet atmosphere for prayer and opening exercises, doesn't it? What a grand time the teachers will have with several forms all packed into one room —and what a lot the children will learn. However, these things will happen in the best of well-regulated schools, but it's thankful I am not to be one of the teachers.

Son just came in and interrupted me with this remark:

"You know, Mum, that bridge must be a whole lot stronger than Dad thinks it is — there are great chunks of ice bearing down on it, and it hasn't budged an inch."

"You mean the Niagara bridge?" I inquired, thinking he had just heard more news over the radio.

"No," he laughed. "I mean our bridge over the creek!"

And then I laughed, too — the comparison was just too ridiculous.

MAY 26, 1938

Well, I have got the better of Hitler Mussolini — I mean our belligerent barnyard rooster. I could never make up my mind whether to call him Hitler or Mussolini, so compromised by calling him both. Things were getting worse and worse. One day I went to gather eggs and stayed in the hen-house about ten minutes because I was scared to come out and face Hitler Mussolini. That was the day I mentioned my problem to Partner.

"Why," said he, "you don't want to let a rooster boss you like that. Go after him — chase him around — take a stick to him. Anything so long as you don't let him come after you."

"I do take a stick sometimes," I answered, "but I generally forget about the wretched bird until he flies at me."

"Well, you don't want to forget — you want to start chasing him before he chases you," advised Partner. "And you will soon find he will let you alone."

Although I was a little skeptical, I thought the advice was worth trying, so next time I went out I armed myself with a fly-swatter — that, I thought, was a weapon that would sting but break no bones.

Near the hen-house I spied Hitler Mussolini strutting around as proud as you please. I went straight for him and gave him a good whack across his back. He immediately spread his wings, poked his head forward and was ready for battle, but before he could move I got in another blow. He squawked in protest, and then, without more ado, he turned and fled as fast as feet and wings would take him. I followed him in hot pursuit, cornered him in a fence corner and gave him another whack before he flew over the top of the fence.

And now, if you'll believe me, I can come and go in peace and Hitler Mussolini takes no notice of me whatsoever. He neither comes for me nor runs away, so I have come to the conclusion he is just a mean-spirited bully, ready to boss anyone who is silly enough to let him. All that was necessary was to call his bluff, and then it was quite a different story.

I tell you this because it is quite possible that someone else may have a cross rooster — and where there are children it is dangerous to have one like that around. I remember when Son was about three years old we had a rooster with a quarrelsome disposition, and one day I heard Son screaming and found the rooster had knocked him down and was standing on top of him pecking at his face. It was the axe that cured that bird.

I have to laugh when I think of my battle the other day. It would have looked funny, wouldn't it, if someone had come along unexpectedly and seen me flying across the yard chasing a rooster with a fly-swatter?

One day just recently I had a grand treat. I went to Hamilton with a friend, and on the way in we visited the Rock Garden. What a marvellous sight it is! And yet I still hear of people in this district who have never yet seen Hamilton's beauty spot. I don't think I ever saw the Garden looking more lovely — but then I think that every time. It was an absolute riot of colour — yellow saxafras, mauve ground phlox, a funny little purple flower which I believe belongs to the weed family. There were soulful-looking pansies and huge patches of snow-in-summer and clumps of bright blue caught our eye and we wondered what flower it could be.

"I really must find out what it is," I said to my friend. So we climbed up the steps — and there were plenty of them — and when we reached the nearest clump of blue we found the flowers were forget-me-nots — but a much deeper blue than any we had seen before. Later on we saw some very similar in the market and I bought some for my little garden.

During the afternoon I went to see a friend who has been in the hospital for a long time. Two months *is* a long time away from growing things. When we are able to move around and go where we will, we take all the beauty of spring very much for granted, but those who can only get a glimpse of it from a hospital bed by the window — they are the ones who really appreciate the fact that when God made the world He made it such a beautiful place for us to live in. And he also gave to man intelligence that he might make of barren places such lovely spots as the Rock Garden of Hamilton.

In the years to come there should be no lack of scenery along our highways. Certainly the way the boulevards are being laid out along the new Middle Road and the way the trees have been saved wherever possible shows that considerable forethought has been given the matter in order that the natural scenic beauty of our country will not be sacrificed for the convenience of the travelling public.

And speaking of trees — I made a point of finding out how the Royal Oak, planted in our County Town last Coronation

Day, was coming along. I found it alive and flourishing, with several little shoots on it. A very small tree at present, but it will mean a lot in the years to come.

JUNE 24, 1938

Attention, all you who raise poultry with the idea of selling dressed chickens for market. Some of you, I know, enjoy looking after your birds, but I never heard of anyone yet who was particularly enthusiastic over picking chickens. So I thought this little piece, taken from a United States farm magazine, might interest you:

"An electric dry-plucking machine which will pick a freshly killed chicken in exactly forty seconds was recently tried out in New York City and found practical. The major parts of the machine are a high powered suction fan and revolving plucker plates. The fan ruffles up the feathers and the plucker plates yank them out."

Now, what do you know about that? If we had electricity I am sure I should be making inquiries about this wonderful invention but as we haven't the power to work it, such a machine would be about as useful to us as the fifth wheel to a wagon.

In the same magazine Henry Ford is stated to have said, "The milk cow is going to vanish from the face of the earth." Mr. Ford says more efficient sources of nourishment can be found than is possible from milk and meat. "The same nourishment can be obtained direct from grain and other field crops."

Personally I believe Mr. Ford is looking to a very far distant future. Right now our Bossies are something we don't want but can't do without. Partner often feels if it were not for the cows he could get out to the field so much earlier. But then the cows bring home the bacon — or at least they provide the means whereby bacon — and other commodities — may be bought.

Well, time marches on and here we are right into the strawberry season again. At nine cents a pint we are not likely to be buying many, but Rusty and I go out after wild ones and we have quite a lot of fun. The first time we went out Rusty could smell there was something around that was good to eat so he kept nosing the ground until he found the strawberries. After that it was a race to see which of us would get them first.

I have been wanting to tell you about our Institute birthday party — so here goes.

Our branch, I would have you know, is five years old, and to celebrate the occasion I thought it would be a great idea to have a birthday tea. So we did and I was simply amazed at the way our members turned out to it. There were only a few absentees — some were sick and others had duties that made it impossible for them to leave home.

Our chief visitors were the two ladies who were District President and Secretary at the time our branch was organized. We had our regular business meeting and then a résumé of the activities of our branch during its five years of life. The visiting ladies gave us splendid addresses, following which the meeting closed with 'Auld Lang Syne.' After the meeting, we had a contest in which the ladies were asked to see how many words they could make from the Institute motto, 'Home and Country.'

I had chosen as a prize a lovely tuberous begonia, in full bloom, and the winner was one of the visitors — our former District President. We were so glad.

Tea was served on the lawn — no elaborate spread, but one thing I did try to have especially nice was the birthday cake. It was a six-pound fruit cake, and I made it three weeks ago. But what a time I had to find anything suitable for decorating. I combed the local stores and later the department stores in the city and all I could raise were a few gold leaves. There were decorations galore for wedding cakes but nothing very special at all for birthdays.

However, I managed all right by spacing the gold leaves around the edge of the cake and placing mauve jelly candies in between in the fond hope that they might be taken for thistles. In silver bullets I printed 'S.C.W.I.' — Scotch Block W.I. — and then right in the centre I stuck a Scotch thistle, which I had made by crocheting the green part and making the thistle itself with purple wool. There were two thistle heads and three green leaves.

It really did look rather good. Of course Partner had to laugh at it, and he tells me the reason no one else did was because they were too polite. Oh well, I had lots of fun doing it and all the ladies seemed to be having a good time.

There were around fifty here, and while I was playing hostess, some of them took to the dishes, so that there wasn't so much as a cup and saucer left for me to do. Next day, the flowers which had been used for decoration in the house I took to the cemetery and placed on the graves of members who had passed away.

So that was our Institute party — just a happy little get-together at which, I hope, everyone enjoyed herself. Daughter was home for the occasion — came home on her bicycle — then went to the Junior Farmers' Strawberry Social that same night, and was off on her wheel again by 6:30 next morning.

July 8, 1938

So the *Acton Free Press* has had its sixty-third birthday. Many happy returns to you, A.F.P., and may your pages never grow less nor the interest of your readers diminish.

My, but you're hale and hearty for your age, aren't you? A regular high stepper in fact. I sincerely hope that when I am sixty-three I shall be just as much alive and as interesting to all classes of people as you are to-day.

And we notice the Editor is promising us something new for your sixty-fourth year. Well, I haven't had word yet that he wants 'Ginger Farm' to drop out. If he does, wouldn't that be just too bad, because I really have a very friendly feeling for you A.F.P., even if I do not always do you justice in my column. Right now, I feel as if you were saying to me on this your birthday, "Grow old along with me; the best is yet to be."

Well, I expect there were a good many disappointed people on July 1st, when it turned out to be such a wet, disagreeable day. Dear knows farm crops needed rain badly enough, but had we been given the choice we would have been quite content to wait for it until Saturday.

Partner even took a bit of a holiday that day — an almost unheard of thing for him. Not that we went away any place — Partner just slacked up enough to get in a little extra reading. How that man does love his paper. I often think he must know more about Parliamentary affairs, both English and Canadian, than some of the members do themselves. Besides our daily paper, we have the *New York Times* passed on to us every week now, and anyone who can wade through the *New York Times* is doing something.

You know, it is really rather convenient when two people have different interests, even in regard to a daily paper. Partner, for instance, would never think of reading the Fourth Column of Judith Robinson's witticisms. But I do, and when anything crops up that I know will interest and amuse him, I pass the information along.

Partner, in turn, keeps me well informed with Mitchell Hepburn's lashings and R.B. Bennett's criticisms and other current topics. It saves me a lot of trouble because I do like to keep abreast of the times without spending too many hours poring over newspapers. One might almost call it our co-operative intelligence program.

One thing I read this week and found particularly interesting was a lengthy press report about Grey Owl. I rather fancy in the course of time he will stand out as the most romantic character in modern literature. What a man! Personally I cannot help but admire his amazing audacity. And yet

I don't think of him as an imposter, but rather as a man who longed so intensely to be the character he acted that he finally reached the point where he really believed himself to be the character.

I shall always remember Grey Owl as I saw him at the Book Fair in Toronto, striding backwards and forwards, forwards and backwards across the platform, fired with restless, nervous energy, pleading earnestly that the right to live a natural life might be granted to 'his people.'

Whether Grey Owl was English or Apache, the Indians were undoubtedly 'his people' — his by virtue of adoption — and, except for the environment in which he was born, I would say Grey Owl had far more right to call himself an Indian than has many a native-born Englishman or Canadian to call himself English or British, if by his conduct he has proven himself disloyal to his country.

And now for a more homely problem. I was talking the other day to the mother of one of Daughter's girl friends, whom we will call Lucy. That isn't her name, but I never know who is going to read what I write, so it is just as well to be on the safe side. Well, Lucy's mother and I were talking, and of course I inquired after Lucy, who is two years younger than Daughter.

"Well," said her mother, "I don't know what's come over her lately. Lucy was always easy enough to get along with until just lately, but now she's that cranky and irritable I don't know what to do with her. If I ask her to do anything, she grumbles, and if I don't give her anything to do, she just moons around and gets irritable."

I am ashamed to say I laughed. Having just come through the mill myself I knew exactly what she meant, so I tried to comfort her by saying it is a stage all girls reach sooner or later, and that she will get over it just as younger children get over measles and chicken pox.

Why girls should be worse than boys during adolescence I don't know, unless it is that boys are more active, whereas girls have just reached the age when they are continually being told that they are young ladies now and mustn't do this, that and the other. Anyway, I would rather deal with three boys than one girl when they reach that age.

So cheer up, mothers of growing girls; your daughter's fads and fancies are merely of a temporary nature. In a year of two you will find that she is a real companion to you — a daughter of whom you may be proud.

AUGUST 5, 1938

Here I am, sitting in the garden, a mending basket by my side, in which repose some things recently repaired and others still waiting to be fixed but which I have forsaken, pro tem, in favour of pad and pencil.

Would you believe it, this is only the second time I have sat out in the garden this summer. Maybe I might not be here now if it were not for the men dragging away heavy beams from the wrecked woodshed. Partner has the horses hitched and a logging chain wound around each beam in turn, and as the horses start up there are all sorts of awful noises — crashing, tearing and splintering! If I were in the house I should be running to the door every five minutes to make sure no one was hurt. Being where I can see saves time.

My, such excitement as there was around here last Saturday! An aeroplane landed in a field just back of our farm. Son was out of sight almost before we could get our breath. As soon as we were sure the plane really had landed, Partner and I wandered over, too. We found a comparatively small monoplane — a 'de Havilland Moth,' to be exact — and it carried a pilot and two passengers.

The pilot told me it was a privately-owned machine and that he was the owner. They were coming from Hamilton and going on to Camp Borden. While flying he detected spark-plug trouble and so was obliged to make a forced landing. He had been flying for two years and this was the first time he had been forced down — so he told me.

For about an hour the young mechanic worked with the motor amid an awe-struck group of farm folk — men, women and children. Yes, indeed, when the plane came down, horses were hastily stabled, cars backed out and children came running across the fields from east, west, north and south, anxious to be as close as possible to the scene of action. We all wanted to make sure we didn't miss anything. It isn't every day we have an honest-to-goodness aeroplane land in our vicinity. Beside that, it might have been Corrigan, and surely he would want someone there to tell him where he was.

However, this young pilot, whoever he was, finally gave the propeller a twist and then all three men got into the cabin of the plane.

"Stand back," yelled the pilot to the watching youngsters, "if this propeller ever hits you, it will be the last thing you'll know."

Then he released the wheel brakes, and with a might roar the machine began to roll across the field. Presently she lifted — higher — higher — a little higher all the time, until finally the man-made bird was flying through the air as surely and steadily as a heron on the wing. I say heron because the heron is such a graceful bird in flight and can fly quite a distance with hardly any perceptible movement of its wings.

After the plane had gone we all went back to our various jobs, although I rather fancy, as far as Son was concerned, that only his body came back — heart, soul and mind had gone soaring aloft in the wake of the departing plane.

This has been the week-end of the Canadian Corps Reunion, and, sad to say, Partner has not been among those present. He has been kind of 'touchy' the last few days, and I just know it is because he has been torn two ways. He did not feel he could spare time to go to Toronto, and yet it was quite evident he was longing to be there.

Sunday he might have managed it, but there was no way of going. The Optimist isn't equal to a trip such as that — being somewhat of a veteran herself — and the train and bus service, such as it is — was hardly on a time schedule to suit farmers.

However, there was still the radio. But were we able to listen to the broadcast in peace? Not a bit of it. Just as the bands were playing for the parade after the Drumhead Service, there was a terrible moo-ing in the barnyard. Investigation showed that Nancy had broken bounds and was in the oat field. The rest of the herd were running up and down the lane, trying to find a way through to join her.

So then Partner and I had our own parade — Son was away — and, if you have ever tried getting one cow out of a field while you keep the others from getting in you will know we had a nice little job on our hands. Rusty was well-meaning, but he wasn't much good, because he always barked at the wrong time. However, we got all the cows together at last, and then Partner spent the next half hour trying to find out where Nancy got through.

What a grand sight that Re-union parade must have been. Too bad the heat was too much for Prime Minister Mackenzie King. Hadn't anyone a parasol to lend him, I wonder? When I heard that Mr. King had been overcome, I started thinking of parades I had seen in England during the war — of men lined up for inspection, standing there in the rain or shine, waiting for the official 'Red Cap' to come along.

I remember one time in particular when the Canadian troops, stationed at Sanding Barracks, in Kent, were expecting a visit from General Sir Sam Hughes. The men were assembled at 10 a.m., and for some reason General Sam was delayed, so the men were obliged to stand until early in the afternoon before the inspection took place. It was just such a day as last Sunday — hot and muggy— and many a man must have felt he would give anything to get out of the sun for a while. But no, each man was there — on His Majesty's Service — and could not quit when the command was given.

Come to think of it, Prime Minister Mackenzie King is also on His Majesty's Service ...

It's a good thing to have this Re-union every few years. It's a good thing 'lest we forget.'

AUGUST 12, 1938

It isn't often there is a sequel to my weekly story, but this time there certainly is one.

You remember last week I told you about the aeroplane that landed at the back of our farm? Naturally, after it had taken off again we thought it was the last we should see or hear of the plane or its occupants.

But yesterday, just after dinner, I saw a man walking around in our front clover field. Just walking — that's all — up and down and round and round. I also noticed a big car was parked at the road. Presently the man walked back to the car and then came driving up the lane.

"Could you tell me," he asked, "just where that aeroplane landed last Saturday?"

I thought he was a newspaper man, out for a story, and I laughed as I answered "You are a little late, aren't you?" Then I looked at him again and a light suddenly dawned. "Why, you are one of the young fellows that was in the plane, are you not?" I inquired.

"Yes," he admitted, "and I was trying to find out exactly where we landed — I thought it was in this clover field. You see, I lost my wrist watch while we were down — I think it broke loose when I spun the propeller."

The young fellow's family were also in the car and his mother and father went on to explain that the watch was a good one and had been given to him for his twenty-first birthday. They didn't really think there was much good looking for it but thought possibly someone might have picked it up. I told them I did not think there was much chance of that as I knew everyone left the field as soon as the plane took off.

Son had just gone to town so Partner took the men of the party up to the back field, where the plane had landed. They were gone about an hour, and came back, minus the watch.

I could see they were all rather upset about it all, but I told them not to give up hope until our boy had seen what he could do — I never knew such a boy as he is for finding things — a little while ago he found a lady's watch and chain, which we have turned over to the police to deal with. Just as the car was leaving Son came home, and he was promised a reward if he found the watch.

As you can imagine, a promise like that to a young boy was like a carrot before a donkey. He immediately made tracks for the landing field, asserting he knew exactly where the machine took off. In fifteen or twenty minutes he was back — WITH THE WATCH!

"Call the newspaper office," said Partner. "Those people told me they were going there to put in a 'lost' ad."

Well. I managed to contact my party, and in five minutes they were back again. And were they pleased! Son was given his reward and the promise of an hour's aeroplane ride if he got in touch with them sometime when he was in the city. We did think we should not let him take the money, but after all, he is only a boy, and I am sure they were glad to give it to him. And don't you think that young airman was lucky? Imagine — going for a ride in an aeroplane, losing a watch in the middle of a hayfield and getting it back again.

I am beginning to feel like a real farmer's wife again. Just lately I have been leading the horse on the hay-fork — not for hay, of course, but for grain, as Partner always uses slings to bring home the sheaves. The first time I went out I was greatly amused. Son was telling me just where to let the horse stand while it was waiting and he warned me to keep away from its flitching tail — "If that ever catches you, you'll know all about it," said my son. Then he saw that I was laughing.

"What's so funny?" he asked.

"Nothing, except that you have evidently forgotten when you used to sit on a beam, out of harm's way, while I did the very things you are showing me how to do now!"

Up until this week I simply could not get my courage up to lead the horse again. But now our hired man has gone, and knowing how much longer it takes when there are only two to deal with a load, I volunteered to see what I could do. Having taken off the first load, the rest was not so bad. I knew it was nothing but nerves, but that doesn't make it any easier. Every time the horse pulls on the rope I am ready for it to break — although it is new and perfectly strong.

Or the track might come down, or the swaying fork catch one of them on the head.

Or I might not have strength in my wrist to hold on to the horse if they wanted him to stop suddenly and perhaps cause an accident that way.

Yes, you may think I am foolish, but don't forget there are more accidents that happen in farming than in any other work at all — statistics have proven that to be true.

Now I hear the wagon coming again, so here I go to take off another load. Am I the brave woman!

September 30, 1938

Although I asserted rather boldly a short while ago that 'Business as Usual' is a pretty good slogan to adopt during this critical period when the fear of war is upon us, yet now things are getting so grave I must confess I find it a little hard to concentrate on writing and reading. It is much easier to sweep, dust or sew because then I can let my thoughts wander at will or else listen to the latest press radio news.

However, let's see what we can do. Here is my latest discovery that I have been saving up to tell you. Believe it or not, I have recently discovered that hens can blush! Oh yes, absolutely, there isn't a doubt about it.

Here is what happened.

I thought this would be a good time to sell a few non-laying hens, so one morning at feeding time I carefully looked over my flock with a discriminating eye.

Now, you know a laying hen should be bright of eye and red about the comb and wattles. Lack of colour and a sickly look around the gills are a pretty safe indication that Biddy has quit her job.

"Now then," I said to myself, "here's an anaemic-looking bird. I'll catch her and put her in the pen." But with a hundred acres for a chicken run, 'saying' is one thing; 'doing' is another. By the time I had chased that hen in and out of the hen-house, round the barnyard a few times, back to the hen-house again and out to the kitchen-garden, that same hen was no more anaemic than the red dress I am wearing.

Indeed no — she was positively blushing — and I hope she was blushing for shame, for you would think any self-respecting hen would be ashamed to quit laying with eggs the price they are at present.

Two fall fairs in one week — and ideal weather for both of them — isn't that a record? Unfortunately, we did not get to Acton fair. Partner had such an awful cold at that time, and I did not think it would be much fun going alone. But we were glad to hear there was such a good crowd.

Daughter was planning to come home for this week-end, so on Saturday morning I went down after her. After dinner we all went to our own local fair. There was a real good crowd there, too. The grounds had dried up surprisingly well after Thursday's rain but of course there were a few wet spots.

One of these was close to the race-track fence where we were standing. It wasn't just damp; it was a regular mud-hole but not big enough to attract attention. A race was in progress; people hurried to the fence and first one, then another, would go ker-plunk — right into the mud hole. Men swore under their breath; women walked off hastily, trying to look as if nothing had happened; and children were scolded for not looking where they were going! It was really just too bad, but it was funny, just the same!

Another thing I like to watch is that trial of strength contraption — where men bring a heavy sledge hammer down with a tremendous bang. And the men who puff out their cheeks, get red in the face, stand on their toes and go in for a lot of arm swinging, they are the ones who fail to knock the ball further than halfway.

Son was particularly interested in a model threshing machine and steam engine that was on display. It was really wonderful — an absolute replica of the real thing. And it actually worked. It was made by a man at the CBL broadcasting station. Last night Son was watching the machine in operation and overheard this illuminating bit of conversation.

"That there thing must have took some doing. He was over a thousand hours doing it, so they say."

"A thousand hours. Well, he did d— good; I couldn't have done it in a thousand years!"

Of course, the Women's Institute exhibit at the fair was a great attraction. It was convenient, too. If you wanted to find any of your friends, you would be pretty sure of locating them at the Institute exhibit. But you had to be careful, too — it didn't do to criticize or praise anything too openly, because you could never tell whether the maker of the article thus appraised might be standing within earshot of your remarks. However, there couldn't be much adverse criticism because all the work was so good.

I see Georgetown fair is having a competition for the best woman automobile driver. Now that *is* something! I wonder, would The Optimist and I have a chance?

NOVEMBER 18, 1938

Thursday I went to the International Order of the Daughters of the Empire meeting, where Captain Scott was the guest speaker, and his topic, 'The Crisis in Czechoslovakia.' His address was most illuminating — at least I found it explained many things of which I had previously only had the foggiest conception. Partner also heard Captain Scott at the Canadian Club that same night.

His information was all absolutely up to the minute as he had been in the Sudetenland at the time of the crisis. He told us not to put much faith in Hitler's peace talk, because he thought Hitler would keep his word just so long as it suited his purpose.

Captain Scott's talk was exceedingly thought-provoking, but not at all comforting. For one thing, he did not agree with Chamberlain's foreign policy at all, although he was tolerant in his criticisms, so that in listening one could not help wondering whether Chamberlain was right or it was all a ghastly mistake. Captain Scott cited the case of a working man in Scotland going home at night. His four children met him and cried excitedly, "Daddy, there isn't going to be a war after all!" "No," replied their father bitterly, "not for me — but there will be for you."

According to Captain Scott, the vast majority of people in England are very far from satisfied, and, as if in confirmation of that, the very next morning we received a letter from Partner's sister, living in one of the most dangerous districts in England — the south coast — and she said, "Of course, we are glad not to be at war, but we still think Chamberlain was wrong." The idea back of it seems to be that Hitler was bluffing and if Chamberlain had called his bluff, Hitler would have backed down.

After the meeting I came home, thinking of Captain Scott's words all the time — wondering what was right and what was wrong and whether there was anything that could be done about it. And then as always, I found the only thing I could do was attend to affairs at home for the present, for there, sticking up on the roof were strange looking objects — ladders, brushes, pails and dear knows what else.

While I had been away imbibing knowledge about European affairs, Partner had been busy with affairs at home, and as a result the house roof was in process of being painted. Well, it certainly needed doing all right — in fact it was a case of necessity — unless as an alternative we were prepared to install a regular drip-pan service all over the house.

DECEMBER 9, 1938

One day last week I travelled along the 'King's Highway 25' to the village of Acton, and my opinion of the aforesaid highway was by no means improved as a result of the trip. It is to be hoped when His Majesty King George VI visits this country he will not see what an atrocity has been designated as a highway in his name.

Of course I haven't really given up hope of the Second Line eventually becoming a highway worthy of the name — in fact I quite expect when the next Provincial election is in the offing, the Department will get working in such a hurry the air will be a constant state of reverberation from dynamite charges as they try blasting their way through from one end of the line to the other.

You know, if you think it out, the Government — any government, so far as I can see — is rather like a dormouse. It goes to sleep after an election and doesn't wake up properly until just before the next one. But perhaps I am unjust — I believe the Government Dormouse does break through its hibernation at times — blinks its eyes, shakes itself, sees the necessity of certain things shrieking to be done, for which it puts the working machinery in motion — and then goes to sleep again!

While I was in Acton, the editor showed and explained to me the intricate machinery of his printing office. I don't pretend to understand all I saw and heard, but I understood enough to realize that the type-setting machine, as we have it to-day, is one of the marvels of the twentieth century.

Sometimes I have been surprised, and, I must confess, at times a little provoked, at the things I have been made to say by reason of a misprint. But when I saw the type-setting machine, and realized the expert knowledge required, I marvelled, not at the mistakes that are occasionally made, but rather at the accuracy with which the *Free Press* is usually printed.

Why, it is the easiest thing in the world to get letters back to front, upside down, or even leave out a whole line of print. Dear knows I make enough mistakes in typewriting, so I at any rate should be the last to criticize the type-setter.

And here's another thing. A tremendous amount of work goes into the production of every issue of a weekly paper — and yet we get it all for five cents! That, too, might be figured in as another marvel of the twentieth century.

Our tax bill was so long in coming this year we began to think we were not going to be asked to pay any. But it came at last, and oh joy, it was about six dollars less than we expected — thanks to the School Board in our section reducing the Trustee rate. Township taxation was slightly higher — but not too high when one considers the roadwork that has been done, the increase in relief disbursements and the amount paid in sheep claims.

The county rate is down — and why shouldn't it be, with Old Age Pension and Mothers' Allowance taken care of by Provincial departments? Now if the Provincial Government would just swallow the whole County Council — bait, hook and sinker — there wouldn't be any County rate at all, and we should be saved approximately fifteen mills direct taxation, or about fifty percent of our total taxes. That is, unless my figuring has gone completely haywire.

As far as township affairs are concerned, there are two things we should like to see done, which are entirely within the jurisdiction of the local Council

1. To offer a discount on all taxes paid before the date on which they are due. As a penalty is exacted for overdue taxes, a discount for taxes paid ahead of time seems only logical.

2. To show more clearly on the tax bill what reduction has been made by the government subsidy. A footnote says one mill is taken off, but the account doesn't show it. We would like to see the tax bill made out in full and then the one mill deducted, just as it would be in an ordinary trade account. We think such a way would make it more clearly understood by the public and be altogether more satisfactory. I think it is shown that way in some townships.

Well I guess I've said enough for one week — and I haven't a doubt some of our men folk will say — "Yes, and a darn sight too much!" Well now isn't that too bad!

APRIL 6, 1939

A happy Easter to everyone. But I must confess that as I write it doesn't seem like Easter at all. However, a lot can happen in a week. But cold winds and snow and not being able to wear our new Easter bonnets need not change the meaning of Easter in our hearts.

Looking back over the last few days, it would seem we have passed a week of history-making events. The Spanish Civil War is officially ended, and no doubt those who are still alive wonder what it was all about, and for what purpose women are left widows and little children fatherless.

And surely the Spanish people have reason to wonder why wars should be, more especially when the fighting was within their own country and among their own people. No doubt the common people know little — so very little about what is settled for them by those in authority. They may try to know and to understand to the best of their ability, but they can only know what they are allowed to know. And I don't suppose that is very much. Would it not be awful to live in a dictator country?

Last week there was also Mr. Chamberlain's declaration to the House of Britain's Foreign Policy, and the result is apparently making itself felt in Europe. Mr. Chamberlain certainly left no one in doubt this time as to where Britain would stand should Hitler make one more false move. But what will be Canada's stand in the event of war? No one seems to know. The Federal leaders keep harping on conscription or no conscription — why, goodness only knows. Surely all any loyal Canadian wants to know is whether Canada will be wholeheartedly within the Empire, or will she stand aloof when it comes to a showdown.

Why should we worry about conscription so early in the day, when even England is expecting to depend first on voluntary enlistment? And wouldn't there be volunteers in Canada, too? Of course there would, because every intelligent person is beginning to realize that Canada would be none too safe if aggressor nations made any headway in Europe. The fact that Hitler made a bid for an air base in Iceland should be of particular significance to Canadian people, even though the attempt was foiled. Canada's rich mineral resources would be a nice, juicy plum to any ambitious, power-loving dictator.

Well, maybe you think I have turned politician or something. It isn't exactly that. Fact is, I have started house-cleaning and it is easy to let your thoughts travel here, there and everywhere, when your hand is wielding a paint brush. Painting requires very little conscious thought, providing the subconscious mind is looking after the cracks and crevices and taking care that no brush marks are left.

And there is also plenty of opportunity to listen to the radio. Saturday I happened to tune in just in time for the ominous silence that came after the beginning of Hitler's speech. It was a queer feeling. One wanted to know so badly what was happening. What was Hitler saying? Was the silence accidental or intentional? We know now that the cut-off was by no means an accident.

MAY 28, 1939

We have seen the King and Queen! Yes indeed — after having said so definitely a few weeks ago that we had no intention of making any attempt to see them. Of course we were just scared there would be such a crowd we would not see them anyway. However, we went back on our word and scurried off to Toronto like a lot of other people.

It all started when the SOS came over the air for ex-service men to volunteer for duty to help look after the children in Exhibition Park. That was enough for Partner — he accepted it as a call to duty. When he decided to go he thought I might as well follow suit as there was to be a reserved area at the Park for veterans' families, I knew I should be sure of a good location, so I went.

Most of you will have read or heard descriptions of the Royal Tour, but nothing you can read or hear can give you quite the same thrill as *seeing*. Watching the King and Queen pass by only lasts a moment, but it is a moment that will live in our hearts and memories for the rest of our lives.

Waiting for the parade you grow weary, whether you be sitting or standing. Watches are looked at every little while, but as the hours pass by and the all-important time grows nearer, you forget your aching feet, your tired back and the numbness of your limbs. The King and Queen are coming.

Look — there's a movement down the line! Children are closing in; little flags are flying; voices are raised in cheer after cheer. It must be the King and Queen are close at hand. Yes, here comes the motorcycle escort. The Queen bows and waves her hand, first to one side of the road and then the other. The people burst into wild applause, and one hears on every side, "Isn't the Queen lovely?" "I think she is the most beautiful woman I ever saw."

More Dragoons follow the Royal car; other automobiles come after the Dragoons and you catch fleeting glimpses of Prime Minister Mackenzie King, the Honourable Albert Matthews, Lieutenant-Governor of Ontario, and Mrs. Matthews, Mayor Day, Chief Draper and other notables. You realize important people of the day are right in your line of vision, but you don't give them much attention. You can see Mr. Mackenzie King is looking very pleased — whether with himself or with the acclaim of the people for their Sovereign, you don't stop to figure out. You are too busy trying to recapture details in connection with the Royal couple.

What was the Queen wearing? I couldn't tell. All I remembered was an impression of blue, an off-the-face hat and a beautiful complexion.

The King, to my mind, looked terribly tired, and older and thinner than his pictures show. I could also see a striking resemblance to his brother, the Duke of Windsor. I wondered if his arm ached and if he were hatless for that reason — tired, perhaps, of continually acknowledging cheers from the crowd.

I watched the cavalcade disappear, carrying away a Royal couple who, I felt, should circumstances permit, would talk with you or me in as friendly and informal a manner as our next door neighbour.

Added to the delight of seeing the King and Queen I also found pleasure in sensing the reaction of the crowd. There is always humour and pathos in such a gathering. One woman looked at her watch and exclaimed, "Another half-hour to go!" Her friend laughed, "Well, what's half-an-hour when you have already waited four?"

Came the time when we watched several companies of veterans march by, apparently at full strength. Then came a mere handful of men not more than twenty. The sight was too much for one old soldier sitting on the curb. "Look what's comin' 'ere," he shouted, "must be the Lost Battalion!"

And for pathos! There were the limping men, the armless officer, the scarred and withered faces, the devil-may-care attitude of hundreds of the men hiding God knows what agonizing memories of the last Great War. Men marched past doing their utmost to keep in step, trying to recapture with pitiful mobility something of the courage and vigour that was theirs in 1914-18.

There was one casualty near us — an ex-service man. He just quietly collapsed. It took First Aid men from fifteen to twenty minutes to bring him round. Then he insisted he was all right, and the men wrapped him in blankets and placed him on a chair in the front row so he should not miss seeing the King and Queen. In ten minutes he had crumpled up again. This time they took him away on a stretcher, just before the Royal procession came by.

June 25, 1939

Thursday, you remember, was the day the King and Queen bade good-bye to Canada. I was in Eaton's at the time of the broadcast and heard Their Majesties' farewell speeches from the store's loud speakers. The reaction of the listeners who gathered on the ground floor was something to remember. As long as the studio music was filling in time, people loitered here and there, with a few doing a little buying.

Then came the toast to the King. Sales clerks and customers alike all stood motionless, many of them at attention, and most of the men with bared heads. The expression on nearly everyone's face was serious and thoughtful. The rapt attention with which people listened was the most spontaneous act of loyalty and affection that one could ever wish to see. It was really marvellous. And, of course, the same thing happened after the toast to the Queen.

Then came the speeches. Everyone listened to the King with marked respect and interest. But when the Queen spoke and the crowd listened to Her Majesty's simple, heart-warming, never-to-be-forgotten message of farewell, there were women who furtively wiped their eyes and men who moved away after the broadcast with a far-away almost wistful look in their eyes.

Seeing things like that leaves one with little doubt as to the loyalty of the average Canadian citizen.

The Department of Highways is really doing things. Last week on this road, Highway No. 25 — don't forget — there was a truck and four men. And they were really busy. The men were painting the mail boxes white. They also dug a hole and re-set our neighbour's mail box post that the snowplough had scooped out last winter.

You have to hand it to the Department — it takes everything in its stride, even mail boxes. They made a wonderfully fine job of the painting considering there were only four men to do it. This week they are busy again cutting weeds along the road — not with a mower, but with scythes, and I don't know how many men there are this time, but I am sure they are working very hard.

There are still persistent rumours to the effect that the road will be graded this summer and stone laid down. There are little sticks all along the road anyway — whether they are meant to be grading stakes or whether they are meant as little tombstones for the county road this used to be, it is hard to say. Like Mr. Asquith, we can only 'Wait and See.' To ask questions is useless — nobody ever knows anything anyway.

But no, I'm wrong. If you want to know what the Liberals are doing or intend doing, ask the Conservatives. They will tell you. If you want to know what the Conservatives have done or intend doing, ask the Liberals. They'll tell you. And the answer in each case will probably be "*nothing!*"

P.S. — Monday ... Warm day ... Partner haying ... Potato bugs hatching!

SEPTEMBER 3, 1939

A day to remember for many years to come. A day of disaster which we hoped would never dawn. But it has come and what can we do about it?

Dear people, if you read this column at all, you will understand that I write as one who knows something of what we may be called upon to face. It takes more than twenty years to obliterate my memories of the last war. I also write as one having the utmost sympathy with women who have husbands young enough to be called upon for duty, sons old enough for military service or daughters ready to serve wherever the need may seem greatest.

Already in Canada there are people who wait with terrible anxiety for the casualty list of the torpedoed 'Athenia' to be made known. On the other hand, here are others who will never cease to be grateful for the safe arrival in port of the 'Queen Mary,' with her cargo of human lives.

Great Britain and her Dominions beyond the seas are at war. Perhaps some may say, "England may fight but why should we?" The only way to find an answer to such a question is by intelligent consideration of the causes which led to the war and the consequences should Hitler become the victor. Don't ask other people why Canada should help England. Reason it out for yourself and you will come to a better understanding.

Those who know that loyal Canadians must come to Britain's aid at whatever personal sacrifice will be asking themselves the question, "If, in spite of our willingness to do other work, we must stay at home, what can we do that will help Britain to win the war?"

Dear people, there is a lot we can do.

You have heard and read a good many times during the last few weeks that the present conflict is 'a war of nerves,' and you know that this war of nerves started long before hostilities began.

Nerves are not entirely within our control, but if we exert sufficient will power they can be kept pretty much in hand. The morale of a nation depends upon its resistance to nervous tension; therefore, to save your nerves, don't have the radio droning away incessantly. Don't listen to every newscast that comes over the air. Press reports will soon confirm which stations are authentic, and which sensational. CBL is giving us excellent service in this crisis.

Don't get panicky in anticipation of a food shortage. Government officials have assured us that such a shortage is extremely unlikely, and so to go rushing out buying sugar, tea and what not, is nothing short of nerves. If nerves were not the cause of this anxiety to buy, would any decent person be guilty of such downright greed?

What right have you or I to buy up supplies that we may be better fed than our neighbour?

Then we come to the hardest lesson of all that we may be called upon to face: that of seeing those we love leave for active service. If ever we have need to keep our nerves under control, it is then.

We must remember that to worry and fret cannot possibly help our men. In fact, it can do a lot of harm because a worried wife or mother cannot write the cheerful letters which are so necessary to the men folk. The day is past when men must work and women must weep. Weeping will never get us anywhere. Women have their work to do these days as well as men, and in a war of nerves it amounts to something more than knitting socks for the soldiers.

Let us keep our lives as normal as possible, do what we can to help Britain fight against the domination of a relentless power and thank God we live in Canada.

SEPTEMBER 10, 1939

A History-Making Week in a World at War

THE WAR IN BRIEF

This week has been one that has had events crowded into it that have rocked the world. After months of international negotiations, efforts to preserve peace have failed, and the world has been plunged into another Great War by the German dictator, Hitler, whose policy would rob the world of freedom, and suppress all democratic forms of government. A brief summary of these nerve-wrecking days shows them to be days of darkness in the history of the civilized world.

FRIDAY

Britain's final ultimatum was forwarded to Hitler, and a time limit set for a reply from the German dictator. France also delivered an ultimatum, with an expiry time a few hours later. Both countries demanded that Germany cease its unproclaimed war and invasion of Poland and made it clear that failure to do so would bring these countries to fulfillment of their pact with Poland.

SATURDAY

A day of waiting for the answer from the German dictator. The invasion of Poland continued. Another of those unproclaimed wars was being waged. No answer was given to the demands of Britain and France.

SUNDAY, SEPTEMBER

At six a.m. Britain proclaimed war against Germany. France followed with a similar proclamation a few hours later. That afternoon, King George VI addressed 'my peoples, both at home and overseas,' in a world-wide radio broadcast.

That same afternoon, Prime Minister King, Hon. Ernest Lapointe, Hon. Norman Rogers and Hon. C.G. Powers addressed Canadians in a radio broadcast, to deal with the war situation.

President Roosevelt addressed the great American people, stating the neutral position the United States would assume in the war.

MONDAY

A German submarine torpedoed the British liner 'Athenia' carrying 1,400 passengers bound for Canada and the United States. All but 44 of those aboard were rescued before the liner sank. Shots were fired at the sinking vessel by the submarine as it left the scene of the disaster.

TUESDAY

British aeroplanes showered Berlin with 6,000,000 leafle The German advance into Poland continued, but was stu bornly fought against by the Polish all the way. The Frer army was reported as moved into position and in contact w the enemy on the western front. Reports from this sect were very meager. British planes made a successful raic battle cruisers in a German harbour.

WEDNESDAY

British troops were reported as landing rapidly in France. The offensive on the Rhine was well advanced into German territory, and first line defences of Germany were reported captured. The German offensive into Poland steadily advanced.

The Canadian Parliament assembled. Hon. J.L. Ralston has been appointed to succeed Hon. Charles A. Dunning as Minister of Finance.

DECEMBER 26, 1939

This is the day after Christmas. At Ginger Farm it is a quiet day. The hub-bub and excitement of the last few days — the extra work, the preparing for Christmas dinner, wrapping presents, the comings and goings — have all simmered down to this quiet, after-it's-all-over feeling.

Daughter and her girl friend are out visiting other friends. Son is trying out a Christmas present set of wrenches on his car. Partner just came in with a plucked chicken that had been ordered, and then we sat and talked for a while.

And I, well, at present I am busy writing, fortified by the presence of a two-pound box of chocolates, a present to Partner and myself. Yum — and are they good! I just told Partner he had better come in and help himself to a chocolate occasionally because, when I am in the house most of the time, I am liable to succumb to temptation rather frequently and thus get ahead of him.

Outwardly, yesterday was much the same as other Christmases. With breakfast over and the chickens sizzling in the
oven, we sat and listened to the King's stirring Christmas
message. Then we had the Christmas tree, a tree that was not
as well laden as usual because several parcels were missing.
There had been no mail from England, not even a card. We
are frankly worried, fearing anything that has been sent may
be lying at the bottom of the ocean. For ourselves we do not
mind, but we hate to think of our friends in England spending
money, which, probably, they can ill afford, and then have it
all spent for nothing.

And so the war has far-reaching results, even if to other
people missing our presents may seem of a minor nature, to us
the significance of the missing presents had the effect of casting an unacknowledged gloom over our homely festivities. We
wondered what they were doing over in England. Would there
be air raids, or ships blown up by a mine? Would they have
enough Christmas cheer to make it seem like Christmas?

Thinking all these things, Partner sent Son down to the
Post Office for our mail. But there was nothing — nothing
that is, other than the paper.

We have also had other family problems, so that Christmas 1939, will not be recorded in family history as the happiest Christmas we ever spent. However, we have much to be
thankful for, and there is a New Year dawning!

May I thank all those readers who have remembered us
this Christmas by sending greeting cards. It is heartwarming
to know you think of us sometimes. Thank you very much; we
appreciate your kindness more than I can say. And in return
for your Christmas wishes, may I wish you one and all a Very

Happy and Prosperous New Year. We also hope you had a lovely Christmas with all your family around you.

That is really what makes Christmas, don't you think? It isn't the presents or the feasting, is it? It is the thought behind the giving of the presents, the getting together of the family or clan and the friendly feeling we all have for one another. In other words, the spirit of Christmas.

I don't think there is any time I like better than the beginning of a New Year. With the work and worries of the old year behind me, I feel myself possessed of new energy. Energy to attack jobs that loomed like mountains towards the end of the old year and which now appear as little things I can just take in my stride as I go along from day to day.

Have you ever considered how monotonous life would be if Time were not divided into weeks and months and years? Imagine Time as one long succession of days! It doesn't sound very alluring, does it? There is something almost inspirational in starting a new week, a new month, and particularly a New Year. It is adventurous. Anything may happen.

And as we approach the end of 1939, in which so much has happened, we look forward to the future, hoping against hope that 1940 may bring reason and understanding to the hearts and minds of covetous dictators, that the suffering of innocent people may come to an end and that enmity in the human understanding of all people may come to an end, and that, in those living under the British flag, may arise a new realization that personal sacrifice from everyone will help more than anything else to bring about ultimate victory.

Don't let us forget, if we want peace we must work for it! And so, a Happy New Year to everybody.

Part III

Serving on the Home Front

1940–1943

January 4, 1940

Yes, this is New Year's Day, also municipal election day in this district. Partner and I have done our duty and now we must wait as patiently as we can for the result of the election. We always take an interest in local politics. But this year our interest is keener than usual, partly because of the close competition among those seeking election and partly because we know that whoever gets in now is there for two years or longer. Naturally, the longer the term of office the more necessary it is to have the right men fill the various offices. So here's hoping the best men win! Now that tells you a lot, doesn't it?

Since coming home, I have stripped the Christmas tree of its trimmings. It was such a big tree and took up so much space that I was almost obliged to get it out of the room as soon as possible. And yet I hated doing it. It was a grand tree, and it looked so pretty. This year I invented a new way of decorating it, which I thought made it look much brighter and daintier. Incidentally, it took about half as long as usual.

The trimmings off, I called Son to take the tree out of the room and then turning to Partner, I said, "Couldn't we leave the tree outside by the front step while it is nice and green? It seems a shame to throw such a lovely tree away. Christmas is over, but the tree is just as green and shapely as the day it came in."

"I guess it would be all right," Partner agreed. And so Son took the tree outside, and there it stands, right by the corner of the house.

Last Wednesday we had quite a busy day. Maybe you remember how cold it was that first Wednesday after Christmas. Well, that was the day we took Daughter and her friend back to Toronto. Son came along, too, partly because we had shopping to do for him, and partly for driving experience. He had never driven in the city streets and was most anxious to try it out.

We did not have to go down town at all, as lately I have been going in by Dundas to St. Clair, leaving the car at my brother-in-law's, and taking the street car down town.

And believe me, we did shop. Among other things, I wanted school pants for our young man. We knew exactly what we wanted, but finding it was a different matter. However, we were eventually successful.

Then Son wanted to browse around in a big store on Yonge Street where they sell motor repair parts. So that is where we went next, and we were so amused in this store to see the salesmen scooting around the place on roller skates! Apparently all the show cases are on the main floor and cover a large area of ground space, and so, I suppose, the salesmen save a vast amount of time and energy by this novel way of getting around as they work. And they even climb step-ladders and run up and down stairs with skates on as if it were no trick at all. It was really quite funny to watch them. I was told, afterwards, that roller-skating salesmen are quite common in the United States.

It was nearly ten o'clock when we reached home that night, later than we expected, but we found Partner quite happy because the English mail had arrived and he had letters from home. The next morning, Son was away to the Post Office bright and early to fetch home our Christmas parcel from England, which had actually arrived safe and sound. Everything was there, nothing had gone to the bottom of the deep blue sea, so everyone was happy. There were letters, cards and parcels posted on December 1st, 2nd and 12th, and all arrived by the same mail.

My sister-in-law gave us some interesting figures on food prices in England. She naturally gave them to us in English money, but I will quote them to you in dollars and cents.

Eggs, 75 cents per dozen. Controlled butter, 32 cents per pound. Back bacon (when they can get it), 50 cents. They gave $1 for a three-pound chicken, but the average price is from 32 to 33 cents per pound. Steak is 33, 35 and sometimes 50 cents per pound. The writer also said that farmers are given a subsidy of $10 per acre to help them out — this, of course is paid by the Government, to encourage production.

JANUARY 18, 1940

It was at a time when there had been a record snow storm. It had been storming for three days and the snow lay inches deep on the ground. Then came a quick thaw and as far as one could see there were flooded fields.

I stood on the front step of our farm home and watched the swirling waters. Presently, above the roar of the water rushing towards the creek, I heard another sound —the low hum of aircraft. It grew louder and louder, and then, in the distance, I saw a squadron of planes flying in V formation. I watched them with interest, and, as they flew directly over my head, the leader dropped lower, and, to my horror, I saw, not the Canadian ensign, but the German Swastika.

I stood rooted to the spot, and, even as I watched, the foremost plane took a sharp nose-dive and as it dipped discharged an aerial torpedo. I followed the torpedo with my eyes as it quickly descended to earth. I saw it plunge into the flooded field ahead of me and disappear from sight, but without exploding.

Then it suddenly penetrated my consciousness that this was, or would be, a German air raid over Canadian soil. I got awfully scared — not for myself, but for the Canadian people, because I knew that few of them knew anything about air raids and would not realize what was happening until it was too late. I thought of people out shopping, of children going to school — they would look up, and seeing the planes would think it was just a practice flight of our own machines.

I wanted to run out and tell people. I wanted to run in every direction at once. But how *could* I, how could I reach anyone in time! The telephone — but aeroplanes travel so fast — I must do something, I must ...

And then I heard a voice. And it was Partner saying, "You had better wake up if we are going to Toronto to-day."

And, oh, how glad I was to wake up! It was the most re-alistic and the most connected dream I have had in years. It seemed to hang over me like a cloud all morning, and the worst part of it all lay in the thought that the air raid was tak-ing people entirely unawares, and they would be absolutely defenceless with no chance to seek shelter anywhere.

Well, after that nightmare or dream, whichever you like to call it, I got up and soon found plenty to do because Part-ner wanted to get some glasses. Not the kind you drink out of, but the kind you wear. There was a cheap rate by train that day — only eighty-five cents — so we thought it would be just as cheap going that way as going by car. And a lot safer and easier, so we thought.

However, it wasn't as pleasant as it might have been be-cause there was quite a crowd travelling and Partner had to stand all the way to West Toronto. I managed to get a seat in the ladies' wash room. Reaching Toronto, we walked from the station to the City Hall, then Partner got his glasses fitted, and after that we thought we would go and see 'Hardy and Son,' showing at Loews. "Standing room only," said the girl at the ticket office.

"Good night," exclaimed Partner. "I've stood enough for one day! Is there anything else you specially want to do?"

"Yes," I answered, "I would like to go to the leather warehouse and get some black glove leather. It's down on Wellington some place — I'm just not sure where."

So we walked, and we walked, and we walked. At last we reached 145 Wellington West — and the store was closed! So then we started walking again. Finding ourselves at University Avenue, we went along there and up Queen. It was all new ground to us because any time we have been in the city we have either ridden in a street car or an automobile. And what does a person find out about the city that way?

Our little exploring trip reminded me of other days, when we use to tramp the streets of London, England. Partner and I were comparing notes just the other day and, while he was living in London for several years, whereas I only stayed there for short holidays, yet we each of us knew places which the other had never visited at all.

Coming back from Toronto, we did manage to get seats on the train, which was fortunate, as the train was thirty minutes late pulling out from the station.

To-day we haven't moved out of the house any more than we had to. Certainly I haven't had the inclination, because with all this ice around I might start out on my feet but it's problematic how long I would stay there.

And were we glad to see the rain! Imagine — water running in the creek again before our water-hole had really gone dry. It sounded too good to be true. We cannot be too thankful.

I can smell my soup, and it's for supper, so I had better scram. The first of the year, and burnt soup for supper — wouldn't that be a bad combination?

May 30, 1940

It is very, very difficult these days to write of anything that has not direct connection with the war. In fact it is impossible; the war over-shadows everything. And so I make no apology if, in this column, everything I write about eventually comes back to that same topic: the war in Europe.

A few months back, a person could, if they so desired, forget that a war was in progress. But not so now. And perhaps it is just as well, because it is only when a full realization of the seriousness of the situation becomes generally understood that we can expect a united effort from the general public.

And yet, even now, I don't think the women of Canada are doing one half, or even one quarter, what they might be doing. Some are doing wonderful work, putting every ounce of strength and energy into whatever war work they are doing. But it isn't enough. In this country of ours, where we live in comparative safety, we don't want a few women to give all their time — we want all the women to give some of their time. That, in the end, would bring far better results.

Every woman could, if she would, give a certain amount of time each day to whatever kind of work she is best fitted to do. It is largely a matter of habit. Most people these days have a radio, and nearly every woman has some special program or other that she likes to listen to. Some work while they are listening — others just sit! I think if those that 'just sit' would make a habit of having a little bit of pick-up work always handy, they would soon be surprised at what might be accomplished in these odd times.

Now there are some women who will say, "Oh, but I never have any time to spare. I am on the go from dawn to dark — I never have time to sit, either to listen to the radio or anything else." When I hear anything like that I always want to ask, "For heaven's sake, what do you do with your time?"

All farm-women are busy, particularly in the summer season. There are chickens, turkeys and other poultry; flower gardens; vegetable gardens, berries and asparagus; cows to milk, calves to feed; and lambs and little pigs to care for. All the chores in connection with these various lines of farming have to be attended to, but they are not generally all found on one farm. So we find each farm-woman is busy in her own way and I will admit it *is* difficult for her to find very much time to spare during the day.

But yet, supposing the telephone rings, as it frequently does, the farm-woman certainly takes time to answer it. If there are many calls, the time spent on telephone conversations mounts up during the day. Or if a neighbour, or any other visitor, drops in unexpectedly, you know very well the farm-woman always finds time to sit and visit for a while, maybe for fifteen minutes or maybe an hour or longer. Yet in spite of these hindrances — which, by the way, are usually very welcome — the work, somehow, gets done just the same.

And that, I think, is how a lot of war work might be done, too. Just by taking the time out to do it, however busy we think we are. Another way might be to give a little more thought to our regular jobs — give them the once-over, size them up, figure out their relative importance as compared to war work, and in that way we might find occasions where work might be simplified, meals served which would be just as nourishing but take less time than some we are accustomed to serving.

Yes, I am sure there all kinds of ways and means by which time might be saved so that we could have more time for war work. But, even more necessary than time, is the *will to work*. If we have the wish to work and the will to carry it through, then time will surely be forthcoming.

Just recently the Red Cross has been appealing for refugee clothing. Is it any wonder? Think of the hundreds and thousands of women and children forced to flee from their homes with nothing more than they can carry along with them. Who is going to help these unfortunate people if we don't? When they reach their temporary shelter what is there for them? Nothing, absolutely nothing, except what is given to them by the Red Cross or by generous people more fortunate than themselves.

Surely we can give a little of our time each day to sew or knit or make over for these helpless victims of war. It takes so little material to make dresses and panties for wee folk. And while we are making them, let us give some thought to our work. Make the little dresses pretty and dainty, just as we would for our own, so that even in this small way we may help to bring back a little pleasure and brightness to those from whom all pleasure and brightness has been ruthlessly wrested.

JUNE 27, 1940

These are anxious days for everyone and particularly for those who have people living in the Old Country. It is only natural when we hear by radio of air raids over England and Scotland that we should wonder if our own folk are safe. And even if those we know are spared, we still hate to think of the peace of our familiar country being shattered and desecrated by murderous bomb and shells.

To every Old Country person, there is some particular spot that is especially dear. Perhaps a little bit of Sussex downs, the hills and peaks of Derby-shire, of Suffolk meadows, or it may even be the old familiar streets and suburbs of London: Highgate, Peckham, Rye, Finchley or Hampstead Heath.

> *God gave all men all earth to love.*
> *But since our hearts are small,*
> *Ordained for each spot should prove*
> *Beloved over all.*
>
> — Kipling

And then we think of the children — the little innocent children — being moved back and forth from one place to another. How is this war affecting them? Shall we in Canada be able to make these little ones happy, to help them in some way to bear the parting from mother and home?

At least we can try. We can love them and care for and

treat them like our own. For the poor wee souls will need all the loving we can give them.

Yesterday we sent two cables to England, one to Partner's people and one to my married brother, offering a home to any of our young relations that they might like to send over to us. We have no idea whether any of them will come, but we feel more comfortable now we have made the offer. If none from our own families arrive, then we shall be prepared to take any little strangers who may need a home and make them as happy as we can.

Yes, we in Canada will soon find plenty of work to our hands.

On Monday the budget comes down and here's hoping nobody blows up when its contents become known. I rather fancy there has already been barrels and barrels of gasoline sold just recently in anticipation of an increase in price. Now, isn't that patriotic? If gas should go up — and nobody knows whether it will — but if it should, isn't that extra tax a means to raise funds to win the war? That being so, how shall it profit us to evade the tax?

What was it Churchill said: "I have nothing to offer but blood, toil, tears, and sweat!" In each instance, we in Canada have been fortunate up to the present even to casualties. According to the BBC there have been only twenty-one Canadian casualties, and none of these were killed in action.

As regards toil and sweat, we have been clamouring for the chance to work. For weeks and months the cry has gone forth, "Why doesn't the Government do something? Why don't they speed up recruiting? Why don't they make more guns, aeroplanes, tanks and ships?"

Well, the Government is doing something now — and for that, glory be — but whatever is done has to be paid for. And so we have the budget — and it is up to us to show how well we can take it.

And here's a thought! Surely the people who have been belabouring the Government so mercilessly for past inactivity, surely they couldn't be the same ones who have been laying in a supply of this, that and the other against a possible increase in prices when the budget comes down! That wouldn't be logical, would it? And yet — I wonder!

Well, the war in France is over — at least one phase of it is over. The peace pact has been signed. "Peace." What a terrible misinterpretation of the word. Rather should we say: fighting has ceased. Now, at last, Britain knows where she stands, with only her own soil to defend, and we all know how bravely she will do it.

Our immediate problem just now is wet weather and what to do about haying. Also the budget has been made known, and it is no worse than one might have expected. I haven't a doubt we shall be able to bear up under it.

A little while ago, we had a reply to one of our cables. The message ran, "Deeply grateful — matter under consideration." So now we wait further developments. The funny part of it is, we have been away from England so long we really don't know how many small relations we have. So we may find ourselves with quite a family, if all goes well.

JULY 11, 1940

Have you heard of the 'B' that can be plainly seen on the oat leaves growing in the field? That was what a neighbour asked me the other day. She also said the oats were marked in the same way during the last war. The B, of course, stands for British and is, presumably, a sign from heaven that the British nation will win this war as it did the last.

This theory regarding the marking of the oat leaves was all news to me, and it certainly excited my curiosity, to find, sure enough, one leaf after another with a capital 'B' marked on it as plain as day. Since then, the phenomenon has been very much discussed. Some claim the marking is just coincidence, others say the leaves are probably marked that way all the time, while still others assure us most definitely that the letter 'B' was seen on oats in 1917 and 1918, but never before or since.

In the old Bible days, miracles were accepted without question by the faithful, but in this modern day and age we are all inclined to be more skeptical of signs from heaven. And yet, why shouldn't miracles happen now just as much as they did in the old days?

No doubt there are often signs from heaven for us to see; the trouble is we don't recognize them or understand them. The best we can do regarding anything unusual is to speak of it as 'co-incidence.' So, whether the letter 'B' on the oats means anything at all is not for me to say. At any rate it is there, and is at least interesting. Some say there is a 'V' on the wheat, 'V' for 'Victory' but I haven't been able to find it yet.

Here is another theory, but of quite a different nature. A friend told me that if, when a mosquito alights on any part of your person, you can take exercise sufficient self control to leave it alone, it will not leave any poison behind to cause you discomfort. The insect may sting, but not poison, if left undisturbed.

Well, I am ready to try anything once, so while I was out picking berries yesterday, a mosquito alighted on the back of my left hand: the hand that was carrying the berry pail. With one eye on the mosquito, I went right on picking berries, and, believe it or not, that mosquito was busy dining for exactly four minutes. I could not feel him biting or stinging, in fact I did not experience any discomfort at all, so I really began to think there might be something in the theory.

I thought that until night time. I thought it until I found a hard, red swelling on the back of my hand, the size of a fifty-cent piece, while all the other bites were no more than a quarter-inch in diameter. So there you are — that's another theory exploded. Next time mosquitoes come buzzing around, they won't use me for a parking lot — not while I can stop it.

You will notice I said, "I went to pick berries," and you may remember I have said that berry-picking trips were definitely off for me, on account of trouble I was having with my feet. Well, that trouble got worse. In fact I could not keep on my feet for more than an hour at a time, and the pain, at times, was dreadful. Partner was worrying me all the time to go to the doctor and I was saying there was nothing to see, and to go for, and there was nothing the doctor could do anyway.

But one day I was down town, and, twice during an hour, I had to get into the car and take my shoe off to relieve the pain. So I finally visited the doctor's office, and, after having my foot twisted and pulled and pummeled, I was told the metatarsal muscles were completely relaxed and a special support would have to be made for them. Then the doctor bandaged my foot and ankle as a temporary measure, and the relief is worth a hundred dollars.

To-day for the first time in weeks, I was able to get all my work done before dinner. And yesterday, as I was telling you, I went to pick berries.

I have told you all this in detail because I know there are dozens of women who have foot trouble, and perhaps they are suffering needlessly even as I was.

Here is another of last week's experiences. Every morning I found dead chickens in the chicken pen. At first I thought they were just dying a natural death but later, a few mutilated bodies convinced me a midnight prowler was at work. So I carefully shut up hens, chickens, cats and dogs and laid bits of bread and butter, spread with strychnine, in front of the chicken pen. The next morning, stretched out beside the pen, was a full-sized skunk — dead. Since then I haven't lost a chicken.

July 18, 1940

Last month, after the collapse of France, we sent a cable to my brother in England, offering a home to my young nephew, if they liked to send him out. We had a cable in reply, followed by a whole sheaf of letters, which arrived last week. My brother's letter was written while an air raid was in progress, and it seems to me the tone of his letter reflects the spirit of the people over there. Of course we read much the same sort of thing in the paper, but somehow it seems a little more real coming from one's own family.

My brother Eddie writes: "Just by way of diversion, let me tell you that at the moment we are all sitting downstairs. The time is 12:45 a.m., and half an hour ago an air raid warning was sounded, so down we all came and now we are sitting in the safest place in the house, I have just composed a ditty, sung to the tune of 'So Early in the Morning.'

> *O darn old Jerry Hitler*
> *O darn old Jerry Hitler*
> *O darn old Jerry Hitler*
> *I want to go to sleep.*

"It is just too awful to think that after 'the war to end wars' this terrible thing should happen, and so far it seems that everything that could go wrong has done so. However, everybody here is full of admiration for the way in which Canada and the rest of the Empire have spontaneously come to the support of the Old Country, and we are fully confident of final victory.

"Now that France has fallen out, it remains for the British Empire to hold and beat the Hitler hordes and vassals — a mighty task, indeed, but we all feel confident that it will be done.

"I know a number of children are being evacuated to Canada and the U.S.A., but when you really come to think of it, the risks of staying in England are not so very great. In the air raids quite a number of people will doubtless be killed, but the individual chance of death is remote, and I am glad to say Desmond is not at all windy. Then again, the chance of any large-scale invasion is remote.

"It is very unlikely that Hitler can get any number of troops here by sea, thanks to the British Navy, but some measure of invasion by air is a possibility which I feel confident is doomed to failure.

"I hope I am not unduly optimistic about the future, but if I should be we shall certainly reconsider your offer. In any case your action has proven what a mother, sisters and brothers can mean to each other and also that the hand of true love for one's own and one's country can reach across the widest sea and ocean.

"Just after midnight last Tuesday the Nazis dropped a 'stone' in Cambridge, wrecked eight cottages and killed nine people, most of them women and children. Following this, I arranged with my neighbour to build an air raid shelter. Our house is not far from the railway bridge, and naturally in that position cannot be regarded as particularly safe. But still —

"Are we downhearted?

"*No!!!*

" 'There'll always be an England' — and a Canada.

"Well, it is now 2:15 a.m. We have had two hours of this and no pom poms — not a sound — rather dreary and uninteresting.

"You might like to know Jerry hasn't starved us yet. We get plenty of grub and that is the truth. There are none of Hitler's Gestapo here to look at our letters to see that we write just the right thing."

At the end of this letter there is a postscript, which says: "4 o'clock a.m. The 'all clear' has just sounded. Hurray!"

My sister-in-law, in her letter, says: "At times we can hardly realize there is a war, but now France has given up, we shall doubtless have more than our share. Everybody here is anxious to do their bit to help. The difficulty is to provide guns quickly enough to suit people. But with all the help we are getting from Canada and other parts of the Empire we shall hope to be ready for Hitler when he comes. Such a tremendous amount of work has been accomplished in such a short time. Everybody is so wonderful and can hardly do enough, so with that fine spirit behind us, we hope to win."

Desmond, age fourteen, writes: "Thank you very much for your invitation, but I don't think it is necessary for me to leave home yet. There are very few boys from our school who are going to Canada. There are over 500 boys in our school. Nearly all our boys have seen at least one German plane brought down just lately. I am getting rather annoyed with these air raids, as they have always taken place late at night. If they took place in daylight they would interrupt lessons at school, which would be much to our enjoyment."

There now, I have not written much about Ginger Farm this week, but I thought you might find extracts from my English mail more interesting.

P.S. I might add my brother is second in command of his local Home Guard unit.

AUGUST 29

Well, the National Registration is over, and I think everyone will agree that it is the best safeguard against Fifth Column activities that we could possibly have in this country. Already it has done good work.

We had quite a time at our registration booth. For a small place I shouldn't wonder but what it was one of the hardest around here, because we had so many foreigners on our list. Of course they had to bring an interpreter, and that made each paper take about twice as long as it would do ordinarily. Not only that, but about two-thirds of the people in this polling division decided to come on the first day.

In the morning there were three of us working, in the afternoon four, and in the evening five. We managed to keep pace with the registrants in the morning, but in the evening we were just about swamped. All the seats in the little schoolhouse were full and I was standing up at the back. And all we could do was keep writing ... writing ... where were you born? ... your father? ... your mother? ... racial origin?

By closing time we were all more than ready to quit. The next day we were busy but not rushed, and the next day was slack — that is so far as registration was concerned. But there was more to that job than writing up papers, so that the other deputy and myself were just about on the jump for at least five days.

But still, it was interesting work, and although we got awfully tired we enjoyed doing it. And of course it was an understood thing that we were doing it free, gratis and for nothing.

I mention that because on the Thursday following the registration I was down town and heard that the deputy registrars were getting six dollars a day! Six dollars, mind you — whereas we were not only doing it free, but I figured I was five dollars out of pocket by taking on the job. Not that I minded that, but it just about burnt me up to have anyone think I was making a good thing out of it. I know, too, that there were others who did no end of running in connection with the job, and as everyone knows you can't run a car on hot air.

At home the harvest proceeds slowly. Partner's trouble with the binder in one field put him back just about two days, so that before he had very much drawn into the barn two threshing machines were in the neighbourhood. Now it is raining again, so although the threshing machines are away Partner still cannot draw in. However, there is hay to cut, so I don't think Partner will be looking for a job.

And how is everyone enjoying the cool weather? I go down town and hear people say, "Oh my, isn't it cold?" But I'm not grumbling. No indeed, why should I? We have a cookstove in the kitchen, an oil stove in the porch and a box stove in the dining-room, and believe me, we light the whole works if and when we think we need them! We don't believe in being cold just because the calendar says it is the middle of summer.

And then, too, this cool weather is grand for getting a few pickles done. Yesterday I did half a boiler of beets. On a hot day I would have been nothing but a grease spot with the stove going steady for two hours. As it was, I was able to work in comfort.

We haven't had any mail from England lately and naturally we are wondering how all our friends are faring. I heard over the BBC the other day that the town where Partner's mother and sister are living was bombed. However, taking it on the whole we are very well pleased with Hitler's 'blitzkrieg.' Pleased because it has not been nearly so effective as he probably anticipated.

But oh dear, how Partner and I wish we were there! It is just dreadful to listen to the radio, to hear all that is happening over there, and yet here are we doing practically nothing that really matters, suffering very little hardship, getting all we want to eat, going to bed and sleeping the night through in absolute safety, while over there they eat, sleep and work in continual danger.

Of course I know that is really a silly way to look at it. Canada is helping, so we, as part of Canada, are helping, too. But it all seems so remote. There are times when we would be glad to go short of this and that, if by so doing it would help the Mother Country at this time.

Some people cannot listen to the radio. They say the war news 'gets them.' It doesn't us. We know there must be casualties, planes brought down and places wrecked. That is war. But we *know* that England will win.

Listen to 'Old Country Mail' on Sundays at one o'clock and you will get an idea of the indomitable spirit of the British People. Listen to the British Israel program at 1:15 p.m. on Sundays and you will be left in little doubt as to the destiny of the British people.

Don't let anyone tell you that Hitler will win the war. He won't while there's an England. And 'There'll always be an England!' Even the German prisoners are singing it. What irony!

NOVEMBER 14, 1940

It seems strange that life should go on so quietly for the vast majority of people in Canada, while, in other parts of the world, history-making events are taking place day after day. Chores are done as usual around the Canadian farms; women shop, sweep, knit and bake; little children go gaily to and from school; teen agers 'step on the gas' with their usual abandon — and all the while things are happening to shape the destiny of each one of us.

Think what has happened in this last week. President Roosevelt returned for a third term and you know how the people in Canada awaited the result of that election with unprecedented eagerness. The average person may not really know why the re-election of President Roosevelt should affect him, yet some instinct tells him that it does.

Mr. Neville Chamberlain died at his country home. Peace, which he loved so greatly, was only possible for him in death. There has been much criticism of Mr. Chamberlain's appeasement policy, but history may yet reveal that, at the time, he was right — and that he was the right man in the right place at that critical job. Winston Churchill stepped in when more aggressive measures were necessary, but it is questionable whether Mr. Churchill, had he been sent to Munich in place of Mr. Chamberlain, would, or could, have handled the situation as well as Mr. Chamberlain. Churchill would assuredly have taken his gloves off and that might have suited Hitler very well.

Another event of the past week: a severe earthquake in Rumania. Oh but that has nothing to do with Canada, you say. No? I shouldn't wonder that it has more to do with the destiny of Canada than any one thing that has happened so far. Earthquakes can do strange things to the earth's formation. Oil fields in Rumania may not prove very productive for quite a while. And Rumania's oil fields were Hitler's newest and greatest asset. If the earthquake has seriously disrupted these fields then Hitler will have less oil for fuelling aeroplanes to bomb Britain and British convoys, less oil to fuel murderous pirates of the seas, less oil to carry on a war where oil is of more importance — to Hitler — than food for the people.

Yes, I think the earthquake, so many, many miles away, does mean something to the people of Canada. And here is something else to remember. This earthquake — Britain's ally — was not the result of a man-made negotiation or pact, but an ally created by Divine Providence. Who can doubt it?

And to-day is Armistice Day, ushered in by high winds and rainstorms — probably our share of the atmospheric disturbances caused by the earthquake. We can stand it.

Last night I went to bed thinking of that first Armistice Day, twenty-two years ago. I may have told you this story before — if so, please forgive me. In any case, you may have forgotten it by now.

I was collecting for an insurance company in England, replacing a man who joined the Forces. My work took me out to the country, through winding English lanes. It was a lovely day, and as I rode along on my bicycle, I thought how lovely the country was and how terrible a thing was war. Passing some fields, I noticed gangs of German prisoners working. Generally they would look up and watch with interest anyone who passed. This day they worked with heads bowed — sorry, dejected looking men. I wondered why.

Wheeling along I presently came to a village. Here the church bells were ringing. Women stood at their cottage doors talking. Men, mostly oldish men, stood in groups here and there, talking — yes — but not excitedly, because English country people are phlegmatic folk and seldom show excitement. I stopped at the little post office, which was also the village store, and asked why the bells were ringing. "My word, ain't you 'eard the news?" the postmistress asked. I shook my head. "The war's over, that's wot. We got them 'uns beat, like I always knew we would!"

The war was over. No wonder the bells rang out with joyful chimes. And no wonder those poor German prisoners bowed their heads. It was not good news to them. There they were well fed, well treated: they did not want to return to Germany.

Yes, that was the first Armistice Day as I knew it. It ended what has been generally known as the Great War. Perhaps history will record it hereafter as the 'Unfinished War.'

DECEMBER 19, 1940

After studying the calendar I have suddenly realized this will be the last issue of the *Free Press* until after Christmas. That being so, I take this opportunity of wishing you, one and all, a very, very, Happy Christmas.

Yes, of course, this is not quite like other Christmases — we cannot help being conscious of that black shadow, called war, that is always with us now. But we might also remember, to our comfort, that the message of Glad Tidings still endures. And will endure to the end of time. And we have so much for which to be thankful. We are still a free people — we also see, on every side, practical evidence of that courage and tenacity of purpose that will keep us a free people. We have a right to be happy and to wish each other happiness: it is one of the principles for which our Empire is fighting. And so, war notwithstanding, I repeat: A Happy Christmas to everyone!

Just at present I still find it a little hard to believe Christmas is so close at hand. It took me some little while to make up my mind as to whether I should make a cake this year. I finally decided I would, because I don't really think Christmas cake is an extravagance, as it goes so much further than any other kind of cake. So, about a week ago, I bought all the necessary fruit, and that's as far as I got. I could not find enough time between meetings, picking chickens and ordinary work to get my cake made.

To make a busy time extra busy, we suddenly got word that the threshers were due to arrive any time. Threshing always means work, but threshing this time of the year is worse than that. Of course the men start late and quit early, so that makes more meals to get. The machine finally arrived, about eleven o'clock Saturday morning. After dinner they threshed the stack, moved into the barn, and were in to their supper by five o'clock — four o'clock Standard Time.

Was I ready? Indeed I was. I am prepared for any eventuality these days, and had the potatoes on by three o'clock. It so happened I did not have any help with my meal. I could have done, but I didn't think it worth while. Monday, we shall be at it again, and there will be dinner to get. After that perhaps I shall get my cake done. And there will be the Christmas tree to get!

My young nephew, from Toronto, is coming down for the holidays. We don't know yet whether Daughter will be home or not — it may be that she will not be able to get away. Last year I had a feeling that it might be the last Christmas we would all spend together. The time when there is a vacant chair comes inevitably to all families. Children grow up and have interests outside their home, work prevents their home-coming, or they marry and must take it in turn visiting the homefolk. And right now there is the war. Some of the boys cannot get leave, others are too far away. Whatever the reason, there is that break in the home circle — a break which we feel so much more at this, the best time of all the year.

I hope it won't be that way with too many of you.

I hope to most of you Christmas will be a time of re-union and happiness.

At our Institute meeting last week, each member was supposed to bring at least one article of clothing suitable for a refugee bale. There was a splendid response — a good many members bringing not one but several articles of clothing. These things will be parceled up and sent off to the Salvation Army for distribution in the bombed areas of England. When

I saw the lovely big pile of good, useful things that had been brought in, it did my heart good. It was just one more instance of results from a united effort. When a group of women get together and each brings one article, even a baby's vest, a pair of mitts or a scarf — when all those things are put together, just think what it means.

I had a letter last week from the school friend in England who wanted to send her daughter over here. She did not come because the British government had temporarily suspended schemes for the wholesale evacuation of children to Canada. My friend's letter was as cheerful and full of fun as if war was an unheard of thing, although they apparently spend night after night in their dug-out. Here is what she says:

"As a matter of fact, we have had a pretty hot time here recently. Whoever thought we would sleep in a hole in the ground — that's what we have been doing since the bombing of London! When Horace, Bill and Betty built our shelter, at the commencement of the war, we thought we might have to use it for an odd ten minutes or so, consequently it wasn't made too large — about 6 feet deep, 6 feet long and very narrow. But since we have had to spend night after night in it, and all night, Horace has decided to enlarge it. Since then the wretched weather has done nothing but rain, so that we can't get it finished. Several bombs have dropped in and around our old home, but, fortunately, very little damage done."

Of one thing I am certain, and that is this: Most people in England will try to celebrate Christmas — even if they do it in an air-raid shelter!

MAY 15, 1941

Last week I had a happy time trying to get this column worked in with my other work. This week I had it ready on Thursday but did not mail it, and by Saturday it was so out of date I just popped it in the fire instead of in the post office. So now I am no further ahead than I was before.

Each week I think, "Well, when we get the next few days over things will be easier!" And then some sort of unexpected job turns up and away we go again.

Last Tuesday, we had a great time hunting rats, and caught seven! Wednesday, I had to make a hurried trip to Hamilton. Thursday, Partner had a good big order for seed barley, and I stayed home from our Institute meeting to help him put it through the fanning mill. Friday, I took chop to the mill, and waited two hours for it. Saturday, I went to an auction sale in the afternoon — and the week was gone.

On one of my trips to town I bought paper to paper our son's bedroom, but when I shall get it done dear only knows. Another nice little extra job these days is washing the cream separator, as with five fresh cows in all at once we naturally have more milk than our quota calls for. And next week, I must go to the city. I shall be walking in my bare feet if I don't. You see I have a very special pair of feet that require a special kind of shoes, and a special kind of cheque to pay for them!

We have been getting quite a bit of English mail lately, for which we are very thankful, even though the news therein was not of the best. However it is such a relief these days to know your friends are still alive that other things they may tell you don't seem so important. Bombs were dropped in the street near Partner's home and the house was badly damaged, but not beyond repair. Fortunately, mother and sister-in-law had moved to another district and were thus unharmed.

From quite another part of England I got word that German dive bombers machine gunned people in the streets of the city where my brother and his family live. It was the first letter I had received from my sister-in-law for a long time. Not because she had not written, but because she had been putting 'Perth County' on the address to me. I suppose she knows someone in Perth and had got the two mixed up.

The last time a letter did reach me, Gussie, I mean my sister-in-law, was awfully worried because she had such difficulty in getting a maid. In this last letter she doesn't even mention the subject, so I suppose by this time she has come to realize that a maid, in war time, is a person she must learn to do without.

One part of the letter reflects what we know to be the spirit of the people of the British Isles. And here I quote: "The enemy has done everything possible to scare us but we intend to fight and stick it out to the very end. We have been working like mad to make all the machines we require. This is a war of speed, and if we do not have the very utmost help now, Heaven help us."

And here is news from a cousin in Suffolk. "At home they had a terrifying experience last week. Two land mines were dropped and exploded near 'The Broom' [a farmhouse Partner and I know well]. Mum says it was absolutely terrible.

'The Broom' is now nothing but a shell. From end to end of the village damage was done. Roofs blown off, windows broken, and ceilings down. But no one was hurt, not even a pig, so that's a miracle!"

Partner's mother says: "I am very thankful you are all out there because there is not much peace here. The siren goes once or twice nearly every night but we have been saved up to now. The town people take no notice and business goes on as usual. The Home guards are no good — work Sundays, as well as evenings after they get home from work. We are able to have a friend in sometimes to a nice cup of tea and bread and butter because of the parcels that come from Canada."

'Tea' and 'butter' are both underlined.

And this is from Partner's sister. "We were very pleased with the onion salt. Someone could make a fortune with it here, as most people are without onions and, as one woman said to me in the butcher's shop, 'what is the good of bones without onions?'

"I wish you could send your eggs over here, we pay 2 1/2d each (5c) and 4d (8c) each in the winter. We pay 4 1/2d a pint for milk (9c). But Uncle Tom is always asking if we have enough to eat and is surprised that we do so well. It has been such a cold spring. I have just been out in the woods picking primroses, but it was too cold to enjoy it so I picked up firewood and brought it home with me instead."

One thing we noticed in all four letters: a closer bond of friendship than ever before. People who had drifted apart now want to know what each other are doing. Any little treat that comes to one person is shared with others. Hitler may lay waste a thousand homes, but houses in ruins serve only to bring together the people of those homes in a unity of unselfishness and love.

News has just come through of the reported capture of Rudolf Hess! Can it be true, and if so, what does it mean? What was he doing? This war is not without its startling, drastic events and the unfolding of this latest mystery is one we shall follow with interest.

MAY 22, 1941

"Did I say that?" No, I am not referring to the radio quiz program. It is last week's 'Ginger Farm' column that I'm worrying about. You may remember I gave a few extracts from letters recently received from England, and in the paper I appear to have said: "The Home Guards are no good."

Now I wonder did I say that? If so, it was an appalling mistake in typing. That sentence should have read: "The Home Guards are *so* good." Just one letter, not even three words, and the whole story is changed. My goodness, to say the Home Guards are 'no good' is enough to brand one as a Fifth Columnist. I sincerely hope anyone who read the mistake will also read this correction.

Just before I finished typing last week, news came through about the Rudolf Hess affair. Since then, everyone has had a wild time trying to figure out just why the Nazi leader flew to Scotland, but it is quite possible the whole story may never be known until after the war is over. I have a feeling that the Hess trip did not turn out according to plan. I believe Hess had a very definite objective in view when he flew to Scotland, and that it failed. I think he also had a cleverly built-up story all ready to tell if he should fail to reach that objective. And I also think the trip was made with the full knowledge and sanction of Hitler.

But now that the whole scheme has proved a flop, its failure must be covered up by arrests and propaganda. And of course, Hitler isn't likely to hesitate in betraying the man who was his closest friend and confidant for fifteen years. Would any man, even a German, voluntarily leave his wife and small child the way Hess would like us to believe that he did, unless the whole thing was prearranged and their care arranged for? Of course we hear now that Frau Hess has been arrested. Well, that may be cover-up work, too. One thing is certain, we British people have learnt to be Doubting Thomases where the Nazis are concerned.

Oh well, let's talk about the weather! How do you like this return to winter, or rather near-winter? My sympathy is with those overzealous people who, a week or two ago, decided that houses no longer needed artificial heat. Of course, it is easy enough to put on a little bit of a fire in a furnace, but if you have stoves and have taken them down, then I'm thinking the dear old kitchen is going to be a very popular place these days.

Last year we kept one stove, as well as the kitchen stove, up all summer. This year we are doing the same thing again. There are plenty of nights, even in summer, when a wee bit of fire is a comforting thing to have around. A stove isn't exactly an ornament in a room but, 'Ease before elegance,' that's what I say.

My chickens are in an outside pen now, still with the one hen. I counted them very carefully when I moved them and found there were seventy-nine survivors, which I don't think is too bad under the circumstances. They are all cockerels, which means I did not pay much for them, and thus the loss in cash outlay will not amount to much.

We are still worrying about rats, and since they are also bothering other people I will tell you what we have done. We were told of a certain product, guaranteed to kill rats, which is harmless to humans, animals and poultry. This rat poison is put up in tablet form and its principle ingredient is syrup of squills. Syrup of squills, as you may know, is also used in cough medicine for children. But while it helps coughs, it kills rats because, with rats and mice it has a peculiar action on their hearts and so the rats just naturally die of heart seizure.

The tablets must not be handled with bare hands, otherwise the wary old rats will get the scent and shy away. Our method has been to put a shingle in the hen-house, sprinkle a little grain over it, and with a spoon drop three or four tablets in amongst the grain. And then we place a chicken coop over the whole works. Thus the hens cannot reach the bait, but the rats have free access to it. I also dropped tablets down any rat holes I saw around.

The first night we used this stuff one tablet disappeared, the second night two, so we are really hoping that we have found something at last to exterminate these pests, and something that is not too risky to use. We understand that this poison is also used quite extensively at our local flour mill.

Last Sunday, Andy Clarke on the radio spoke of the growing season as being two or three weeks ahead of schedule. It may be in some places, but not in this district. Partner says he doesn't remember a year when growth has been so slow. And we need rain so badly. One thing is certain, if we get light crops there won't be the same worry regarding farm labour shortages later on.

SEPTEMBER 25, 1941

"Do you want to see something wonderful?" asked Partner the other night as he came in from milking.

"Of course," I answered, "but what is it?"

"Come outside and you will see," continued Partner.

So out we went and there were the Northern Lights, more magnificent than any display we had ever seen before. And we have seen plenty of marvellous displays too when we were living out in the West.

I stood spellbound for a minute, then I ran into the house to telephone two friends in case they might be unaware of what was taking place. Beauty like that should be shared, I thought. After contacting my friends I went out again and Partner and I stood watching that glorious sky for fifteen or twenty minutes. We had never seen the Northern Lights rolling up in clouds as they did that night, nor had we seen that peculiar cone shape effect, the peak of which seemed to be directly over our heads.

Partner thought the fleecy clouds of light which seemed to come from nothing and disappear into space, looked like gunfire as he had seen it during the last war, while I kept wondering if these apparently celestial lights held some hidden meaning. Science, of course, has an answer to almost every phenomenon but sometimes one is tempted to discount science and cast about for a more primitive explanation.

One thing we have noticed, our radio has been working better since that wonderful night than it has done for weeks. It was working all right for local stations but we occasionally like to get WKBW and for weeks we have not been able to get it at nights because of the terrible amount of interference. Now it is as clear as CBL.

And by the way, has everyone realized that we can now get CBY on our radios without any trouble? You know they increased the power of that broadcasting station so now we can get programs which are given only over SBY, such as addresses to the Canadian Club, many of which we have previously missed because it was impossible to get CBY.

This has been a busy week, so busy in fact that I did not even get to Acton Fair, a splendid event which I hardly ever miss. However, this year I just couldn't make it. There have also been things happening in the district which have been very disturbing.

Word was received last Wednesday of the first casualty of the war for this district: a young airman, well known and well liked, killed in action, presumably over Germany. Naturally it is not for me to say what his death meant to his parents, but I can say what a great shock it was to the district, and it probably did more than any amount of press news to bring the war home to every-day folk. The thought in everyone's mind seemed to be: "This is our community's first casualty, how many more will follow?"

A depressing thought no doubt, but unfortunately one from which we cannot escape. While this war lasts, men must fight: on land, on sea and in the air. And as long as men fight, there will be casualties. That fact we have to face, and hope for the best.

Another loss to this community was caused by the death of our rector. He had been ill for three months and although we knew he was dangerously ill, yet because he had lasted for that length of time it was hoped he might ultimately recover. But it was not to be.

Of course I need hardly tell you that with our boy away in the army thoughts of him have been mixed up with all my work. Since it is all so new to him, it is only natural to wonder how he is getting on and I kept looking for a letter every day, a letter that never came! As the week wore on, I concluded he hadn't written because he would be home.

From Saturday noon I looked for him, and listened for his cheery whistle. But he didn't come. On Sunday I began looking for him again. He will get out about twelve-thirty, I thought, and if he is lucky in getting a ride he should be home by two o'clock anyway. Two o'clock and three — and still no sign of him.

Partner said, "Maybe he is walking the highway." "That is just what I am afraid of. There might not be many cars coming up from Palermo," I answered. So then we decided to go along the road a-piece, just in case. It was so hot for anyone to be walking, and such waste of time. So we set out and half-a-mile from home our boy stepped out of a car. Well, and happy and very brown.

"Why didn't you write?" was naturally one of my first questions. "Write? Well there wasn't anything to write about, and I was coming home anyway!" Time, apparently, had passed quickly for him.

AUGUST 28, 1941

That was a grand speech of Mr. Winston Churchill's! Yes, a grand speech for all peoples of the Americas to hear: it meant a lot to us but how much more it must have meant to the unfortunate folk of Nazi-dominated countries. Of course, everything would be done to prevent conquered peoples from hearing such a cheering message, but there would be some who would find a way. And those who didn't hear the speech would get word of it afterwards.

Imagine yourself in a Nazi-occupied country and hearing Churchill's words meant specially for you: "Have faith ... have hope ... deliverance is sure." I said, "imagine yourself in a Nazi-occupied country," but of course you can't, none of us can. If we only could, if we could know for even one hour what Nazi domination really means, how much it would speed our war effort. Oh, I know Canada is officially doing her part, and our much criticized Government is endeavouring to make our war effort something really worth while, but how much does the average person know of war?

Mothers with little children feel they have all they can do in looking after their families. Some say, and no doubt quite truly, that they have no time for work. And yet, do they ever stop to think of the future for their children if Hitler should win? Isn't it more important to young married people than to the old and middle-aged that we should win this war? The young have a normal expectation of many years of life: the future is of immense importance to them. From a personal angle, the outcome of this war is not so important to the old and getting-old.

But fortunately few look at it from a personal angle, and so the war is waged for our country's sake and that those who come after us may lead normal lives free from Nazi persecution and domination. It is useless for older people to deplore the thoughtlessness of the younger generation; they cannot realize what war means, that is, the ones who are still in civil life. To them a gallon of gas is neither here nor there. The young airmen, the soldiers and sailors, and the nurses — young men and women of their own generation who have gone overseas — they could tell them a different story. But telling is of little avail; it is experience that counts.

Life has been pretty easy in many ways to the youth of to-day and I don't think it will do any harm if those who are left in Canada have to do without some of the things to which they have become accustomed. The curtailment of gas will help a lot. Nearly all young people have formed a habit of being in an awful hurry to go nowhere in particular. There is a lot of time being wasted that might be put to better advantage. Boys and girls these days have plenty of energy and they will realize before very long just where and how that energy should be applied.

The war isn't over and I have a hunch that we shall all learn a lot before it is. I rejoice whenever I hear there is a shortage of this and that. We should go short of things, we should be glad to take our share of hardship and deprivation with the people of the British Isles. Why should we worry about silk stockings when 'over there' they must give coupons for everything they need to wear. Why should we worry about the goods we cannot get at the grocery store when there is plenty of stock from which to choose a substitute? There is so much for us to do. Nothing that might be used should be destroyed. Salvage is the civilian's greatest war weapon.

On the farms there is work for us to do all the time, work that will help Canada's war effort. Don't grumble at egg-grading regulations. You may think there is no sense to them, but if you aim at bringing your eggs up to the A Large standard you will find there is little to grumble about. Don't gather your eggs just once a day, take a trip to the hen-house four and five times a day. Grade A eggs are to your credit, grade B eggs, or even C, might come in jolly useful!

We might also pay careful attention to what storekeepers tell us in regard to what they can and cannot get. If there is a shortage of something, don't raid the town and buy up all available supplies. Don't be a 'grabber'; leave such tactics to Hitler. At the same time, if there is something we really need, don't delay buying it until the last minute. If we can't get exactly what we want, suppose we use a little ingenuity and get the next thing to it. And for heaven's sake, let's forget about the Joneses! You don't need to be afraid of losing them. You may lose sight of them during the war, but they'll be back again. You can lay your hand to your heart on that!

DECEMBER 18, 1941

War developments moved a little quickly last week, didn't they? But now we have got used to the idea of Japanese popping up, with characteristic treachery, in the most unexpected places. I hope we have all had time to size things up as we see them and have come to some decision as to how and where we can best do our part in the tremendous struggle that lies ahead of us.

In order to do this, we need to know why and in what manner our ordinary every-day life will be affected so that we may use a little forethought and economise in material that will be urgently needed. There are certain things that will soon become non-existent for domestic use and we must either learn to do without them or find a substitute. In this land of plenty we have become all too thoughtless in the value we place upon things, and far too careless in our use of them, and of course in that class I include ourselves.

Without warning, the sale of automobile tires to the public has been prohibited. At first the Government did not tell us the reason, but a glance at a geography book supplies the answer. A lot of Canada's rubber is imported from the Dutch

East Indies, and, until we have cleaned up on the Japanese, how are we going to get it, especially with the 'Prince of Wales' and the 'Repulse' at the bottom of the sea? What supplies of rubber and rubber goods are available must, of course, be held in reserve for the fighting forces. So it behooves us to take good care of any tires we may possess, drive less, and we shall save both tires and gasoline. There are also numberless household articles it will soon be impossible to procure, even to the indispensable plate scraper.

And how else will the war in the Pacific affect us? Well, let's take a look at our imports. Canada apparently is dependent on other countries for her supply of raw sugar, spices, tea, coffee, raw silk and cotton, tropical fruit — and rubber.

Where do these things come from? I suppose we must have been buying a certain amount of sugar and spice from the Dutch East Indies, tea and coffee from Java, oranges and sugar from Jamaica, best-quality raw cotton from Egypt, and at one time raw silk from Japan. We don't need to think very hard before realizing that the supply of those ordinary everyday commodities is in future bound to be limited, even though some of these imports may be obtained from other places. As to that, I am not sufficiently well-informed to know where or to what extent. In any case, it seems fairly obvious that we shall have to economise, substitute or do without many things which we have hitherto taken for granted.

And you know, it is really possible to get quite a kick out of seeing how well we can manage. It can be fun trying to make just as good a cake or pudding with some of the necessary ingredients left out.

Here is an instance. During the last war, when I undertook to cook and bake for twenty-five people in a boys' boarding school, one of our 'stand-bys' was bread pudding, and, 'though I says it as shouldn't,' my bread pudding was good. The original recipe called for stale bread, shortening (dripping and butter), milk, eggs, mixed fruit (raisins, currants and peel), sugar, and spice.

First of all butter and white sugar were rationed so I substituted lard and brown sugar. Presently sugar and fat rations were still further reduced, and I used all dripping and treacle. Eggs were hard to come by, so I used custard powder instead. Then the supply of fruit gave out until finally my bread pudding ended up with stale bread, shortening (which was part dripping, part suet), milk and water, treacle, spice or caraway seeds. That was our war-time bread pudding, and the boys still came back for more and were glad to get it. Not so the Principal; he didn't like caraway seeds! But he had to eat at least one helping. The boys had their eye on him!

And now in Canada to-day this new war has brought about still other results. Partner and I realized this when our boy came home on Saturday and said he would soon be 'on the move.'

"Where to?" I asked.

"Borden, on Monday. After that I don't know — the coast likely. Anyway, we'll soon be going places, I guess.'

That's quick work if you like. The boy has been in the army only two months and isn't nineteen yet. And now, since there is no conscription, it is evident the boys who have enlisted voluntarily must be rushed through now the need for men has become increasingly urgent.

Of course our boy is quite happy about it, that is only natural, and we are, too, if we could be sure that those who have volunteered will not be left stranded for want of reinforcements.

Major Power's announcement last Saturday about 'selective service' may have been just a 'feeler' to prepare the public for more drastic things to come.

May 21, 1942

Anyone who has helped in sorting salvage knows it to be the most conglomerous collection of things imaginable, but I think the salvage we have here beats all records, for in it I found a real live collie pup!

I had just returned from town and on my way from the garage I took another look at the collection of rubber. And there, if you please, snuggled down among old rubber boots, tubes and hot water bottles, was a wet and shivering black and tan collie pup, apparently about two months old. I really thought I was seeing things for at first the puppy did not move. However, as I got nearer he wagged his tail, blinked his eyes and wriggled along on his tummy. So then I knew that this salvage problem hadn't really deranged my mind and that I was actually looking at an honest-to-goodness living puppy.

The poor wee mite of a thing — it looked so cold and pitiful. Of course I had to pick it up, carry it into the house and get it warmed and fed. As I did so, I certainly wondered who could have been so callous as to put a puppy out with their salvage. I kept wondering until Partner came in to supper and then he solved the problem for me. It appears that during the afternoon, while Partner was sorting papers and bottles, a neighbour's dog came down to visit and brought the little pup with her. After a while the mother dog went home leaving the puppy behind.

So during the evening, young John took the little dog back to its mother and there was a joyful reunion in the canine world.

Our community scrap pile is getting bigger and more complicated all the time, with Partner spending every minute he can spare sorting and straightening the stuff as it comes in. And we are by no means through. Right now we are busy melting down various small cans of fat that have come in and running it into large candy pails. So far we have about fifty pounds of grease. One load of scrap iron was sent to the city on Saturday, and the results from the sale of it were very satisfactory. It will boost our Institute funds considerably and we shall have the satisfaction of knowing the iron is where it will do the most good.

We also feel that by the time we get through with the paper, rubber, rags, fat and bones, this community's salvage will prove a very worthy contribution to our country's war effort. And if a collection of salvage such as we have here is being picked up in every community — and I certainly hope it is — then who can say how far reaching may be the results?

Did you hear the story of the woman at a meeting who asked, "What more can we do to help win the war?" And someone in the audience answered, "Stop yapping and start scrapping!" Very impolite of course, but how very much to the point. Action, that's what we want.

Last week we had the best spring rain we have had for many years, but it started at a very awkward time for some people. We were having an Institute meeting here and the women, some of them walking, had just nicely got away when the storm started and the rain came down as if it were from a cloudburst. It flooded our garden and low-lying spots in the barley field; it filled the cistern to overflowing; it started the creek running; and it made the kitchen ceiling leak in several places. It rained most of Thursday night and nearly all day Friday. It made it very wet and disagreeable getting around, but it was a grand and glorious rain for which we cannot be too thankful.

Partner has not as yet turned his cows out to pasture, and for that we are very thankful, too, because with the ground so soft what grass they didn't eat would have been trampled underfoot. Partner debated for some time whether he should turn the cattle out or buy hay, and finally decided to buy hay so as to give the pasture a better chance. And that is the second time only that we have had to buy hay since we came here. I thought it was the first, but Partner says no, we bought one load of hay some years ago.

Hay, you know, is one of those things that are simply grand when you have it to sell. But when you have it to buy, ah, that's quite another story. Start buying hay and your milk cheque vanishes like chaff before the wind!

JULY 16, 1942

I like new experiences, but you would think after twenty years farming, more or less, that there would now be very few new experiences. That is not so; we are always running up against the unexpected and that adds zest to farm life.

And what is it now? Well, we are going to start drilling for water on Monday. Nothing exciting about that? Oh, but there is.

First of all there was the problem of choosing a site. Partner knew where he wanted the well, but the question was, would it be the right place to find water? However the man we have engaged to do the drilling thought the chances were good. He also gave us the name of a 'well-witcher' if we wanted to get one in.

Neither Partner nor I come from Missouri, but yet we do occasionally have a skeptical streak, and faith in water-witching is one of them. Later in the week we had a man come along who is to look after pump fixtures, and he, too, mentioned the same witcher as had the well-driller. Then Partner and I began to sit up and take notice, and we decided that it wouldn't do any harm to have the man in anyway. So we phoned him and he came.

We all turned out to see him do his tricks. He brought several thorn tree forked branches along with him, and paced backwards and forwards over the spot where we wanted to drill. Sure enough the branch began to turn, but the man shook his head. "Yes, there's water there all right but I don't like it — the spring's not strong enough."

So Partner took him to an alternative site and he began pacing the ground again. Presently the stick began to move — gently, gently — and then it took a quick downward twist and pointed to the ground. "There's your water," said our well-wizard. "That's a pretty good spring — I don't think you would make much of a mistake in drilling there."

By this time, I was quite fascinated and picked up one of the forked branches and walked along where the man had been, holding the branch in the prescribed manner. But did it move? Not a bit of it. "Look at that," I exclaimed in disgust, "the stick won't budge for me."

"No, but it will if you hold my hand," said Mr. Witcher. "Come 'round here and I'll show you."

So the well-witcher took one end of the forked branch and I took the other and we walked hand in hand.

"Hold it — hold it hard. Don't let it twist," he said. And I did hold it hard — I held it as tight as my will and muscle would let me. But slowly and surely I felt the stick turning as surely as if someone were pulling it away from me, and presently it dipped in spite of me.

My skepticism is all gone — I believe now that certain persons have it in them to witch for water. I think Partner is also convinced, but I don't think he was as skeptical as I was in the first place.

This man also claims to be able to tell, within a few feet, how far it will be necessary to drill to tap the spring. In our case, he says, anywhere from forty-five to fifty feet. By this time next week we should know as we start drilling on Monday.

We were talking about wells in general, and he told us some interesting things. He said, generally speaking, all springs run from west to east — only very occasionally is a spring found to run from north to south because all springs follow a natural course to the lake, and if by a stroke of ill-luck two persons tap the same spring the one who is nearer to the lake gets the water and the other fellow's well goes dry — or next thing to it. He said it was quite possible something like that may have happened to the well we are now using, since at one time it had abundance of water and now if we water the stock from it for more than two weeks it goes practically dry. Distance apparently makes little difference as the man who taps another fellow's spring may be five miles away and neither know anything about it.

I am wondering how much extra work I shall get done next week because I shall certainly want to be outside in my spare time watching that drill at work. Partner doesn't get nearly so excited about these things as I do; maybe it's because he has been around and seen more of it.

AUGUST 27, 1942

Last Thursday came news for which we had all been longing and waiting: news of offensive action in Europe. Press dispatches as they were first given sounded thrilling — unbelievably exciting — and we felt the whole raid was a real blow to German prestige. Then came more details of Dieppe, and as we listened we began to count the cost. Yes, listening to the stories of heroism and skill, we began to realize that every wife, every mother and every sweetheart who has a boy 'over there' would be wondering with icy fear in their hearts, was he in that raid ... was he safe, or was he one of those included in that first brief communiqué: "it is believed that there were considerable number of casualties"?

Now, those of us who know that no one belonging to us took part in the raid, must surely feel that our rejoicing should be tempered with a humble spirit, especially when discussing the raid with those whom we meet, for, as yet, we do not know 'for whom the bell tolls.' And so, although we may be justly proud of Canada's splendid officers and men, we remember, too, the price of victory, and remembering, our hearts go out in sympathy to those who have lost in action someone near and dear to them. For them, war in its grimmest sense has become a stark reality.

Meanwhile life on the home front goes on much as usual. Come good news or bad, we have little time these days to sit down and think about it. Harvest and threshing are still very much the order of the day. I think threshers must be hounded to death this year for, from every farmer, comes the cry, "Can you give me a day's threshing pretty soon? I can't get another sheaf in the barn!"

Some farmers, who had every intention of stook thresh-ing, found it impossible to get a machine in reasonable time and have stacked their grain instead. I passed one farm yes-terday where there were three such stacks, and no doubt the barn was full, as well.

Farm-wives are having their own troubles these days try-ing to put up a decent meal with such a small sugar allow-ance. But I haven't heard yet that any man has gone home hungry!

And speaking of rations, I have been surprised and decidedly disturbed at the attitude taken by some people in regard to sugar, tea and coffee rations, and from quarters where it was least expected. But, let me hasten to add, it was not in this immediate neighbourhood.

They say, "There is plenty of sugar in Canada; the storehouses are bulging with it" "Why can't we have more tea and coffee? They have more than we do in England and in the States they can buy all they want." "Well, I tell you, I can't quite see through this rationing business — it seems to me someone is getting a rake-off somewhere!" "An ounce of tea — it's ridiculous."

All those and similar remarks are what I have heard. Why, oh why! At this critical hour, cannot people reason things out for themselves? Perhaps there is plenty of sugar in the country — I hope there is — but who can say how long it may have to last? No one knows yet how much this year's raw sugar supply will amount to. And still less does anyone know what labour will be available to handle next year's sugar beet crop. It is quite conceivable that this country's reserve sugar supply may have to be eked out for several years.

Then as regards tea and coffee — both commodities are imported to Canada. Here again the amount we are allowed to buy naturally depends upon what reserve stocks are in our warehouses. Future stocks depend, not upon Government, but upon what happens to cargo boats carrying these supplies. A cargo boat, laden with tea, may start out upon its perilous journey. If it reaches Canada our tea ration is assured again for a little while. If a torpedo, or Jap planes, get a lucky strike at the boat, our future ration may sink to the bottom of the sea — and with it possibly brave lads who man the boat to bring us our favourite beverage.

So, in heaven's name, don't let us grumble, but remember in humble gratitude that lives are being risked to bring us every ounce of tea we use. Use less and spare the merchant marine.

SEPTEMBER 17, 1942

This week, as you probably know, all women in Canada, with certain exceptions, must register, if they are between the ages of twenty and twenty-four. The purpose of this registration is to make sure that every employable woman of that age is given the opportunity to work at a job for which she is best suited — in Canada — so she can take her share in the fight for freedom.

In Vichy, France, women between the ages of twenty-one and thirty-five are also required to register, but they must go where they are sent, and must work at whatever work is given them. The general interpretation of this order is that French women are to be sent to Germany to work for Hitler!

Could there possibly be a more striking comparison? And of course, the same thing applies to the men.

In Canada to-day there are many worried mothers whose sons have been called. The attitude of both mothers and sons in response to the call varies considerably. Which is no more than one might expect. In a peace-loving country such as Canada, people, generally speaking, have raised their sons to take their places on the farm, in the factory or in some profession — not as aggressive soldiers, sailors or airmen. And it is hardly to be expected that mothers can change their attitude overnight. And yet, if Canada is to do her part, a change of attitude is absolutely essential. We who are mothers must see to it that we do not become bottle-necks. We have a part to play.

Let us think this thing out. Supposing you are a mother whose son is of military age and you are hoping and praying that he will not be called, or if he be called that he will not pass. Why do you hope these things? There are so many reasons, aren't there? Quite apart from the fact that Dad probably needs the boy at home you are also worried because you feel that Jim would not be happy in the army. You don't like the thought that he may be sent a long way from home, perhaps to another country; he might be ill and need you, or, and this is a thought you admit only to yourself, he might not come back. Wherever he goes or whatever he does, you somehow have the impression that his life will be in constant danger. Isn't that so?

A lot of your fears may be quite reasonable but yet contradictory if you take a wider view. Your son in the service may sometimes, not always, be in danger for the duration. But, if we win this war, there will come a day when your son, if he is spared, and your entire family, will be normally free from danger. If we don't win this war, then remember, your son, your family, your children's children, will always be in danger. There would be no peace, or happiness, or safety, under Hitler. And the outcome of this war is of greater importance to the young generation than to us who have raised them. It is their future at stake. If we allow selfish, misguided personal fears to stand in the way of their going, whenever or wherever they are most needed, then we are living under a delusion. Home life is not longer a safe life, and will not be a safe life until Germany and Japan are crushed.

Not all men are fitted for the services but fortunately many men rejected as medically unfit are still perfectly able to farm, and they are badly needed. But, when a boy or man is called, and passes A1, surely nothing — that is, no personal objection — should be voiced to stop him going.

We need to think of it, too, from the boy's point of view. When a boy is left behind after seeing his chums enlist or called, he may be feeling pretty badly about it. If he is fit that makes it so much worse. If he finally goes of his own accord or is drafted, it doesn't make it any easier for him to know that his family is worrying about him day and night. Tears and fears never won a battle yet. Courage and a determined cheerfulness as we say good-bye will help our fighting lads far better than we know.

A cheery smile and an aching heart are a combination hard to achieve, but that is our part — the part of every mother whose son leaves home to help win this war.

And to those who are left behind? Let us be slow to criticize, quick to sympathize: for them serving on the home front may be the harder way. It is not given to every man to serve with the armed forces, but, at home or abroad, we all have a part to play, and a war to win.

JANUARY 7, 1943

To the *Free Press* reader who gave our soldier boy a ride last New Year's night I would like to say 'Thanks a lot' and I can't think of any time when a lift was more appreciated. Perhaps, for the benefit of those who don't know what I am talking about, I should explain that our son was on his way home from Quebec, and, according to the time he left there, he should have been home at 9:30 New Year's morning. But, due to the bad storms in Quebec which you have probably heard or read about by this time, the trains were running twelve hours late.

Bob got to Toronto some time New Year's night and started out to walk home from the Queen Elizabeth Way after getting a ride that far. I think he had already walked about eight miles when along came this good Samaritan with whom he was given a ride right to our very gate.

It was two-thirty Saturday morning when we heard his step in the back kitchen. And he had to get some sleep and some feed and start his long journey back to Vancouver that same day. It was quite a scramble, I can tell you. Not that our son was at all worried — far from it — he took it all in his stride. What a thing it is to be young!

Yes. Christmas and New Year are over once again. On Monday I shall really get to work in earnest and my first job will be to divest the Christmas tree of its trimmings and burn the tree. And it won't be a day too soon, believe me. The tree we had this year was a balsam, or is it larch? I'm really not sure. Anyway it is very pretty with very fine needles that drop all over the place as soon as the tree loses its natural moisture. We had this same variety of evergreen once before, and don't I remember it! The needles were everywhere: in the cracks and crevices of the woodwork, under the edges of carpets and rugs, sticking to cushions and drapes; you just couldn't move anything without finding needles somewhere.

That was my first experience with balsam, but this time I know what I am up against and shall work accordingly. It will also give me something to think about as I work, because at best this putting away of the trimmings of Christmas is a rather sad business. You cannot help but wonder what life has in store for you, or rather I should say for the nation as a whole, before the Christmas season rolls around again.

However, melancholy musings don't get us anywhere; there is work ahead for us to do. And the more we work and the less we grumble the nearer victory — what then? That is what everyone wants to know, and I think we are all agreed that we want better world conditions than have prevailed in the past. In the meantime we have to put up with things as they are and be ready to accept whatever inconveniences the future may bring.

After all we haven't suffered too much for lack of material things up to the present. Even the butter shortage didn't kill us. But there is no doubt we shall go short of quite a number of things in 1943. Wholesale supplies of various stocks and commodities are rapidly being used up, and when they are exhausted we are really going to know it.

Some of the restrictions are really funny. Imagine buying teacups without handles! Did you hear the answer given by an official of the W.P.T.B.? He said, "Anything too hot to handle is too hot to drink." Do you agree with that? I don't. Try it out sometime. It seems to me that tea you could drink from a cup that was cool enough to hold in your hands would be a mighty tame beverage.

So let's hang on to our cups, girls; don't let them slip from your hands when you are drying them. What we have now may have to last for the duration. Maybe the time will come when there will be no tea to put in them, but there will be something, don't ever worry, even if it's only hot water. And hot water is awfully good for you, isn't it?

Right now I am not worrying so much about cups and what goes into them but how to get this letter mailed when it's done. I can't get through the lane and it is a question whether the mail man will ever get around. Oh well, here's hoping, anyway!

JANUARY 21, 1943

Hardly a week goes by these days without bringing some further restrictions in our daily life, or at any rate a forecast of restrictions to come. Last week we were told that in all probability meat would be rationed on March 1 and that the ration would be at the rate of two and a half pounds per person per week. Well, no one would starve on that! Such an allowance seems to me unbelievably generous.

But, if we should feel inclined to think ourselves hard done by, it might be well to remember that in England, Lord

Woolton warned the people that rations over there would be progressively smaller for the next six months, in order to conserve shipping space in preparation for the coming Allied offensive. Imagine 'Progressively shorter rations' with an egg allowance already at one a month!

Canadians have also been warned that all pleasure driving will be eliminated when the new gas ration books come into effect on April 1. Now that *is* something, especially after Ottawa had recently announced that there was practically no pleasure driving in Canada anyway. When we heard that one, we wondered what sort of blinkers they wore in Ottawa these days. However, the blinkers, whatever kind they were, have apparently been removed.

And now we are wondering how 'pleasure driving' will be defined. For instance, if a business trip to the city for the man of the family is absolutely necessary, will it be permissible for his family to go along to take in a show? Not that I think going to a show is a matter of life and death, but I am wondering how it will be worked out because I believe a great number of people have managed to kill two birds with one stone in that way.

Well, whatever else is or will be rationed, the weatherman is still pretty generous with his winter storms. Believe it or not, I haven't been off the farm since the day after New Year's. That doesn't mean I haven't been out, of course. There are always enough chores around the farm to provide one with the necessary amount of fresh air. And sometimes when Partner takes the milk to the road I get a ride on the sleigh just for the fun of it.

This is the nearest to a western winter we have had since we left the prairie. But it has been far more inconvenient than anything I ever remember in the West. That, of course, is because we have become accustomed to depending on cars to get around. Now when we have to use the sleigh or cutter to go to town, there is no place to tie the horses. There used to be three sheds until a few years ago. Now there is only one. The other two were torn down because they were so seldom used.

And that means that when Partner goes to town I can never be sure he will be able to do any shopping because you can't park a team and walk into a store as you can a car. You must either have someone with you to mind the team or find a place to tie it. However, the man who gets our eggs brings the groceries on a toboggan from the road; the butcher leaves our meat in the mail box; the mailman takes our letters, except when he doesn't; and the car stays in the garage high and dry. The weatherman is an excellent oil controller!

But that reminds me: there is another restriction which comes into force in February and which you have probably heard about. After that there will be no more charging of food, fuel or drugs. It's pay as you go from then on. And that is another step in the right direction. When pay-day can be postponed, people are more likely to buy more than they can afford, forgetting that pay-day has to come sometime.

There was one time I bought something on the instalment plan and I vowed I would never do it again. Pay-day rolled around so fast each month the ink was hardly dry on one receipt before the next instalment was due. Finally I managed to get the last three months paid at one time and then I felt I could breathe again.

Great news has come over the radio this morning. Bombs on Berlin for the second night in succession. Boy if one of them could only drop on Hitler!

September 2, 1943

We have really got some coal at last, and we look on it as something very precious, indeed. Of course we had to take twenty-five per cent of the bituminous variety, but as we do not use our furnace we had the hard and soft coal kept separate as we plan to burn soft coal and wood in the range during the day and hard coal at night.

This bituminous stuff is something we have never had before, so, as the nights have been very cool, and a little heat more than welcome, I have been doing a bit of experimenting. I find the soft coal throws out a good heat, but oh dear, is it dirty! It is just about the nearest thing to pine stumps that I know. Directly it is put on the fire, it sends up a dense black smoke, and in a little while the under part of the stove lids are fringed with thick strings of soot.

The coal also seems to coagulate into a solid mass and burns away until there is nothing left, that is if a few sticks of wood are put with it occasionally to keep life in the coals. It does not clinker, and it is cheaper than other coal, but believe me I think we need to watch our flues and pipes to keep them clean. And certainly I'll not be burning soft coal on a windy day in winter.

I have just come back after shutting up the hens and chickens. It is a lovely night: quiet, cool and restful. As I walked towards the barn I noticed how the evergreens were in silhouette against the afterglow of the setting sun. It was very beautiful. Instinctively those lovely lines of Robert Browning came to my mind:

> Where the quiet-coloured end of evening smiles,
> Miles and miles
> On the solitary pastures where our sheep
> Half-asleep
> Tinkle homeward thro' the twilight, stray or stop
> As they crop

And then I thought of the devastated areas in so many countries where, not trees, but gutted homes and shattered buildings are in silhouette against the sunset sky. Many a place which, to continue the poem:

> *Was the site once of a city great and gay,*
> *(So they say)*
> *Of our country's very capital, its prince*
> *Ages since*
> *Held his court in, gathered councils, wielding far*
> *Peace or war.*

It all seems so tragic, doesn't it?

And yet it must go on — the bombing of cities and the loss of human life until the day comes when the Axis powers shall be ready — and probably glad — to accept the Allied terms of Unconditional Surrender.

Of course we are already looking for great things as a result of the Quebec conference, but maybe it is just as well for our peace of mind that we don't know 'what's cookin'.'

That was a grand speech of Mr. Roosevelt's last week. The part that appealed to me the most was that in which he implied that after the war there would be no return to the good old days, but rather the development of a better life from the remnants of the old.

Mr. Roosevelt is surely right. We certainly don't want 'the good old pre-war days' back again — we want something better for the boys who come back than depression and unemployment. We want them, and everyone for that matter, to have such opportunities for work and a decent living that our boys will say, "This was worth fighting for!"

And perhaps from the souls of those who fell we may fancy there comes an echo, "This was worth dying for."

I am sure we are all eagerly awaiting Mr. Churchill's speech on Tuesday. I don't know how you feel, but it always does me good just to hear his voice. There is something about the very quality of his voice that inspires one with a new zest for whatever lies ahead. Even when he promises nothing more cheerful than "blood, toil, tears, and sweat" one feels it is a challenge — a challenge that one must accept.

SEPTEMBER 9, 1943

Well, I have shooed the rest of the family off to bed. Now I can burn the midnight oil.

You see I have been sort of caught napping. This column should have been written and it isn't. I was busy at first on one thing and then another, and kept putting it off thinking I really had plenty of time. And yet, I knew it should be done in case we had company over the holiday. But then, as I hadn't heard of anyone coming I thought I might as well take my time. There was no letter from Daughter on Saturday, so I concluded she wouldn't be along — probably couldn't get the time off so soon after her vacation. But I might have known, these young things being as unpredictable as they are!

Came Saturday afternoon and a telephone call from Daughter: if she took the bus Monday morning could I meet her at Bronte? Needless to say I could, and I did. In fact Partner and I both met the bus.

After we got home, there was plenty to talk about, so we talked. Once in a while a guilty conscience would whisper in my ear, "What about your column?" and I would answer back, "Hush, let me alone; Daughter will be going back tonight and then I'll get down to work."

And then, to my surprise, I found Daughter wasn't going back — at least not until Tuesday night. So then my conscience and I agreed that there was only one thing to do, and that was sit up and work after the others had gone to bed.

So here we are, and glad I am to feel a cool refreshing breeze blowing through the screen door after the sticky humid weather we have had for the last forty-eight hours. You know, sticky weather, plus a holiday, really does lead to complications in housekeeping. For instance, if we don't buy enough bread to last over the holiday we naturally run short. And if we buy enough and to spare, then it goes mouldy before we can eat it up.

You people with your frigidaires and iceboxes, you can never realize the difficulties of keeping house without them. A day like this and butter turns to oil, milk goes sour and your ice cream for dessert is soft before you can get your first course decently disposed of.

My, oh my, but going shopping these days is somewhat akin to a Chinese puzzle. I often wonder what takes people to town on Saturday nights, because by that time there is nothing left to buy, that is in the line of provisions, and that is what most of us are hunting these days. As one storekeeper said to me, "Most people do their shopping in the morning now."

Yes, most of the town people. It doesn't take them long to slip up street, get what they want and home again. But farm-wives cannot leave their work so easily to come down town in the mornings, at least not at a time to suit the storekeepers. If we got there at a time that suits us, the stores are not open.

The other day one of our neighbours had been promised that if she got down town good and early the next morning she could get her car greased. So she was there by seven-thirty the next morning and had to wait half-an-hour for the garage to open. To-morrow morning I shall be taking this down to put it on the eight o'clock train, and if I could do a little shopping at the same time it would be just fine. But the stores won't be open, so I must either come home and make another trip later on or hang around for an hour.

Yesterday, on our way home from Bronte, I thought it might be a good idea to take a an ice cream brick home for dessert so I left the car at the post-office and told Partner and Daughter I wouldn't be a minute. I went up street to one drug store, and then another, and then to the ice-cream parlour, but no luck, they were every one of them closed.

Coming down street I met a Jewish gentleman so I thought I might as well do a little business. I suppose I was gone quite a little while one way and another so that when I got back to the car Partner said "Well, where's the ice cream?" "Oh," I laughed, "I couldn't get any ice cream so I sold fifty chickens instead."

DECEMBER 23, 1943

Practically everyone I have spoken to just lately has said," I am nowhere near ready for Christmas — it just seems as if I cannot get my self into the mood for it!" At Ginger Farm that has been our feeling, too, and I have little doubt that whether we mention it or not, it is our war-conscious minds that make it so hard for us to work up any real enthusiasm for Christmas in the traditional way. And then, Prime Minister Churchill's illness came as a great shock to all thinking people and has been responsible for much additional anxiety. But I am also sure the fact that he is, up to the date of writing, making satisfactory progress, is the best Christmas present the majority of the world could possibly wish for, and one for which we are all deeply grateful.

And yet, in spite of the war, there are some homes — and I love to think of them — in which the happiest Christmas of the war will be spent this year. I am thinking of one such family where two of the boys have been overseas for some time. For a while one of the boys was reported missing — later he was known to be safe. That boy is back from overseas and home for Christmas. What his homecoming meant to his family we can only guess. And now the other boy is also expected home along with his English wife and baby. What a family gathering that will be! I was speaking to the mother just a few days ago, and the look in her eyes was something to remember.

If only such happiness could come to every home.

Last week was a very worrisome week on the farm — cold weather, pipes freezing, cows calving, all kinds of extra business one way and another, until at the end of the week we seemed to have accomplished nothing. And that, as you may know, doesn't give one a particularly good start for another new week.

Then came Sunday and a candlelight service at our church. Partner couldn't go — he was still at the barn when I came home — but I went and took a friend along with me.

Have you ever had the experience of being harassed and bothered about your own little every-day problems and then suddenly felt as if they had all been spirited away?

Well, that is how it was with me almost as I entered the church. There in every window were the flickering candles against a background of cedar sprigs. Large evergreens filled each corner of the church. Lighted candles in red and white were the only illumination in the choir stalls. On the altar, upon either side of the Cross, were tall, tapering candles, from whose flickering lights shadows came and went. And there, high up above the altar, a single star shone clear and bright, just as a star must have shone many centuries ago.

The church when we first entered was fully lighted. Then the bright lights were dimmed and only the soft glow from the scores of small candles illumined the church and the congregation as it waited reverently for the service to begin. Softly the strains of the organ filled the church to accompany the white-surpliced choir as they came slowly, two by two, singing their way up the centre aisle towards the chancel.

Then as the congregation knelt in the flickering light, the thought came to me: "This is Christmas. This is something, which we feel in this church. This is the real Christmas, which neither hate, nor fear, nor brutal force can ever destroy."

The song service went on, young and old singing the familiar hymns and carols in unison. Then came the sermon: the story of the Nativity, illustrated every now and then by the choir singing exactly the right hymns at the right time. The rector, a splendid preacher, said, "The test of a service is after you have left the church." How true, and what a pity it isn't more generally realized.

As for this particular service, there was little doubt in my mind that, unless a person were deliberately unresponsive, the beauty, the solemnity and the promise conveyed by the entire service, and which it was naturally intended should reach the congregation, would certainly do so and would stay with them far beyond the confines of the church walls.

Last week I found it difficult to send you a Christmas message, but to-day I can wish you a Happy Christmas with all my heart, because I know a happy Christmas is possible even in the midst of war.

Part IV

REACHING THE
HOME STRETCH

1944–1946

JANUARY 6, 1944

After over four years of war isn't it wonderful to start a new year with a really definite hope that this is to be the year of victory? Oh yes, I know we have 'hoped' that same thing before, but we hoped because we were afraid to do anything else. There was very little conviction behind the hope, was there?

But now we can feel the end of the European war is in sight anyway, the Allied forces are ready to strike and I am sure everyone feels that, however great the price, victory is assured.

And doesn't that thought spur you on to greater effort? Don't you actually feel, "Well, what does this matter, or that matter, so long as I have more opportunity to do things, to go without things, that will help our boys along and bring them home again that much quicker?"

And just think how Mother Nature is helping us out and making things so much easier! No matter how much snow and cold weather we have from now on, it can't be as bad as it was last year because it will have started later. And how this mild weather has helped the fuel situation. Sure, it is still bad enough, but it could be a whole lot worse.

And it has its funny side, too. Have you ever been in town after any one of the coal dealers has received a carload of coal? It was quite funny the other day to watch the trucks buzzing here and there like so many bees around a hive. Big trucks, small trucks or any kind of truck the dealer could get hold of to unload the car and make coal deliveries to customers anxiously and hopefully awaiting their turn.

Down from the station came the trucks with their precious loads: one ton, half a ton, or whatever it might be. In a little while the empty trucks would go rattling by again and up to the station for another load. It looked as if the truck-drivers were just as anxious to get coal to the people as the people were to get coal.

And isn't it nice, now the hustle-bustle of Christmas and New Year's is over, to get down to our ordinary every-day life? The mail comes along at the right time; work that we had put on one side 'until after Christmas' can be brought out again; receipted bills can be sorted out and put away for safe keeping; and we might even take time now to read the daily paper and keep ourselves abreast of the times.

We might also have time to enjoy visitors and to do our little visiting ourselves, and of course we would take our knitting along with us. We wouldn't just sit and talk and do nothing the way the men do! You know, I really think knitting should be encouraged among our menfolk, especially in war time. Think what a lot of work could be done if the men took their knitting along with them to their council and school board meetings!

And speaking of visitors …We had a friend staying here last week just for a day and what a time she had. She had to be taken around to see the horses, the cows, the poultry and even the barnyard cats. And she wasn't above looking at Elmer, either. She wanted to know how much milk this cow gave, and which heifer was the daughter of which cow, and she was especially interested in 'Old Cicely's' record.

Cicely is nineteen years old and still going strong. However Cicely is going out before long, so you may meet a bit of her if you buy some bologna about three months from now! Then there was the poultry, how many eggs from this pen, how many from that? Where was the garden going to be this year and did we get that wood off the farm?

Finally we settled down in the living room, she with her quilt blocks and I with my knitting, and I think we both had a very enjoyable time. You see, our visitor was a retired farm-woman, and I guess to a person who has been born and raised on a farm there is nothing he or she likes better than to get back, if only for a few hours, to all the things that they knew and loved in the past. That is, if they did love farm life. There are others, of course, born on a farm who would do anything rather than go back to it.

JUNE 15, 1944

Sometimes we think we have too much work to do, and no doubt most of us have these days, but if there was ever a time when we should be thankful for work, and the ability to work, it is now. Can you imagine anything worse than to have time on your hands, time to listen to the radio, time to sit and think, to let your imagination run riot conjuring up all the possible and impossible things that may be happening on the beaches of Normandy and the battlefields of Italy?

Of course we all like to listen to the news some time during the day; in fact I must confess that when D-day finally arrived I arranged my work so that I could work and listen, too. I had the choice of several jobs that day. I could work in the garden, wash or paint the pantry. I chose to paint the pantry and in that way I was able to listen to the radio most of the day without wasting any time.

There were very few bulletins that I missed, and I was always ready and eager to relay the latest news to Partner any time he came near the house. Incidentally, the band music which was interspersed with the news I found to be a splendid accompaniment to painting. Try it some time; you will be surprised how well your paint brush slips along to the time of marching music.

That same night I went down to the special D-Day service. It was good to see how many people responded to the call for special prayers. I think, too, it filled a need for self-expression for many persons: it was something they could do, a definite link between the battle and the home front.

And now, time marches on. We have more or less got over the initial excitement of the invasion with most of us making some attempt to carry on as normally as possible, hoping and praying for maximum results with a minimum loss of life.

Well, as I was saying, I started to paint the pantry on D-Day and took the rest of the week to finish it. You know how it is: you can't paint the woodwork until the walls are dry. You can't do the 'trim' until the woodwork is dry; you can't enamel the shelves until the trim is dry; and you can't get things back on the shelves until the enamel is dry — four-hour enamel which took longer than overnight to harden. I tried to create some sort of a colour scheme and yet use what paint I had in the house. So, to do the walls I had a very little shutter green and put it into a quart of white and that gave me a pretty green tint.

But colour schemes don't always come up to one's expectations. Take our dining-room, for instance. I didn't tell you about it, did I? The colouring is buff and cream with a touch of red here and there to brighten things up a bit. You know, red in the wallpaper border, red in the cretonne curtains and a red flowered border to the new tablecloth that Daughter had given me. And then I washed the curtains, and believe me, they needed it. The soft coal had made them so black I soaked them in cold water overnight.

I got them clean all right, but they came out of the wash a nice, pretty pink. What am I going to do about it? Nothing — absolutely nothing. The curtains are still quite good and when things are so hard to get one cannot discard anything unnecessarily. So we shall have to look at pink curtains and a red trim for the duration, I guess. Maybe not for the duration of the war but for the duration of the curtains. Unless I dye them. But no — after what happened in the wash-tub there is no telling what I might make of a dye bath. I don't think I dare tackle it.

I suppose all you good people are busy in your Victory gardens? Ours is coming along fine, what there is of it. We nearly always have more garden stuff than we can use or give away so, with future hoeing in mind, we put in less this year than usual. After all, there are only two of us most of the time, and we are neither of us rabbits. Which reminds me, I saw two rabbits in the field quite close to the garden. If they find it ... well, there will probably be even less hoeing than we bargained for.

JUNE 22, 1944

Will you come exploring with me, just you and I and Tippy? You will? That's fine, then let's be going. But wait, we had better take that mosquito dope along — nasty little animals, those mosquitoes; they can sure take the joy out of life. It's pretty warm, you think? Well, yes, but then it's summertime, isn't it, so what else can one expect?

Come along, we will start up the back lane, through the pasture field, across the bush and over to the track. Yes, you guessed it; we're to go exploring for wild strawberries.

What wonderful growth of grass there is in the lane — that's because the cattle have not yet been pastured here. Next week it will be a different story, and the walking a little easier. See how well the spring crop looks ... yes, there are thistles there and chicory, too, along the fences. We don't like the look of them at all but still there is a limit to what one man and his wife can do on a hundred acres. Look, do look, over there near that blackthorn tree. Did you ever see a wild canary quite so yellow? Hear how sweetly he sings.

Now we must hunt for that place in the fence where we always get through to the track. How the years fly. Such a little while it seems since Daughter and our wee Son came exploring with me. And how soon they tired of picking berries. The creek was a much greater attraction. There was far more water in the creek in those days, and in it both the children learnt to swim. Right here at this bend — we called it 'the raspberry corner' — is where Bob nearly drowned. He was about three years old and was playing happily at the edge of the creek while I was teaching sister to swim. But he didn't stay there, and he went down twice before I reached him.

Well, here we are at the track. Mercy, where's Tippy? I hear a train coming, it will scare the life out of her. "Here Tippy. Come here little dog. Yes, we'll pick you up and hold you good and tight until the train has gone by. Don't tremble so, little dog, nothing is going to hurt you. See, there's the engine driver waving to us."

Well now, we had better start looking for strawberries in real earnest. After all, that's what we came for, wasn't it? Or was it?

And so it goes. We wander around, picking where we can, climbing fences where we come to them, swatting, every now and then, at mosquitoes which persist in attacking us despite our attempts to repel them. We are enjoying our rendezvous with nature, and we don't want to go home. But we must. There are hens and chickens to feed, and, on a hot night like this, Partner will be looking for a drink while he milks. Come to think of it, we could do with a drink ourselves.

How many berries have we got? Is that really important? Well, if you must know there are enough to make a good feed for two people for dinner to-morrow! Was it worth while, did you say? Wouldn't it have been more practical to slip down town and buy a quart, even at 35 cents? Well, that depends on one's sense of values. Out here, as one looks towards the far distant horizon — which doesn't seem so very distant after all — earth and heaven seem to merge into one. There is a 'peace that passeth all understanding' and one's faith is once more restored. Faith that somehow, somewhere, all the ugliness and suffering that is in the world to-day will come to an end. That out of the maelstrom of human misery there will emerge a better world in which all men may live in peace.

You see what I mean? One cannot buy hope and a new faith with a box of berries from a store, but one can find them out where the wild berries grow, out where the birds sing songs of freedom for all who wish to hear.

NOVEMBER 9, 1944

Well, it was nice while it lasted, wasn't it? That marvellous warm weather, I mean. Imagine 68 degrees in November. Did you make good use of it, doing jobs that you wanted done but never expected would be?

I was afraid to lose a minute. Partner and I were painting the outside of the house, and you know windows take a long time to do, what with puttying and two coats of paint. But it is such a satisfaction to have them done. The fresh white paint looks so nice against the red brick. Only one needn't expect other people to notice what has been done, at least not the menfolk. Actually we had a man come in one day and I asked him what he thought of our paint job. "Oh, have you been painting — I really didn't notice!" and then, to cap it all, after Partner had been down for the mail one day I asked him how the house looked from the road and he said: "Gosh, I forgot to look at it!" These men …

Working so much outside has led me to wonder if post-war inventions will include portable telephones. Directly I get back to the house I spend half my time answering telephone calls and every person starts off the same way, "Where in the world have you been? I've been trying to get you all week!"

Well, anyone who rings now will find me right at home. I haven't the least desire to be outside. There is a cold wind, snow flurries and a decided drop in temperature. It makes one begin to think of Christmas.

Christmas … another wartime Christmas. And so many people thought the war would be over by fall. Partner and I never thought that was possible. In any case, don't you think it rather unwise to let oneself speculate very much as to when the war will end? Such thoughts are bound to have a slackening effect on our work. Unconsciously we begin to think more about our own personal affairs, and perhaps let down a bit on whatever we have been trying to do in war-work activities.

Don't let us fool ourselves. There is no easy time ahead. The day will come when the war will end, be it late or soon. But to war there is always an aftermath, and in that aftermath our work, our faith and our courage will be taxed to the limit. So, if we must speculate as to the end of war, let us think of it only as the end of fighting and bloodshed, not as the end of work and worry to ourselves. There will be plenty of both, but we are Canadian women, descendants of a fighting stock. We shall surely accept the challenge. Isn't that so? From the prairies and the towns, from the cities and the farms, Canadian women everywhere will surely prove they can work for peace as well as for victory.

We have just got a letter from our son. He is at a camp now which is recognized as the jumping-off place for overseas. At any rate, his letters are censored. He says he doesn't know how long he will be there or where he will be going, and that if he did know he wouldn't tell us. "Don't look for any code messages from me," he writes, "because you won't get them. There is altogether too much of that kind of thing going on. I know you wouldn't tell, but then how is anyone to know what might happen to the letter, whether it might go astray or into whose hands it might fall?"

He also mentions the number of times he has been given a lift and the questions he gets asked, which, he says, are no doubt generally prompted by no more than a friendly interest. But in speaking to strangers, how can anyone know who might be an enemy agent?

Well, I guess our son is on the right track and if all the boys would be equally careful it would be all to the good. What about that merchant vessel that blew up in the St. Lawrence last week? Apparently no one yet knows what happened. It may have been a submarine or sabotage, and either could have been helped in their work by idle gossip. Who was it said, "Any fool can talk, but it takes a wise man to hold his tongue"?

MAY 10, 1945

The week-end of May 5th, 1945, is one that will long be remembered. Even though, officially, fighting has not yet entirely ceased, we know that an announcement regarding the end of the war is likely to come at any hour — in fact it has been expected since the afternoon of May 3. And what of the outcome?

Well, it seems to me that is something too big for you and me to even consider at this stage.

As for celebrating — I imagine the ones who do the most celebrating will be the ones to whom the war has brought very little in the way of worry or self-sacrifice. All thinking people are thankful that the slaughter of human lives is nearing an end, but one remembers, too, that for many families the end of the war will have come too late.

Yesterday I was down town and I met many persons who looked happier than I had seen them for some time. That haunted look was gone from their eyes. They wanted to stop and talk about where their boys were and what they were doing, and possibly for the first time in months they talked without restraint and without fear. It was good to talk with them.

Yes, it is easy to rejoice with those who have reason for rejoicing. But what of the others? On the eve of victory what can one say to the widow whose only son was killed when his plane crashed just a few short weeks ago, or to the father whose nineteen-year-old son was recently victim of a sniper's bullet, or to the family who, as yet, have no knowledge of the whereabouts of their son reported to be a prisoner of war in Germany. Least of all, how can one find words to sympathize with the young wife and mother, who in the midst of general rejoicing, received word that her young husband has been killed in action?

Perhaps these are not very cheerful thoughts; nevertheless one should remember there are hundreds of such cases in our midst — and if one remembers, then naturally one takes care that those who have suffered greatly will not be wounded still further by tactless and over-exuberant celebrations if it is in our power to prevent it.

Happily, there is another side to the picture. The long looked for return of the 'five year' men. Husbands who must learn to court again the girls they married. Fathers renewing their acquaintance with the kiddies who were mere toddlers when Daddy went away. And who can match the pride of the father who sees his son or daughter for the very first time?

Some of these happy family re-unions are taking place day after day, and now that the war is so nearly over, every mother, every wife and every sweetheart, whose loved ones have been spared, will feel that at last she can really hope — hope without that nameless dread — that the time will come when the boy, or boys, who went away will be marching home again.

Yes, but we shall need to have patience and fortitude. Wars

are not settled overnight. Fighting may cease, but there is still much work to be done, and the lads who wear the King's uniform are needed for the job. And there is still Japan!

As for us — particularly for the women who wait — we have our work to do. There is no room for idleness or relaxation while undreamed of distress prevails in Europe, but we can go forward with hopeful hearts, doing the job that is nearest, helping, each in our own small way, to build a new world, making our homes and our communities places that our boys will be glad to come back to and remembering always that it depends upon us whether the boys will say upon their return, "*This* was worth fighting for!"

P.S. — This was written before V.E Day was announced. And now all that we have longed for over so many years has come to pass.

May 31, 1945

After several days of fine weather, complete with warm, drying winds, our thoughts were hopefully turning once again to spring seeding — only it would seem more like summer seeding at this late date. However, call it spring or summer, it doesn't make any difference, for it is raining again just another good old soaker. So that is that.

Yesterday we had a houseful of family week-enders and we all went for a drive. It is said that misery likes company, but I can assure you that it didn't make Partner or me feel the least bit better to pass farm after farm in no better condition as to field crops than our own. Some of the wheat wasn't too bad, but we didn't see one field of spring grain that showed any promise at all. Unless a miracle happens, the result is bound to be serious.

Our drive took us to Malton Airport — a place that we like to visit about once a year anyway. We remember it from the time when construction work was first started, when there was nothing there at all other than a corner store, a few farm houses and construction gangs and machinery at work.

Now the runways, the various aeroplane plants, Trans-Canada sheds and the dwelling houses cover acres and acres of land. Any time we went there during the last few years we always found the place seething with activity, planes of every description coming and going all the time.

Yesterday it was very different — in fact the place seemed dead. It certainly looked as if the war was over. Trainer planes were conspicuous only by their absence. A lone Lancaster took off, circled around a few times and then landed again. One Trans-Canada Airliner was pushed out of its shed, given a warming-up and then left alone.

Around five o'clock a plane came in from Chicago. Ten passengers alighted — as nonchalantly as if they were stepping off a street car. The plane was re-fuelled, mail and baggage put aboard and in about twenty minutes she took off again, this time for Ottawa and Montreal and with only six passengers. And how I wish I had been one of them. I hope it may yet be my good fortune to go up in the air at least once before I go underground.

To review events further back in the week, we had a letter from son Bob, at present stationed in Germany — and if you think the Nazis are completely subdued take note of this, and remember it was written eight days after peace was declared. I quote from the letter:

"So far I just carry on, dodging mines as usual — and bullets too. A Jerry sniper put a bullet into my instrument panel yesterday. I got away pretty quick, I can tell you, and told the M.P.'s. I don't know whether they got the guy or not. I sure hope so as he had shot four of our guys that day already. It happened as I was driving through a German town. The bullet came through the back of the cab — and I'll swear it made a detour around my head before it smashed into the instrument panel. Now I have another hole for fresh air anyway. Half an hour later I nearly piled my truck up because I had to take to the ditch to avoid hitting a Jerry civilian. To-day a Jerry asked me for a cigarette. I opened my case, took out a smoke, lit it myself and just looked at him. I never said a word but he caught on pretty darn quick."

When one gets a letter like that and realizes that our boys are still at the mercy of death-dealing snipers, one gets rather disgusted at the verbal sniping that is going on in our own country, particularly in political circles.

Well, it is time for me to feed my chickens. In this worrisome spring they are the one bright spot. They flourish and grow like nobody's business, come rain or shine. I have lost fewer this year than in any previous season — and I have taken bigger chances. The little ones are not yet three weeks old and they are getting along very nicely without any help at all.

Perhaps I should not say I am taking a 'chance.' I am really experimenting on the theory that heat and damp weather produce disease. Keep the heat down, and while one may lose a few chickens that are not too hardy, those that survive the Spartan treatment are healthy and thrifty.

JULY 19, 1945

Please forgive me if this week's 'Chronicle' should be a trifle disconnected. So much has happened since last I wrote that I find it really hard to concentrate. You see we have our son back home again, alive and well. There is no need for me to elaborate on that statement — every parent with a son on active service knows very well what that means.

Yes, our boy has returned to us, but even at the moment of his arrival my heart ached as I thought of those families so much less fortunate. I am sure that to see other boys returning, and know that your boy lies buried in a foreign field, is like turning a knife in an old wound. But that, unfortunately, is one of the fortunes of war. Our good luck might easily have been yours — your misfortune, ours. Probably only a sniper's bullet made the difference.

And as I sit listening to the war talk between the men of my family, I am amazed that our son ever managed to come home at all — in fact that so many come back alive.

Bob came over on the 'Queen Mary' — you remember she docked in New York harbour last week — and thereby hangs a tale. For some reason which I cannot explain, ever since it was first announced that the 'Queen Mary' was bringing troops home, bound for Canada, I was absolutely certain that our son would be among them. Partner thought I was crazy — especially when the news broke about the riots in Aldershot, where he was stationed.

And then every few days letters would arrive — the last written June 30, in which Bob said he was getting another short leave. That increased Partner's conviction that his return soon was impossible.

I didn't argue — because logically speaking there was nothing to argue about — but my hunch stayed with me just the same. When the 'Queen Mary' docked I stayed as close to the house as I could, waiting for a possible wire to be relayed by telephone. And it came — it really came — followed in half-an-hour by an official card from M.D. 2.

I ran to the barn — and after telling Partner the good news I reminded him that it is sometimes better to trust a woman's intuition rather than a man's reasoning.

Of course it wasn't long before I phoned Daughter, and so sister met brother in Toronto. They spent the evening together, and then Bob continued his journey home on the 'midnight.'

And since then, well, the next few days can hardly be described. There is so much to talk about, so much to explain and describe. Bob wants to know all about everyone he ever knew in this district; we want to know all about the folks back home whom he visited.

We are careful not to ask too many questions about his experiences in Europe, but we hear plenty just the same. They leak out in the ordinary course of conversation. We hoped he would bring home a few souvenirs to hand around, but he brought home very few. The reason was that most of the time he was either in Holland or Germany and he says Belgium is the place to buy souvenirs. In Holland there is nothing left to buy.

However he did have a few relics: a collection of Dutch and German coins, a German belt, a watch purchased in Belgium when he first landed, a pair of wooden shoes — in miniature — and a solid brass cover for a memorandum pad which he picked up in Germany. He also had an Iron Cross which a young German boy had offered him when the Canadians first took over, but which somebody later 'swiped' from his kit-bag.

All these things are quite interesting, but the best souvenir he brought us was himself — and we shall never cease to be grateful that he was spared to come back to us in good health and all in one piece.

As for Bob — I think the farm looks pretty good to him just now. At any rate, he has lost no time in getting out and doing things to help his Dad. And I'm telling you, there was never a time when his help was more acceptable than it is right now.

AUGUST 16, 1945

Concentrating on one's own work has been almost impossible these last few days. Mixed up with harvest and home activities are thoughts and fears of the awful possibilities of atomic bombing. It grips one's imagination, sends shivers down the spine — and is so utterly fantastic as to be almost unbelievable.

Comments from the press, pulpit and public have also been thought provoking, especially those which assert atomic bombing to be inhuman. There is no doubt that such bombing is, of necessity, inhuman, but one should also remember that if it must be either them, or us, and if atomic bombs serve to bring about the end of the war, then surely their use is justified.

What a week-end this has been! Everyone on their toes expecting the news that V-J Day had at last arrived. And then when the news did come, it wasn't true. The whole thing has all the appearance of a clever piece of enemy propaganda. However, I suppose it will be true, sooner or later — and may it be soon.

No doubt those in Canada most interested in the progress of the war with Japan are the men in the services who have volunteered for the Pacific. And of course, friends and relatives of the men are equally interested. We are among that number. Our son's thirty-day furlough expires on Tuesday. And after that — only the powers that be know the answer — and they won't tell!

The month has gone so quickly and son Bob has been busy all the time. And having more help and less worry has made a new man of his father. It will be a good thing when the labour situation is relieved for it seems to me that many men — and women, too — who have passed the age at which they should be taking things a little easier are now working harder than they ever did. At the same time, readjustment to peacetime conditions will be no easy problem to solve. There is bound to be discontent. But it will help if we all try to cultivate a greater degree of common sense coupled with sympathetic understanding.

What our men have been through under shell fire and as prisoners of war is bound to have its effect in the immediate future. There will be times when they will be irritable, restless and moody. I know, because I went through it after the last war. This is a different war, and a different generation, but fundamentally, cause and effect are the same.

The men have done their part, and, for those who return, whether they are able to adjust themselves to peacetime conditions depends largely upon the women in their homes. A woman who matches her husband's irritability with more of the same cannot expect a very happy future, nor can the woman who drags her man around against his will with the idea of giving him 'a good time' and helping him to forget.

I don't suppose many young married folk read this column, but if there are a few war brides who do, let me beg of you to have patience with that returned man of yours, remembering that all casualties are not obvious to the beholder. Generally marriage is a case of fifty-fifty, but the aftermath of war can make it anything — sixty-forty, seventy-thirty, with a gradual evening of the scales according to the courage and common sense with which a returned man's family deals with his every mood.

If a man feels like walking the floor, it isn't going to help if you tell him to sit down and read a book and stop being restless. Far better to suggest that he take it out on the woodpile. Or if he is quiet and moody, keeping up an endless chatter of small talk isn't going to have the effect of cheering him up. It is more likely he is remembering things of which you have no knowledge, and of which he does not wish to speak, so that frivolous, inconsequential small talk can only add to his impatience and may well act as a wedge to drive you apart.

Think it over, war-brides. Your men have fought to win a war. It is your job to fight to win the peace — peace in the new homes of Canada.

May 9, 1946

We were sitting at supper Saturday night. Presently Bob glanced up at the calendar and said reminiscently, "This time a year ago, just exactly where was I? Yes, I remember it was a little place just across the Rhine. I wrote you a letter from there, Mom, did you happen to keep it?"

Yes, I kept the letter; it is even more interesting than when it was written. Here it is, in part:

"Saturday, May 5th, 1945. Canadian Army Overseas.

"I intended to write yesterday, but there was no opportunity nor any official news. Now I am wondering — will this be the day to remember through the years to come? At 4:30 this afternoon we were given the official news of Germany's surrender by army dispatch. What was it like back home?

I am sure no one in Canada could quite realize what it was like out here, but I am going to try and tell you.

"On May 4th the men began to take a new interest in the news, not wildly, but casually asking first one person then another. We had a very long drive that day and occasionally bits of rumour would be picked up along the way and spread around among the boys. There was really no excitement. Life went on just the same as before. Life — and death. Outwardly no one expressed any particular elation.

"Friday evening we were billeted well forward in Germany. Someone started to rumour that peace was to be signed on May 5. It did not create much of a stir, it was accepted casually as just another rumour. Saturday morning we were idle, waiting orders. There were all kinds of rumours: that we were moving back to Holland; that we were to stay put; that we were moving still further up. No one knew anything; no one cared very much."

It was just another day with another detail to be filled. Everyone knew that peace was inevitably near, but no one let up on his job nor did we want to. In the billet here, one group of men were playing cards, another group singing to the accompaniment of a guitar and harmonica. Some were sleeping, some talking and joking, others working on their trucks and one fellow was doing a paint job.

"There was no great feeling of optimism or of pessimism for that matter, yet everyone was happy, happy with a tense sense of expectancy. We moved again, up into Holland. There was no more news. But this morning we were informed we might have the day off, our very first. That, believe me, really brought forth the cheers. But yet it didn't make beds; some fellows went out to hunt new girl friends.

"At 4:30 we were summoned to the Orderly Room and given the news. It was officially announced that Germany had surrendered. There was still no great excitement, no cheering, just the ordinary murmur heard after any lecture. The men went back to their beds. Some read, some talked, some shaved, but there was no great show of feeling. To-morrow our platoon will be out on detail again. There is plenty of laughter going on right now, but no one is so optimistic as to feel our job is done."

Bob looked over the letter quietly. "Yes," he said, 'to-morrow our platoon will be out on detail again.' I remember that all right. It was V-E Day, but we were working as usual. One of our trucks hit a mine. The truck was blown up. Three of our boys were killed. That was what V-E Day meant for them."

Now it is 1946, and we are 'enjoying' the fruits of 'peace.' It is not war in Germany now that is making the headlines, it is strikes and more strikes and we wonder where it is all going to end.

I wonder if anyone realizes what a depressing effect all this industrial unrest has on the farmers. We are urged to grow more, raise more, produce more, but I ask you, what encouragement are we given to do it? Half the time we can't get what we need to work with, or if we can the price is just about sky-high. A farmer working alone doesn't know where his help is coming from to take off the crop.

And yet we carry on — it may be better next year! In the meantime, we have had a million dollar rain, and are we ever thankful for that.

JULY 18, 1946

When a person has lived in a neighbourhood for over twenty years and has had the same neighbours east, west, north and south for most of that time, it creates a feeling of permanency, for ourselves and possibly for the neighbourhood in general. The men are accustomed to 'change work' with the same neighbours year after year; the women visit back and forth, when they have time, at quilting, meetings, teas or perhaps only on a telephone. On washdays as we hang things on the line we notice our neighbours have their washing out, too, and it all helps to give one a comfortable feeling, a sense of unity with the rest of the community.

That is how it has been here anyway. Insofar as we are concerned, I must admit we have not visited back and forth very much, but yet we always knew, that should the occasion arise, as indeed it has a few times, we had only to ask for help and it would be given graciously and willingly.

Of course there have, unfortunately, been gaps left in our neighbourhood by the work of the Great Reaper, but there has been very little moving away from the district.

And now, like a bolt from the blue, comes news that two of our neighbours have sold their farms. It gives one a queer sinking feeling. It is hard to get used to the idea that in a few short months these same farms will have different owners, and we shall have different neighbours.

What will they be like, these new neighbours? Will they be of the 'dirt farmer school' or will they incline towards ultramodern methods of highly mechanized farming? Will they be congenial neighbours, good mixers, or will they endeavour to live unto themselves? Those are questions to which only time can give the answer. At the same time, we can't help wondering — and with a little trepidation — because one's neighbours are so important, especially to folk who live in the country.

And the people who are moving away? In one case the place was acquired, but in the other, the lady of the house has lived there all her life. One can only imagine the heartache it will be to pull up stakes and go. I am sure that as the day of departure gets nearer, anyone so placed would find every tree, every shrub, almost every nail on the wall had some special significance. The well-worn path from the house to the barn along which so many well-loved feet have trod, the pump by the kitchen door which has provided water summer after summer, the view from the kitchen window, and oh, so many things — such little things that may never have been of any great importance up to now. But to leave them, ah, that's a different story.

But isn't that the way of life? Sometimes we must lose a lot in one direction to gain a little in another.

On the other hand, if we take a change we sometimes lose a little but gain a lot.

In the meantime, there is still seasonal work to do on all farms: haying to finish, and wheat to cut. And speaking of wheat, I have mended our binder canvas. But I didn't mend it with needle and thread. This time I pasted the patch on the canvas. Whether it will be a success has yet to be proved. I am hoping it will be, because it was a lot less work anyways.

This week-end we thought we were going to be alone. Yes — actually! But around six-thirty Saturday night the telephone ran and a meek little voice said, "Hullo, Aunt Gwen, can I throw my hat in for the week-end?" Of course there was only one answer to that question. But then we didn't see much of our visitor, because on Sunday afternoon Bob took her to Toronto to see other relations. And then the house was so quiet I could not sit still, or was it because I was reading a very disquieting article on the Soviet Union — an article which proved beyond a doubt that Communistic organizations are unhealthily active in Canada and the U.S.A. Is it any wonder we have strikes and yet more strikes?

AUGUST 15, 1946

It has come at last! "What has come?" did you ask? Well, if for weeks, in fact months, you had been hoping by day, and dreaming by night, for just one thing, then you wouldn't need to ask 'what.' Of course, it is my electric stove I am talking about. Yes, it actually arrived, last Tuesday to be exact, and this time it was not damaged in transit.

Wednesday morning a couple of electricians came in to fix it up, and by eleven o'clock it was ready for action. And so was I. We had an extra man for dinner that day as they were trying to finish clearing the barley field. What with the stove, the electricians and extra field help, I really felt somewhat rushed that morning.

However, one thing was clear in my mind: I mustn't be late with dinner. You don't mind telling your own men dinner will be ten minutes late, but you feel you have to be on time for extra help. I was on time all right! Everyone had been warning me that, at first, I would think an electric stove was awfully slow.

With this in mind, and to be on the safe side, I set the grill and put the pork chops in right away, at eleven o'clock! In twenty minutes they were done to a turn. Then I didn't know what to do with them. I tried shutting off the grill and leaving them in the oven. But the blessed things went right on cooking. In desperation I tried the warming oven. That, at least, didn't cook them, but by noon my nice, fresh meaty chops were just as dry as chips.

Fortunately the vegetables were all right and I managed a pie filling without disaster, but those chops: they were really something to remember!

After dinner I experimented with some baking, but of course, before doing it, I spent no end of time studying the directions. I did so with fear and trembling because a friend had told me how very careful you have to be in setting the oven or the whole system of automatic heat control would be thrown out of order. She knew because she had done it!

And I am not surprised. Operating the oven, at least on the type of stove I have, is just one of those things: simple enough when you understand it but as complicated as a whole bag of tricks until you do. As a matter of fact, before night came I was so on edge I was ready to bite. I was wishing to heaven everyone would clear out and leave me to do my experimenting in peace. But you don't catch Partner doing anything like that. He always seizes any opportunity to tease. If he came in and the stove wasn't in use he would say, "Why aren't you using the stove? What's the good of having one if you don't make use of it?"

If I was using it then I would hear, "What are you using up all the power for? Just because you've got a stove, you don't have to keep it going all the time!"

Is it any wonder that I had to take an aspirin to cure my head ache?

And I thought an electric stove would mean the end of all my baking worries. For a few days it was only the beginning. But I am learning — learning fast — the hard way. So far I haven't ruined anything other than the pork chops, and the family hasn't died of indigestion. Occasionally I turn on a burner to boil the kettle, go out to feed the chickens, come in again, and find the kettle hasn't boiled for the simple reason that the burner I turned wasn't the one under the kettle. This stove has all solid plates and it isn't until you feel the heat from them that you are sure which burners are alight, that is supposing you are green and dumb like I am.

However, in spite of all my worries I am already convinced that an electric stove is a great convenience and time saver. To say nothing of being able to bake in hot weather without being reduced to a grease spot. Some of our week-enders were here again and they were properly enthused.

And speaking of week-enders, this is really getting to be somewhat of a madhouse. Our young nieces collected barley stalks, complete with head and beards, thistles, a small quantity of gravel, a flesh brush and a cold 'hot' water bottle and dumped them all between the sheets of Bob's bed! What a riot there will be next week when Niece Joy arrives on the scene.

Isn't it great to be young, or failing that, to be where young people are!

Part V

LIFE GOES ON

1947–1952

July 17, 1947

Something seems to tell me that this is summer. At any rate, it is the time of heat and haying, sudden storms and summer visitors — but not necessarily related — and times when everything seems to happen at once.

Saturday, for instance. The men were working like fury trying to clear a big field of hay before threatening storms could stop them, or the close of the day bring a normal end to field and barn activities. And between them they did it. Partner took over the chores while the boys stayed out in the field.

One load they brought in just about had me quaking. I was sure the wagon would never go into the barn or that John would be decapitated in the process. The load swayed crazily on the rough ground and as it approached the barn I stood watching. John crouched lower and lower, the horses lugged their way into the barn, the beam over the doorway caught the top of the load until it pushed a few forkfuls of hay back and back and finally over the end of the rack. Except for that the load did go into the barn.

Having reassured myself on that point, I moved 'the Greening' out of the sun into the garage. Maybe my mind was on the load, or maybe it was the heat, anyway when I wanted to go to town a couple of hours later I found the ignition was still on and the battery worse than useless. I thought to myself, "Well, that's something for Bob to deal with, and will he be mad!"

After supper I told him the worst, and he wasn't mad at all. In fact he took the opportunity to do a little experimenting. Instead of towing the car or getting a store battery, he jacked one wheel up and then turned the wheel just as he does the fly wheel on the tractor, and presto, away went the motor as slick as you please.

Then came Sunday. Both the boys expected to be away most of the day and as Partner and I were not looking for any visitors, we intended to make the most of a quiet day and rest up a bit. Incidentally there wasn't too much to eat in the house because in humid weather I try to keep perishable food supplies down to a minimum rather than have them spoil.

Of course you have guessed what happened! Yes, we had visitors all right —visitors from a distance — for dinner, afternoon tea and supper. But don't think they starved. On a farm there is always something one can rustle up a meal with in a hurry, but until one has thought it out one does have a few bad moments! And believe me, short rations notwithstanding, we were pleased to see our visitors.

Then came Monday. Carpenters were here first thing in the morning to repair the hayfork track. Partner left the boys to help with the job while he went out to mow. While all the men were thus occupied, a truck came along to pick up a veal calf we wanted to have butchered for the locker; then along came another truck for two veal calves that were going to market, and of course each time I had to hunt a man to handle the calves. Sometime during the morning, John came to the house and looking for bolts in a box at the barn he disturbed a bee's nest. By the look of John's arm, one bee had shown active resentment, the others were buzzing around angrily just near the driveway in the barn where the horses had taken their load. As everyone knows, bees and horses in a barn don't make good companions. I fixed up Johnny and then after I had given the bees time to quiet down a bit, I fixed them, too. Thank heaven for DDT — it can sure save a lot of work and misery on a job like that.

Back to the house and my baking — at least that's what I thought. But no, the phone rang and a Jewish gentleman asked if the chickens were ready that I had promised him. That was the last straw. "No," I answered — and probably I was a little short — "it is too hot to crate chickens to-day."

Well, I did eventually get four pies baked and my meat and vegetables cooked, but by dinner time I was certainly too hot and tired to help eat them. But that didn't matter, the men were fed and that was all I cared.

Now I am looking forward to our four o'clock tea — that's what I enjoy more than any of the regular meals. The kettle is on and while I am waiting I am writing this by a open window looking on to the hayfield. There is a lovely fresh breeze coming this way and I am hoping my men are getting the benefit of it, too. The chickens are having their siesta under the shade of trees and shrubs; even the robins are waiting until the sun goes down before raiding our cherry trees.

The news says, "Hot again to-morrow" — oh-oh — and to-morrow my sister-in-law is coming to stay!

NOVEMBER 13, 1947

So, it's here at last: cold, stormy weather, and how much we would like to know if it is here to stay. We would know then what to do about a number of things. Whether to shut up the pullets for good, and whether the cows should be stabled — they have all been running out so far in the hope that we might cut down a little on the feed bill.

Oh, that feed bill! Four bags of laying mash that cost $10.80 in September is now $15, and fattening mash that used to be $2.50 now costs us $4 per hundred. And yet the price of eggs and chickens has dropped. Dairy concentrate, without a doubt, is correspondingly high but so far we haven't bought any. Buying concentrate, supposedly, increases the milk flow, but then what a farmer gets for the extra milk is used up paying for the concentrate. The same applies to poultry and poultry feed. How long farmers can continue to rob Peter to pay Paul is questionable. Rumour has it that milk is due for another price increase. We would rather see the price of milk stay where it is and some of the things we have to buy go down.

How long families with small fixed incomes can stand the high cost of living is something we are all wondering.

However, I read the other day that according to statistics we have just about reached the saturation point. I don't pretend to know much about it but I like that expression, 'the saturation point.' It sounds as if a huge, dry sponge had been thrown into our economic set-up and was absorbing the life-blood of the nation. But now if the saturation point has been reached, or nearly so, then a change must come, and it would seem that the sponge must be squeezed to release to the public some of that same life-blood that has been so readily absorbed.

Which is worse, I wonder, austerity or inflation? An austerity program such as Britain is experiencing to-day is hard on everyone, but yet that same fact creates a common bond of sympathy. People have a way of realizing that many have troubles greater than their own, and they set about trying to help each other if they can.

Inflation produces inequality and discontent. Those who already have much, get more; those with little, get less — and if there is a surer way to breed discontent I have yet to meet it. There is also distrust, jealousy and certainly a great deal of ignorance concerning the other fellows' problems among the various types of wage earners.

Farmers lose patience with striking industrialists, while wage earners have an idea farmers are sitting pretty, living off the fat of the land with little or no expense. White collar men consider their inadequate salary — at least, to them — and figure they would be better off laying bricks. Store keepers, builders and plumbers grumble at the high cost of trucking; truckers complain at what they must pay for tires, licence, insurance, repairs and labour.

And housewives — well, there is no limit to their budget worries. However, no more sugar rationing certainly gives us a wonderful break. I have a feeling it won't please the bakers quite so well.

No one has really suffered under sugar rationing but without it house-keeping is certainly going to be a lot easier. Home-made brown sugar syrup comes in very handy at times, and is much cheaper than corn syrup. Poured hot over stale sponge cake or rice pudding you have a dessert that children love. And of course it will take the place of the more expensive maple syrup to serve with pancakes. Fudge also is now a possibility instead of eight cent chocolate bars. Incidentally what could be better for packing in boxes for Britain than home-made candy?

And speaking of boxes for Britain: I had a grand little job passed on to me last week. It was to deliver seventeen boxes for Britain to Tamblyn's drug store. Twelve were from our own W.I., four from a small country district and one from a private party. The manager of the store nearly dropped when I told him how many there were to bring out from the car. Of course you all know these boxes were in answer to an appeal from Mrs. Kate Aitken, broadcasting for Tamblyn's stores.

NOVEMBER 27, 1947

It would be interesting to really know which created the greater stir last week — Princess Elizabeth's wedding or Canada's 'austerity' program. Personally I thought one counter-balanced the other.

I suppose it is hard for some people to understand the British reaction to that wedding — many think it was a dreadful waste of money — money that shouldn't have been spent with Britain lacking so many of the necessities of life — and they wouldn't listen to the broadcast for that reason. I don't think people who have that opinion know very much about real hardship. It is easy to criticize under those circumstances. Naturally people who are hungry want food for the body but if people are hungry long enough they also crave food for the soul so that they may endure their physical discomforts more easily.

Princess Elizabeth's wedding gave the British people — and many Canadians — colourful, heart-warming romance, that is, food for the soul. Listening to that broadcast did something to a person — one was conscious of a tightening of the throat. One forgot the bride was England's future queen, at the moment she was just another girl, marrying the man she loved. And that, I think, was also the feeling behind the cheering crowds on that memorable day.

Elizabeth not only symbolized the British throne, she symbolized romance. I am sure there were many persons who went back to their homes that day and ate an insufficient and uninteresting meal with less resentment because of that little bit of colour that had come into their lives. And after, if the Princess had been married in a cotton dress, would it have added one ounce to the average person's ration?

And now, what about Canada's austerity program? That is not so easy to figure out, is it? Personally I think the description 'austerity' is a travesty of the word and almost an insult to people who really know what austerity means. On the other hand, it is a little early yet to really appreciate what the outcome will be. It will probably affect the farming class less than urban citizens, but even in the country it may have unforeseen repercussions.

I know it has brought a sudden end to one of my fond hopes for the future — that is, an electric refrigerator. And, oh dear, how I was hoping that next summer I might be spared that ever-lasting running upstairs and down with food to and from the cellar. But I suppose what has to be, must be — and who am I to grumble? Certainly I shall go without a refrigerator a little longer rather than pay an extra hundred dollars to get one.

One gets used to disappointments these days. Last Saturday, for instance, Daughter had bought tickets for us for the Royal Winter Fair, then Partner developed some eye trouble — the inflammation just about closed one eye — and I had a touch of neuralgia so that little outing was cancelled. By Saturday night Partner was in bed and I was listening to the hockey match — the fact that the Leafs trimmed the Bruins was a little consolation. Then on Sunday morning, Daughter came home for the rest of the week-end, and that helped still more.

Well, it looks as if winter is trying to pay us a visit at last. So far we haven't done too badly. Son Bob has got all his ploughing done and the worst is over insofar as our new highway is concerned. It will be even better if we get a frost. To walk down the road means carrying about ten pounds of clay on each shoe. That is hardly conducive to comfort.

Why mothers turn grey! Daughter decided to stay until the 7 o'clock bus Monday morning. I set the alarm and had everyone up at six except Partner. But you know girls and their last minute fixing! While Daughter was swallowing her apology for a breakfast — and doing several other things at the same time — I thought I would check on the bus time table. It left at 6:45. Thanks to her brother she made it, but only by stopping the bus on the road. It was really the advertisement in our local paper that saved the day. Does it pay to advertise? I don't know, but it pays to read them — preferably a little ahead of time!

December 18, 1947

How many seasons in a year? Did you say four? I think there are five: spring, summer, autumn, winter and Christmas! Don't you think that is right? And don't you think it is wonderful to have Christmas come right in the middle of what is often the longest and dreariest season of the year — a season within a season, as it were? A season with weeks and weeks of wintry weather with more darkness than light, and days of blizzards followed by blankets of snow, sleet, rain and frost — and then more snow.

But then in the middle of this austere weather, and just as we are getting terribly fed up even at the thought of it, along comes Christmas with all its colour and story; with its beautiful traditions and spirit of goodwill, and if we are wise, we forget all about the elements and set our hearts a-singing. Away from home, who lets the weather worry them anyway? We say, "Aw shucks, I'm going home no matter what!" And if we are among the stay-at-homes, we look forward to our folks coming for the Yuletide season; we work and bake and scheme; we trim the tree and wrap the presents; and, although just about tired enough to drop, we greet everyone with a cheery, "Happy Christmas!"

And have you ever noticed, friends, that with every Christmas greeting that we give, some part of it comes back to ourselves? We just can't go around wishing other people happiness without sharing in it, too.

And another thought: just as we welcome Christmas in the middle of winter, isn't it also possible to experience an even greater sense of gladness when we remember that in this troubled world with its threats of still more war, its strikes, disunity and its millions of hungry people, there is yet always Christmas, steadfast as a rock, now and forever.

Oh, I know that in many homes Christmas will be little more than a name — the presents, the fun, and many of the accustomed good things to eat will be absent. Ah, but even in such homes there will be mothers telling little children about the Christ-child that was born many long years ago to bring peace to a troubled world. And perhaps as she tells it, there will creep into many a mother's heart the peace that passeth all understanding. Thus will she find hope again.

Friends, let's not let bitterness spoil our Christmas. Let's not think, "What's the use ... all this unrest ... all these high prices ... where's it going to end?" Let us give ourselves a Christmas present of faith in the future, and let us be content with the little things in life — the friendly greeting, the little unexpected kindnesses that come our way, and the happy, comfortable feeling that comes to us with the spontaneous desire to help make Christmas a little easier, a little brighter for someone else.

And where better can we start than with the children — not just our children, but children everywhere. Christmas and children surely belong together. Happy the family where young, excited voices and merry, carefree laughter mingle with the deeper tones of the grown folk. Let us make this Christmas — and every Christmas — one for the children to remember. Whatever our troubles we can surely forget them for a while so that the children may be happy — and in their happiness probably find our own.

And so friends, in all sincerity, may I wish you a very happy Christmas. May you be light-hearted and gay, the better to enjoy your friends, your children and *yourself*. In short, have a good time and enjoy your Christmas. There will come other days — days when we can fuss and fret and stew, if we must. But this is the Christmas season, this is the time to cast dull care aside and say to everyone we meet — "Happy Christmas, everybody!" Yes, and mean it.

Ah, what a thought! If a share of each greeting comes back to oneself what a lot of joy is coming my way, because, here am I, sending a message to literally hundreds of people. Now what do you know about that? A Happy Christmas to you *all*.

MARCH 2, 1950

Some weeks go by as quiet and uneventful as drifting clouds on a summer day. But not last week — anything but! There was plenty doing both at home and abroad — the British election, our belated Canadian winter, installation of a milking machine, and my one-woman quilting bee.

Dealing with these events by virtue of their importance rather than their natural sequence we come first to the British election, because what happens in Britain, either politically or economically, certainly affects Ginger Farm and the rest of Ontario. Like most people we went to bed Thursday night expecting the British Labour party would be returned to power with a good majority. And we were a little fearful — fearful that the Socialist government in its headlong nationalization plans would be taking the people too far out on a limb, in a way so far removed from British traditions it was hard to imagine that it could be a success.

But first thing Friday morning the trend showed signs of a change, and by noon — well you know the story. When Partner came to dinner I turned on the radio. "Listen," I said, "listen to the news!" Partner listened with growing incredulity. "But what happened — I thought Labour was in with a big majority?"

And what did happen? That is what everyone would like to know. And the end of the story is not yet. In fact for quite a while the rest of the world will be watching the British political crisis with increasing interest.

Well, while the British Isles were getting 'hot,' Canada was getting cold with its first prolonged spell of winter weather. It snowed and it snowed; the wind blew and the mercury almost lost itself at the base of the thermometer. Highways were blocked, sideroads impassable and most farm lanes plugged as tight as could be.

Then as we started watching our coal bins, the news of the coal miner's strike in the U.S.A. did not make us feel any warmer. Our lane filled in with snow and Bob was obliged to leave the car at the road. But when the wind dropped he borrowed a snowplough — that is, a tractor with a blade attached to the front of it — and it did a real good job of ploughing out the lane. Now we can drive in and out with the greatest of ease — at least if we want to be out driving — which I don't. And it's thankful I am to have someone at home who can get the bread, pick up the groceries and bring in the mail.

Last week was also eventful at the barn. Another chapter written into the history of Ginger Farm: the installation of a milking machine, no less! This, of course, is entirely Bob's venture and only after plenty of consideration, pro and con. We heard all kinds of stories: a milking machine produces mastitis; if the cups are left on too long they draw blood; some cows won't let their milk down at all. And we also heard of several farmers who had bought milking machines and after a while gone back to hand milking. Granted all these instances were true, Bob figured they were in the minority as there were on the other hand hundreds of farmers, even in this district, where milking machines were used to advantage and without injury to the cows.

Came the night when the milker was used for the first time. I was just itching to go down to the barn, but concluded the fewer people there were around the better. So I stayed in the house, waiting and wondering. Since not one of our cows had ever seen one of these mechanical contraptions, there was no telling what their reaction would be, and I knew the nervous tension would be hard on Partner.

At long last, the men came in for supper, including the agent from whom Bob had bought the machine. And everything was wonderful! Not one of the cows offered to kick at all, and one cow which had always done plenty of stepping around stood quiet as a lamb and gave more milk than usual.

I thought everything was fine. But during the evening Partner got deathly white. He was cold and his stomach became upset. I was alarmed until Bob figured out that it was a case of mild shock. Partner had been more keyed up then he or any of us realized watching the cows, ready to deal with them should they become obstreperous. And then nothing happened! It was a complete let down — and the reaction produced the condition I have described. Bob said he had seen the same thing happen dozens of times during the war.

So Partner went to bed, and in the morning he was his usual self. Since then everything has been all right. Of course it is Bob who runs the milker, but I suppose the time will come when Partner will want to have a go at it, too.

Space all gone — guess my quilt story must wait until next week.

June 1, 1950

"If only it would rain!" That is what we were saying this time last year ... and to-day we are saying it again. Everything is so dry: the fields, pastures and gardens, yes, and also the dust on the roads, most definitely! We made our annual inspection trip to Malton Airport yesterday, and we swallowed bushels of dust all the way over and most of the way back. But we forgot it all at the Airport as we looked over the wonderful improvements that have taken place since our last visit.

The old offices and waiting room have been converted into a modern airy restaurant. Over in the new building there are spacious waiting rooms and offices and over the whole structure there is an observation roof, which, I would imagine, would accommodate a thousand people. From it you can observe at close quarters planes coming in for a landing or taking off for distant points east and west. You can watch the ground crew crashing around like so many ants — except that these ants travel by jeep and tractor.

A plane lands and immediately a little tractor maneuvers a runway into position for travellers to alight from the ship. Another tractor, trailing three to five little trolley cars, is loaded with passenger baggage which it totes around to the Customs Office. Passengers alight as nonchalantly as they would from a street car: men with brief cases or golf clubs; fashionably dressed women, some with rather bored expressions;

mothers with babies in their arms, or youngsters toddling at their side — the children excited, the mothers too occupied to be bored. And, last to leave the plane, the stewardess and the pilot and co-pilot.

Then another ground crew takes over: the big ship is refuelled for its next take-off, and baggage is brought up by the little trucks which also carry a loading escalator, one end of which is elevated to the baggage compartment of the plane. The escalator is set in motion, and up goes the baggage without benefit of Red Caps. Then a jeep comes along with a box-like container carrying refrigerated food supplies. The entire container is raised to the level of the ship's receiving door by means of an invisible hydraulic hoist.

In a little while loud speakers announce the number of the flight and its destination and presently passengers fill the ship again, helped by a trim young stewardess receiving them at the door of the plane. Then the pilot and co-pilot, upon whose skill and integrity the lives of so many people depend, once more take over at the controls; the ground crew finish their jobs and the big silver bird roars into action again.

As it wheels around for a take-off down the runway, those on the Observation Roof hang on to their hats and catch their breath as wind created by the four whirling propellers swirls around them. I don't know why, but a visit to the airport always increases my conviction that to travel by air is about as safe and pleasant a means of transport as one could hope for in this day and age. And I never see a plane take off or fly over our farm without wishing I was one of its passengers. Who knows ... some happy day maybe I shall be!

But right now we at Ginger Farm are not so much concerned with what happens over our heads as we are with what goes on underfoot. You see, right through the centre of our farm, and also through the two farms east and west of us, there are little stakes here and there, complete with flags, indicating that the Department of Highways is at work on a new surveying job. The whole neighbourhood is agog with curiosity because rumour has it that a new four-lane highway, running from Montreal to Windsor, is being planned, and will probably angle right across country leaving us with 45 acres on one side of the road and 55 on the other.

Well, having had dealings with the highway department before, we know it moves mighty slowly its wonders to perform, so at present we are just sitting tight and awaiting further developments.

Other changes have already taken place around here which are of more concern to us at the moment. We are saying goodbye to our tried and trusty horses and also to our big high-powered oil-burning tractor, and in their place we have a small exceedingly mobile tractor that will, we hope, take the place of the horses and yet be equal, on a smaller scale, to do the field work that was formerly done by its big brother tractor.

With all this going on, we have also been entertaining. One of our nieces, who is now a nursing sister at Sunnybrook Hospital, spent a few days with us last week. Saturday night Bob took her back to Toronto and then came home, bringing with him Daughter and a friend. And I am still busy with the paint-pot!

AUGUST 16, 1950

This is definitely the morning after! The morning after the end of a hectic week. More rain, of course. Then when the weather cleared, the men decided it would be better to stook-thresh than to draw the wheat to the barn. But the day the threshers were to come we had another heavy shower. More delay. By the time the weather had cleared again and the machine on its way another threshing machine had moved in to one of our neighbours, so that made it bad for both of us.

In the meantime, there had been an Institute meeting I couldn't miss. For one thing Edna Jaques was speaking — and I had been given the little job of introducing her — and was also on the lunch committee — three good reasons for not staying at home. However, the meeting over I was soon back to making pies and apple sauce, and figuring out the rest of the meals, ready for threshing either Friday or Saturday.

Then Daughter phoned: she and friend J.J. would be out to help us if I would meet them at Bronte (15 miles) at 9 o'clock Saturday morning. She was sure the help they could give would make up for the time spent in meeting them. There was logic in that, so I went. And you know, that drive was quite a relaxation — the fresh morning air, dew glistening on every leaf and cobweb on the fields and pastures all a-sparkle as if they had literally been sprinkled with diamond dust. It was very beautiful.

So we threshed on Saturday — all the wheat and half a field of oats — and we had 12 for dinner and 14 for supper, that is, including ourselves. It was our first experience at threshing without horses — without horses of our own, I should say; one neighbour brought his team. All told, there was one team along with three tractors in the field.

That naturally led to a discussion after the threshing as to the relative merit of tractors versus horses. Partner and Bob were in favour of tractors; Johnny, who lives with us and helps Partner, was loyal to the horses. If he was farming on his own he "wouldn't have a tractor on the place!" Strange to hear a young fellow talk that way.

Partner and Bob like the tractors because it is possible to get closer to the separator and quicker getting back and forth to the field. Several times this summer, Partner had said how glad he was he let the horses go. Pasture problems have been bad enough — they would have been worse with the horses to worry about. But of course there are disadvantages to the tractor, too. There is $15 to pay out every few weeks for gas. Horses might actually cost that much to feed if you figured the pasture out in dollars and cents, but you wouldn't notice it because it wouldn't make any difference to your bank account. In changing from horses to tractors, it is very necessary to take a long range view all the time.

There are certainly fashions in farming just as there are fashions in hats and dresses. Our first threshing on this farm was with a steam engine. We had to have a good pile of rough wood ahead of time as fuel for the engine. Then there was water to draw for the boiler before we started threshing, and again while the men were having their dinner. Then came the tractor-driven separator — with a team to draw the separator up into the barn. Later the thresher had some kind of contraption by which the separator could be pushed into the barn by the tractor. The tractors were big and powerful, but slow on the road.

Now our thresher has a Diesel tractor that travels along the road almost as fast as a car. Not only that, but he's here and he's gone without any extra work or worry to the farmer — except paying the bill. And yet, although threshing machines seem to have reached the last stage in mobility and efficiency yet they have more competition now than they ever did. The combine is certainly giving them a run for their money. More and more farmers are realizing how much a combine saves them in time and labour. Some farmers already have their own machines, others hire them.

Which is the more economical way of harvesting is very much the $64 question. There is no denying the fact that, with the present shortage of farm help, a combine, followed by a baler, certainly solves many problems — and no threshing meals to worry about! If farming gets much more mechanized farmers' wives will be able to pack up in summer time and go away for a holiday. That will be the day!

What do you say, friends — think we could take it? If country women took a holiday, where would city folk go for their vacations?

JANUARY 10, 1952

This column is being written as I sit at the kitchen table while keeping one eye on the stove where I am searing our weekly roast in the pressure cooker. To look at that roast is to laugh, as indeed I did when I bought it from the butcher yesterday! Three dollars and so help me you could wrap it up in the dollar bills I handed over to pay for it.

Not so very long ago, the same amount of money would have bought enough meat for a threshing. "But," said the man who served me, "see what you get now for your cattle when you sell them." "Yes," I answered, "but we sell a cow only about once a year; meat we buy every week."

No doubt many people will say, "Why don't you use your own meat and put it in a sharp freeze locker?"

That sounds like a reasonable suggestion; in fact, we did just that for about ten years. But as our family became smaller, we found we were further ahead to buy our meat as required and thus get more variety.

It takes a long time for a family of two or three to eat a quarter of a beef or half a pig, and how sick and tired you get of it before it is finished. And yet, to have less than that put away is hardly worth bothering with.

And then again, we have a family who doesn't like fat, and there is a considerable amount of fat and bone when meat comes straight from the carcass.

So there you have it, and if any of you think the high cost of living doesn't affect the farmer then I wish you could take a peek at our steak roast this morning. I called it "our weekly roast," but actually it will do well if it lasts three days.

And yet, despite the high cost of living which affects everyone, TTC operators can afford to go on strike — it just doesn't make sense. We had a man in here this morning, an employee of a large delivery company, who, after talking about the transportation strike for a while said this: "Now the farmers should go on strike, and that would be a strike to end all strikes!"

"And how would you suggest we go about it?" I asked. "Easy enough, stop selling anything at all," he replied. "A week would do it." This man may be right, but I would hate to see it happen. The untold misery it would cause isn't nice to think about. As in all strikes, everyone would suffer — winners and losers alike. Nor is it likely to happen because it would only be possible if all perishable farm produce were dumped out: milk thrown on the fields, eggs and cream destroyed, and fruits and vegetables left to rot.

No, it just won't happen because to willfully destroy anything is absolutely foreign to a farmer's principle. The farmer is an idealist at heart, and idealists cannot work with nature and then thoughtlessly destroy the products of her bounty.

That, probably, is one reason why a farmer will often go on producing at a loss rather than quit. To quit is to break faith with the good earth he loves. He is also an individualist, which may be one reason why he does not always succeed too well in co-operative enterprise.

And while we are thinking of the farmer as an individualist, let me recommend for your reading a book by A. G. Street: "Gentleman of the Party," a novel featuring farm folk and farm practices in rural England from 1872 to 1936. But let me warn you, the book is mostly in Wiltshire dialect and until you get used to it, it is very hard to read. But once you have mastered the first two or three chapters you won't have to put the book down.

It gives a better picture of comparative farm practices through the years than anything else I have read. What so-called 'prosperity' did to the farms and farm families during the early days of the First World War is wonderfully well drawn, but it doesn't make for happy reading.

Partner was in the army at that time and so saw little of rural England, but I was living in a farming community and saw a great deal of what was being done: farms taken over by military authorities, and men conscripted into the army, and yet I did not realize its significance. Mr. Street also gives a wonderful description of the advantages and disadvantages of mechanized farming: how a farm can be ruined by a too intensive cropping campaign or reclaimed by proper methods. According to Mr. Street, modern machinery can be a blessing or a curse depending upon how it is used. And that, surely, applies to Canada just as much as to Great Britain.

Before I finish this column I would like to say congratulations to the *Free Press* and to the town of Acton for being chosen to represent a cross-section of Canada on New Year's Eve and in heading the list of weekly newspapers to which publicity is being given on CFRB. No one should ever need to ask, "Acton … where's Acton?" By now everyone should know it's on Highway 25 and it's where the *Free Press* is printed!

FEBRUARY 21, 1952

When I began this column the time in Ontario was seven in the morning. The date was February the 15th. From the east, the soft roseate hues of early dawn spread across a wintry sky.

It was a particularly appropriate and beautiful sunrise. The air was quiet and still: a perfect accompaniment for the funeral service broadcast of his late Majesty, King George VI, to which I was listening, while all else was forgotten.

The gun carriage bearing the King's oak coffin arrived at purple-draped Paddington station. The Royal Dukes followed on foot. Bands played. High dignitaries from the British Empire and all over the world arrived to board the processional train to Windsor Castle. And as I listened to the solemn, beautiful music from the various bands, and also to the respectful and sympathetic commentary from the B.B.C., I imagined the lonely Dowager Queen also listening to the same broadcast. A Queen who has known much sorrow as husband and sons each in turn has passed away, until now, in the person of her grand-daughter, she sees a queen reign in their stead.

As I listened to the broadcast I knew that Partner also would be listening to it from his radio at the barn, the while he milked the cows. And Bob would be listening as he drove to Oakville in his car. Thus would it be, all across Canada, people in high places, and in the humbler walks of life, all listening, and waiting, and listening again, as the King was borne to his last resting place in the historic crypt to lie with other great monarchs who have lived and died, even as kings must live and die. But surely among them was none so deserving of the fitting tribute we now hear so often in connection with our late Sovereign, "He was a good King and a good man."

And so as I say, I began writing this column while the original broadcast was in progress, even as the sailor piped their Admiral on board and bagpipes followed with the Highland Lament. I wrote it then because only at the time can one fully appreciate the pathos and pageantry of such an historic ceremony. Too soon the affairs of the day intrude upon our fleeting greater moments.

At 11 o'clock that same morning in company with hundreds of other towns, cities, and villages, there was a Memorial service in one of our local churches with ministers taking part from the Anglican, United and Presbyterian Churches. It was a very solemn and beautiful service and was well attended.

In his eulogy, the minister gave a brief résumé of the life of King George, bringing back to memory incidents which, for many of us, had faded through the years.

He quoted, as has almost every paper and broadcast, that famous Christmas message which the King read to us in those dark days of 1939 — "I stood at the gate of the year ..." — but only once have I heard the rest of that quotation, which the King did not give us, but which must have often been in his thoughts during these last few months when he knew "he walked with Death."

This is the rest of the quotation: "So I went forth and finding the hand of God trod gladly into the night. And he led me towards the hills and the breaking of day in the lone East."

And now, our late King being at rest, we resume once more our ordinary, every-day life. In our time, we shall not soon forget George the Good, who possibly did more than any other Sovereign to connect with the common people, and during the reign of Queen Elizabeth II, we are sure this good fellowship will be increased and solidified.

No words of mine can add to the heart-felt tributes that have been expressed by press and radio, but it would not be fitting if this column were written without some expression of loyalty and regret, even though what I write has been said many times before.

Ginger Farm means nothing to the house of Windsor, but the death of George VI was a personal loss to us who live here. We can only repeat in all sincerity, "The King is dead ... *Long Live the Queen!*"

MARCH 20, 1952

Cold weather is with us again, and yet it doesn't feel as if winter has returned although it is colder than many days we had during the middle of winter. The country has a different appearance. Now the brown fields and bare trees have a 'waiting' look. Perhaps the longer hours of daylight make a difference. Whatever the reason, in spite of the cold, it doesn't feel like winter but rather like a dreary day in early spring with bitter cold winds.

A few days ago I was in Toronto. The lake was more beautiful than I had ever seen it. A wild sort of beauty as the wind whipped the greenish waters into rough, tumbling waves, breaking as they hit the seawall and sending white foaming spray five or six feet into the air.

The lake was not rough to the same extent as I remember rough seas on the east coast of England, but it was rough enough to recall pleasant memories of those by-gone days when I would stand watching the breakers with a fascination that is hard to explain.

An angry sea is always a challenge. Once I attempted swimming — alone — in a rough sea. Swim? I couldn't even stand. The angry waves picked me up and threw me against the jagged rocks. By some miracle, I scrambled ashore, breathless, bruised and beaten. It was the one and only time I challenged a stormy sea.

As we passed along the lake front the other day, a little old lady, sitting next to me in the bus, was recalling Toronto as she first remembered it. There was only one road then along the waterfront, she said, and of course, it wasn't paved. She showed me where farm barns had stood on the greensward just below Sunnyside. She remembered how, when the lake was high, the waters flooded the road and even got into the barns. She mentioned Lorne Park as being a little village, and how often she had gone out, day after day, picking wild berries in the surrounding fields. I wonder how many berries could be found in Lorne Park during the summer in this day and age? So many changes in one person's lifetime. One wonders what changes will take place during the next two generations.

When we came to this farm twenty-eight years ago, we were 'the new people.' Now we are more or less old-timers, most of the farms around us having changed owners several times in that twenty-eight years. This has given us an opportunity to observe many things, particularly how farms can be completely changed under new ownership, sometimes for the good, and sometimes very much the opposite, depending on the experience and financial status of the owners.

Actually, it is very interesting to stay put and watch 'the passing show' as it applies to the country. Interesting, yes, but alas, too often it is also heartbreaking. Many folk start out with high hopes and great ambition, but so often with little actual knowledge of practical farming. The result is a foregone conclusion, as the overconfident seem only to learn by experience.

Yet that old adage is as true now as it ever was: 'a wise man learns from the experience of others, a fool from his own.' And yet, how many of us prefer the hard way every time. With those just starting out in life, it seems almost inevitable. But with older folk, well, you can draw your own conclusions — which will probably be very much the same as our own.

AUGUST 7, 1952

Now it can be told! For the past four weeks we have been very busy getting ready for our daughter's wedding. I haven't mentioned it before because we wanted a quiet wedding — just the family. But somehow it didn't stay quiet that way. There were friends who were going to be very disappointed if they were not invited. So plans were changed and we decided on having a small reception. Not having any help, I suggested it could be held at a nearby guest home. But no, Daughter wanted it at home. That being so, I decided I would manage it somehow.

Then we went to work, painting and cleaning, while Partner spent hours on the lawn, cutting and cross-cutting every few days. There was plenty of telephoning — flowers, cake and refreshments to arrange for — and a trip to the city to get myself a dress.

Finally the great day arrived. The bride and groom and their two attendants went to our picturesque little Anglican church standing high upon a hill, and there they were married. The only guests at the church were those who especially wanted to be present; most of the guests came to the house to await the coming of the bride and groom.

They keynote of the whole affair was simplicity, with formality kept to a minimum. And yet, there was a meaning and a purpose to almost everything that was done. The decorations were pink and white gladioli, grown by one of our neighbour-friends. The two-decker cake was all white, topped by a small vase with real sweetheart rose buds in a lovely shade of pink. The tablecloth used was one specially requested by Daughter because of the wide lace border, crocheted by her late grandmother. Of the two silver teapots that were used, one had been a wedding present to that same grandma, and the other a wedding present to us, when Partner and I were married. The serviettes had written in silver lettering, 'Dee and Art, August 2, 1952' — a nice little memento.

A heavy thunder shower blew up about two o'clock but, by the time the bridal couple returned from the church, the sun was shining.

As a mother, may I be forgiven if I say the bride was love-ly? She was dressed very simply in a two-piece white serge suit with a navy blue shawl collar, and a navy blue picture hat. A corsage of Talisman roses was the only touch of contrasting colour.

Irrespective of the clothes she wears, there seems to be an aura of loveliness about a happy bride that shines through and around her as she stands with trusting feet upon the threshold of a new life. And in this our daughter was no exception.

The bridegroom was, as most bridegrooms are, proud, happy and self-conscious. What did he wear? I haven't the faintest notion. I only know he looked nice and carried him-self well. His parents are no longer living, so the only imme-diate members of his family able to be present were a sister from Toronto, and a brother from Ottawa whom we liked immensely.

Came the picture taking, both professional and amateurs, as guests stood alongside the photographer as he posed us for the group pictures. This over, guests went back to the house moving in and around our rambling rooms, getting to know each other and chatting with the bride and groom until re-freshments were served..

Ah, those refreshments — they were grand! I can say that quite freely because the credit is not to me but to our Scotch Block Women's Institute who arranged it all and did such a wonderful job. There were plates and plates of dainty sand-wiches to suit every taste; a wonderful assortment of little cookies and sweetmeats; punch, flavoursome and refreshing; relish; and radish roses.

All this was brought in early in the afternoon on covered plates and silver dishes, ready to serve. But the ladies themselves did not stay, as some of the Daughter's younger friends were to do the serving. We thought it would be more friendly and informal that way and they would be happier having something to do. (I am telling you this in detail as the information may come in handy for other mothers without help in the house.)

I was a little worried about the tea and coffee problem until a good neighbour offered to look after it for me. And then I knew I had no further need to worry.

All in all, everything went off without hitch, thanks to the W.I. There were twenty-nine relatives and friends. One person was sadly missed — a much loved aunt of the bride who passed away two years ago. But she was not forgotten. Next day, at Daughter's request, we took a big bunch of the gladioli to the cemetery.

And there you have the highlights of the first family wedding to be recorded in the Chronicles of Ginger Farm.

Part VI

WINDING DOWN

1953–1955

March 26, 1953

We shall soon be living on the outskirts of our county town, close to a new industrial plant. That is, unless present plans are drastically changed. Not our plans: I don't mean we are moving off the farm, far from it, it just is that the town is stretching its boundaries and coming out to meet us. Not immediately, of course; things like that don't happen overnight. There will be arguments and counterarguments, annexation by-laws and all that sort of thing. But the change will come eventually: you can't stop progress, even if you happen to be 'agin it.'

Our small county town of Milton has been practically at a standstill for years and years, and now suddenly it looks like we may see a bit of mushroom growth. And why not? The huge Ford plant is only about twenty miles away; Milton airport and its industries fifteen miles; two railways by-pass the town; a big factory, which, until now, was Milton's main industry, can supply every type of screw nail likely to be called for; and there is all kinds of farm land that can probably be bought for industrial sites and building projects.

One of our neighbours recently sold his farm to a steel company to be the site of a new factory. No doubt there will be more farm land going the same way. And there will certainly be plenty of farms sliced up when the new Montreal to Windsor highway goes through this district, crossing No. 25 at an, at present, undetermined point.

Perhaps you think it is a shame so much good farm land should be taken up that way. I quite agree. It seems like economic suicide to thus undermine one of its most productive areas, in what has been generally agreed is Canada's basic industry, agriculture.

But perhaps it is just as well. I guess we have reached the stage when many farmers think the proverbial worm knew what it was doing when it turned.

So, when farmers in this, and other industrial areas, are given a good offer on their property, it is usually accepted. Of course, any farmer worthy of the name hates to see the old place go, to have factories and storage sheds built on his fertile fields, but then on the one hand he remembers the price of cattle and hogs, the glut of milk on the market and the threatening decrease in the price of that same milk to the farmer, to say nothing about margarine and the possible inroads of synthetic dairy products. Very few farmers, however, want to see a ban on edible oils.

On the other hand, the farmer thinks of the fellows who work in industry — of the returns for their labour, and short working day as compared with his own — and he figures he might just as well be getting a share of the big wages himself instead of making a bare living, and, by his hard work adding to the surplus that already exists. Many farmers' sons have already got on the industry band wagon so that the greater number of farms are now owned and operated by older men, and it is these same men that we find only too glad to dispose of their farms if the price offered is good enough.

What will be the result? Maybe ten or fifteen years from now a middle-aged couple — Mr. and Mrs. Rip Van Winkle — will decide to take a run out to the country 'to get away from it all.' They will drive for miles, and all they will see are huge chimney stacks and flat-top factories.

Mrs. Van Winkle will turn to her husband and exclaim in distress, "But Rip, I thought we were to take a drive through the country! Where *is* the country, Rip? Where are all the lovely farm places we used to know with contented cows grazing on tree-shaded pastures? I was even hoping we might find a farmhouse where we could buy some real milk, or perhaps a little cream. I'm so tired of synthetic products. Why is it so hard to get real dairy produce now, Rip?"

"Well, now, that's a long story. A story of supply and demand. Synthetic products caused many farmers to go out of business. There are still dairy farms farther out in the country, but dairy products are now in the luxury class. The general public has to be content with synthetics. They wanted them in the first place because they were cheaper. Now they have what they have asked for, and don't like what they have got too well."

"Well, then, we might as well go home, Rip. We haven't time to drive any farther. And I was so hoping we could have gone home with some real milk," said Mrs. Van Winkle with a sigh. "And, oh my, wouldn't it have been a treat?" she added.

JUNE 11, 1953

The weatherman, apparently, is in the dog house. Very few of his forecasts of late have been accurate, and the general public has become annoyed and distrustful. He promises a fine day, and we get a downpour; cooler weather, and it becomes hot and sticky; clearing skies, and we waken to the steady rumble of thunder. Yes, it is most annoying when the forecasts and the actual weather are so contradictory, especially when farmers, gardeners, fishermen and just ordinary folk planning an outing have come to depend upon the day-by-day forecasts.

In the weather office, as we know, changes in atmospheric conditions are registered on sensitive instruments that have stood the test of years. Using them, the weatherman knows the type of weather that should normally follow according to the disturbances that have been recorded. Then, why have these forecasts suddenly become so unreliable? Well, what about the atom bomb? Until the last few years did the weather bureau ever have to deal with the effect of atomic weapons?

Imagine ordinary, every-day air currents floating around in the ether, just minding their own business, bringing good weather or bad according to normal pressure conditions, and then suddenly they find themselves blasted in every direction by huge atomic explosions, without advanced warning being registered by weather office barometers. And then, the reputation of the weatherman is blasted as completely as the weather he has been so unfortunate as to predict, especially if he promised the next day would be 'warm and dry' and what came was wet and windy! Ah me, who would be a weatherman in this atomic age?

Lying awake the other night, listening, unwillingly, to the crash of thunder, and trying not to watch the lightning, a comforting thought suddenly came to me. Never yet have I heard of a tornado or 'twister' unleashing its fury at night. As far as my knowledge goes, it always happens in daylight. Am I right or am I wrong?

Well, last week this column was written on the eve of one of the most memorable events of our time: the coronation of Elizabeth II. Now that, too, has become history, and time marches on. From 5 a.m. to 1 p.m. on June 2, and then again from 3 o'clock onwards, the radio was never off. I don't think I missed a thing. Nor did Partner, because he was milking the cows and following the procession at the same time on his radio at the barn.

It was such a wonderful broadcast, but such an emotional strain that we were both tired out afterwards. Instead of going down town to enjoy our local celebrations that evening, we were glad to finish up our chores and get to bed a little earlier than usual. But if the broadcast was tiring to us, what must the actual proceedings have been to the thousands of participants, and to the Queen herself? It is beyond my imagination.

Now, as I write, another important event is in the making: the long awaited Armistice in Korea. It has hung fire for so long one is almost afraid to hope. And if an armistice is signed, then what? Time will tell, but we can be very sure whatever happens in Korea will have some impact on the lives of each of us wherever we may live. We hope more attention will be given to a better distribution of the foods we grow so that all nations in the world may benefit, producers and consumers alike, without graft or greed.

From the look of the fields in this district there is likely to be a shortage of cereal grain, but there should certainly be plenty of hay, although everything depends on the weather. The alfalfa is very heavy but at present there is no bloom. I foresee happy days ahead when we start haying!

With so much sap in the stalk, it will take a lot of curing before the balers can handle it. Good drying weather is very necessary as hay has to dry quickly these days. Cut it down, call the baler, draw it to the barn — the quicker the better — that seems to be the idea now.

Haying no longer interferes with what we women want to do. An extra meal or two perhaps, but few women have to stay home now to drive the team to the hayfork. What a hot, dusty job that was, and how heavy the whiffle-trees as we lifted them when turning the horses back to the barn! However, when you're young you take it all in your stride. It is only now, with those days behind you, you remember, and you thank the powers that be that no longer is such work required of you. You can get on with your meetings; the haying goes on whether you're at home or away.

MAY 28, 1953

I suppose the minds of most people these days are, like our own, just a jumble of thoughts: world tension, the Coronation, the tornado that struck Sarnia and London districts, and the damage done by last week's storms in whatever locality we happen to live. We certainly hope the weather bureau has good things in store for the big event on June 2. Sunshine or rain, we know the Coronation will go on as scheduled but it will be so much nicer if a sunny sky does its part towards making this day one to remember.

Children in years to come will tell of the great festivities when Elizabeth II was crowned queen, just as we who are older remember other coronations of the two Georges and in some cases of Edward VII, according to our age and our ability to remember — or our willingness to admit how many sovereigns have come to the throne during our lifetime. It would seem one's age might also be measured by coronations! But then, who cares? Admitting or hiding one's age doesn't make one either younger or older.

I wonder what happened in your district last week at the time of the tornado. Although the twister confined itself to the Sarnia and London area there were other unrelated storms in Ontario that did a considerable amount of damage. We had terrific winds and heavy rain in our immediate locality: no damage that I have heard of, not even power failure, but five miles away it was a different story.

At and around the village of Lowville there were 'golf ball' hailstones that smashed windows wholesale, lopped branches off trees and shrubs, and leveled tulip beds as neatly as a scythe. I have never seen hailstones as large as the ones reported, so until I heard about them from several sources I thought the stories must be exaggerated. I was wrong. One man put a few in his freezer to present as evidence, at another place the farmer's wife measured one of the 'big ones'— in circumference it was seven inches one way and eight inches the other, just about the size of a big double-yolked egg.

Here there was hardly any hail, but the rain was terrific, even the downspout from the eavestrough couldn't carry it away fast enough so that some of it ran down into the cellar, until Partner investigated. He found a few leaves in the connecting pipe were stopping the flow of water. Next day I was along the road and there I saw fields lately sown with spring crop, the low-lying spots nothing but a swamp. Corn ground, some of it sown, some ready to sow, were sad-looking fields. But the pasture and hay fields are wonderful. So, as usual, what we lose on the swings we make up on the roundabouts.

Now I wonder if that expression is familiar in Canada. We haven't been in Canada thirty-four years and yet I still find myself unconsciously using expressions that are unintelligible to native Canadians. A few weeks ago, I happened to mention 'art on the hoardings.' My companion had no idea what I meant, and at the time I could think of no better way to express my meaning. I suppose the common term is 'billboards,' 'advertising signboards' or something similar. I had never given it a thought, because to me all such signs are hoardings.

And speaking of signs, or should I say omens, we know robins always sing their best when rain is in the offing, but now I am wondering about other song birds. Last week, before the storm, Partner and I were working in the garden and I don't think I ever heard birds sing so much.

The weather was warm, windy and somewhat sultry. Usually the birds sing very little in the afternoon, but that afternoon there must have been a complete bird orchestra. Orioles, song sparrows, canaries, bobolinks, meadow larks: they were all there, singing with joyous abandon. Did they sense the approach of the storm, were they singing to exercise their vocal cords, knowing they must soon take to the protective covering of the trees and shrubs?

Strangely enough, the robins were silent, could it be they were jealously sulking? The little hummingbirds are here again. Every evening one wee bird comes fluttering around our japonica bush, while the bumble bees make busy at the lilac. Lilies of the valley are out by the hundreds, but I haven't seen any winged creatures in their sweet-scented vicinity.

Partner has been helping me eradicate an overgrowth of snowberry. One time I brought a root home from a neighbour's. She warned me, "It's bad stuff to spread; mind where you put it." That was ten years ago, and for the last five years I have been pulling out sucker roots everywhere. Some people have to learn the hard way: I seem to be one of them.

August 27, 1953

Friday August 21, 1953, was a day that will long be remembered by members of the Women's Institute in Canada and, we hope, by women from other countries who were also present in Toronto at that time. It was 'Canada Day,' the day which featured the pageant 'Dominion of Destiny' presented by the Federated Women's Institutes of Canada.

Before noon, bus-loads of W.I. members began arriving in Toronto. They came from every part of Ontario and from Quebec and across the border to see this action-story of Canada's history which came as a grand climax to the eleven-day conference of the Associated Country Women of the World.

Twelve thousand women took their seats in the Maple Leaf Gardens Friday night. Many of them were also present in the afternoon to hear the addresses. The chairman, of course, was Mrs. Hugh Summers, President of the Federal Women's Institute of Ontario. The first speaker, the Hon. Stuart Garson, Minister of Justice, Canada, officially opened the program.

It is impossible, in this column, to even give you a gist of the speeches, which included greetings from delegates of every nation represented at the Conference. You have probably been following the proceedings by radio, television and the press, so I will confine myself to interpreting what I think was the 'atmosphere' of the conference.

I was speaking to many delegates from other countries and from different parts of Canada and they all said the same thing: "We are having a wonderful time; the kindness and hospitality we find everywhere is marvellous." But this consideration was not one-sided. Visiting delegates returned kindness for kindness by patiently answering the many questions that were put to them. But they also asked questions about Canada. Even from the U.S. came many inquiries with the repeated remark, "We had no idea Canada was like this!"

However, the answer to many of the inquiries was dramatically given in the pageant itself as the pages of history were turned back and Canada's destiny revealed in story and song.

One end of the arena was shown as a rural setting: a map of Canada against a background of beautiful evergreens, particularly appropriate for the colourful and historic scenes that were presented in proper sequence. The audience was thrilled with the tribal costumes and war-dance of the Indians.

Then came the Vikings, the explorers, adventurers, priests and traders. Cartier, Hudson, Champlain, LaSalle, Frontenac and Madeleine de Verchères were realistically portrayed. Scenes illustrating the growth of Canada, the War of 1812, the coming of the United Empire Loyalists and scenes typical of the pioneer period up to Confederation were portrayed.

Then came the development of the country in ways which to-day we take so much for granted. The establishment of the R.C.M.P., the building of the C.P.R., the organization of the W.I. at Stoney Creek, the development of culture and the progress of art and education: folk dancers from Cherry Hill Farm and group singing from the Junior W.I. of Oxford County.

And so we came to the shadows cast by two world wars: to the rumble of guns and the sound of marching feet. And then the valiant attempt of peace-loving peoples to form the nucleus of the United Nations. The Peace Bridge, symbolic of so many miles of undefended border between the U.S.A and Canada. To visitors from foreign countries this was one of the amazing highlights of their trip.

Said a delegate from Europe, "But do you actually mean you have an entirely undefended border? No armed guards anywhere at all?" It was explained to her that, for extended visits from one country to another, identification was necessary; there were also trade restrictions and customs regulations respected by both countries, but they certainly were not enforced by armed guards on either side. "Wonderful, almost unbelievable!" exclaimed the European delegate.

The last scene of the pageant previous to the finale was a tribute to the Coronation of Queen Elizabeth II, Queen of Great Britain and of Canada. In the finale we saw again the many organizations that had taken part in the pageant and to whom Canada owes so much: the Red Cross, Girl Guides and Boy Scouts, the Y.M.C.A. and Y.W.C.A., the 'Mounties' and a host of others.

And so a heart warming, soul stirring day came to a close, as 12,000 women left the Gardens in search of buses, trains, planes and cars to carry them home. Maybe in the heart of each one there came a sense of pride, national pride, as through the medium of this great pageant came the realization that Canada is a wonderful country and that to be a Canadian is a definite privilege, but a privilege that carries with it obligations.

FEBRUARY 25, 1954

Well, well — it looks as if the rural telephone is in for a little house-cleaning, especially the old party line. Just in case you missed that bit of news, perhaps I should explain what I am talking about. A Bill was introduced in the Ontario Legislature last week to put the Rural Telephone service under a new branch of government, created by the Telephone Act in 1954. The Act is aimed at giving "continuous and efficient service" to the 164,000 rural subscribers in Ontario, the first major change since 1918.

Under this new section, it will be an offence to hold the line if someone needs it for an emergency, such as fire, accident or sickness. Penalty is a $50 fine or 30 days. A similar penalty is in place for the use of "indecent, obscene, blasphemous or grossly insulting language." Eavesdroppers who gossip are liable to a $50 fine — that includes telephone company employees as well as the general public.

Looks as if a lot of ground will be covered by this new Act. Maybe the person who made the recommendations had recently had some experience with rural telephones!

The old party line — like parking — isn't what it used to be. It has changed even more than the old grey mare. Time was when the party telephone was used almost exclusively by farm families living on one road. They all knew each other and recognized a neighbour's voice if she asked if the line was busy, and if your need for it was not really important, you hung up again without saying a word, returning in a little while. If, however, you particularly wanted the phone without too much delay, you asked politely, "Is this line busy?" Chances are you would hear your neighbours ring off in a few minutes — a signal that the line was now disengaged. But, if they held on for another ten or fifteen minutes, you asked again — and waited. That usually did the trick. Both parties would say, "Well, I guess someone wants the line."

If polite inquiries failed — which was very rarely — then you would get husband or brother or son to inquire in a deep, masculine voice, "Line busy?"

That nearly always worked. A woman seldom dared to hold out against a man's need of the telephone — he might be wanting the 'vet' or a repair man, and fast.

Of course, in case of a real emergency, you had only say, "May I have the line for the doctor, please?" — and the line was yours. Not only that, the chances are one of the neighbours whose conversation you interrupted would give you a ring later, ask who was sick and was there anything she could do to help. However, if no one came on the line while two neighbours were talking they would talk on — the length of time they chatted was entirely their own affair, especially if there were only six or eight on a party line. Yes, we really got along very nicely on the old party line.

But how times have changed! City folk have moved out to the country, small town boundaries have been extended and more and more subscribers have been added to the party lines. To many of them, sharing a telephone is a new experience. Having little knowledge of the unwritten country code, instead of taking the hint when another person asks if the line is busy, they go right on talking. The neighbourly feeling on a party line has entirely disappeared — that is, in congested areas. A person at one end of the line may not even have a nodding acquaintance with the party at the other end. Not only that, the rural party line was never intended for business purposes — other than farm business.

It seems to me there should be a printed card of instructions handed out to every party line subscriber, with general directions for using the rural telephone and also how to ring another person on the same line. Some years ago, a new neighbour on our line wanted to give me a ring. She knew our ring was 13, but to this person '13' meant thirteen. So she straightaway proceeded to ring the telephone thirteen times.

I hear it — who wouldn't! — had a hunch what was happening and answered — as well as I could for laughing.

The telephone company in our nearby town is talking of a dial system and we hope it takes in rural areas, too. A few years ago there were fifteen subscribers on our line. Then they divided it and, for a while, there was comparative peace and quietness. But as more and more people moved into the district, more and more were added to our line. Now we are back to where we were before. That is the general pattern so I am sure most rural people will be glad the party line is coming under jurisdiction of the Ontario Government — that is, if it mean fewer subscribers on every line.

APRIL 29, 1954

Last Tuesday I had my first ride on the new Toronto subway. On the whole, I thought it was grand. Just imagine, I boarded the train at Milton, arrived at Union Station, took the subway to College and was able to keep an appointment without once getting out into the pouring rain. It was wonderful.

Now for reasons for and against the subway. I liked the clean, roomy, fast-moving coaches. I liked the mysterious, distant rumble of the train as it approached the platform. I liked the escalators — but I definitely didn't like the steep stone steps. In some stations there are two flights to climb. Actually the steps are my only objection to an otherwise perfect method of transportation.

There were, however, a few things that worried me that could be prevented: passengers standing too close to the edge of the platform and mothers allowing children too much freedom while waiting for a train — children playing too roughly could easily push each other on to the track. With fast trains coming every two minutes, the risk is too great.

Of course, there are still many people every day taking their first ride and some of them don't realize there is more than one door. There are also people keeping away from the subway entirely, having heard rumours of doors that automatically open and close, hardly giving passengers time to get on and off. That is just non-sense of course.

Nor is there any need for what happened to Ellen and Mary who were taking their first ride on the subway. Ellen got on the train, but Mary was left behind on the platform! But even in a case like that there is no need to panic. Ellen had only to wait at her destination for Mary to come on by the next train — possibly a matter of five or seven minutes. But this I must say — it isn't wise to read the evening paper as you ride. Far better to watch for your station on the wall of every platform or, first thing you know, you will find yourself at Eglinton instead of Bloor or College or wherever you intended to get off.

Back to the country. Spring seems to have been so late in coming the last few years. And a late spring makes such a rush job of seeding. Not enough of the right kind of weather for a long enough time is really what causes the trouble. It just doesn't leave any margin. A breakdown with a tractor for even a few hours can mean a week's delay in getting a field seeded if rain should come before the repair job is done.

No doubt this feeling of having to beat the weather is responsible for a few fields here and there not being worked up as well as they might be. A lot depends on the soil of course — and it could be that farmers with clay-loam look enviously on while neighbours, perhaps no farther away than the next concession, work away with very little interruption on their sandy-loam fields. But then comes a dry spell and then it is the clay-loam farmer who reaps the benefit. No one can win all the time. In the long run, the law of averages evens things up pretty well. And that applies to more than farming; it applies to every aspect of life.

We can all think of people we know who are blessed with plenty of the world's good but there may be ill health in the family, dissension in family circles, tragedy or loss of life. Or we may know others who appear to have so little but yet seem so happy. Because of their religious beliefs, or their philosophy of life, to them every day is a new beginning. A beautiful sunset means more to them than a movie, a well written book better than a television show and a friendly call from a neighbour more than a bridge party. There are also people so busy all the time that physical tiredness and a mind at peace with itself brings sound sleep at night. And there are those with too much leisure and too much social life who hardly know what it is to get a good night's rest without the aid of sleep pills. The law of averages again. What you gain on the swings you lose on the roundabouts.

Well, it is raining again, but Partner says there is nothing for farmers to worry about. He says according to what he has heard from old-time farmers, if Easter is early, seeding is not likely to start until a week or two afterwards. And in those days seeding took six weeks. Now our modern tractor-farmers expect to get the job done in two weeks anyway.

Antibiotics, commercial fertilizers and weed-destroying chemicals were unknown at the turn of the century, but I think everyone will agree that the old-time farmer was as weather-wise as a swamp frog.

DECEMBER 23, 1954

The Festive Season is almost upon us. Time to say, once again, "Happy Christmas and God Bless Us Every One."

Christmas 1954! Is it any different from any other Christmas? How many years can you look back? And in those years that have passed, which were the happiest Christmases that you remember? Or the presents that gave you the greatest joy? Was it the doll-carriage that you had always longed for, or the bicycle the family gave you between them? Do you remember the first time you realized that Santa Claus didn't really exist?

You didn't always get what you wanted, but now, I suppose, if you are a foolish mother, you love to give your little girl the very things you longed for and didn't get. Or perhaps it is the first time that you gave you remember even better than what you received — the wonderful pot-holders you made in secrecy to give mother on Christmas Day.

Or is it the first Christmas after you were married you recall most easily? I suppose we all have our memories, and the memories of the past contribute towards the Christmas of each passing year. This Christmas would not mean as much to us unless we could add to it the memory of those that have gone before.

As I look back, every Christmas in my childhood is interwoven with thoughts of my mother and my brothers and sister. My father died when I was three, so there is little that I remember of him. His death meant that mother became the breadwinner for her family of five, one of whom was born after my father died and who left us when he was sixteen months old.

I remember our first Christmas tree. Every family did not have a Christmas tree in those days. It was a token of affluence — a story-book symbol of Christmas. But I had been very ill, and my family pooled their meager resources to give the little girl who had been spared to them the best Christmas ever. I can see that tree so clearly — trimmed with glittering tinsel and real candles. I was propped up on a couch with pillows and blankets right across from the beautiful tree.

I remember another Christmas, or rather, pre-Christmas. We were busily engaged for weeks making paper-chain decorations, presents for mother and for each other that often had to be hastily hidden away. I had two brothers, Eddie and Evelyn. Eddie was very clever at fretwork. This particular Christmas he had worked hours and hours making a fretwork clock-stand for mother, for which he had bought a small clock. It was almost finished and stood about eight inches high, the block being at the top.

On evening my two brothers got into an argument. Eddie was the easy-going type but Evelyn often had most destructive fits of temper. On this occasion he picked up a heavy book and threw it at the beautiful block. It was smashed completely. The unhappy incident marred that one Christmas for us all.

From that time on, I have no recollection of any Christmas that was outstanding because every Christmas was happy and exciting. We used to lie awake on Christmas Eve listening to the Waites playing all the old familiar hymns. Sometimes carol singers would join the Salvation Army Band and go from street to street singing and playing.

Then I remember our first Christmas in Canada, out on the prairie on a farm where Partner was working as hired help. Mail had been delayed and there wasn't a letter, a parcel, or even a Christmas card from our friends in the Old Country. Christmas morning we got a phone call: there was mail at the post office. There was no delivery along prairie trails, so Partner walked in for it — at 30 below. Fortunately he had only to walk half a mile. He came back with letters, cards and small parcels. It was a Happy Christmas then, believe me.

I remember, too, our next Christmas on the prairie as we were at last in a home of our own. Wee Daughter was eleven months old. We had balloons and gay streamers hanging from the ceiling near her cot. When she woke up Christmas morning the wonder of it kept her cooing for hours.

Then came our first Christmas at Ginger Farm. Our ten-room house was sparsely furnished and very cold. All our money had gone into stock and implements. But we were happy. We had our baby with us, our Son whose life for the first nine months teetered perilously on the borderline between life and death. Dee was nearly four, a happy healthy little girl. We did not know then we were heading into a depression that would mean a lean Christmas for many years to come.

And now, to Christmas 1954, which we hope will see our family united once again. As we grow older, we are thankful for each Christmas that finds our family circle still complete. All being well, our children will be with us, and our grandson as well. Christmas will take on new meaning with little David around. No doubt we shall spoil him badly, and Dee and Art will have a sweet time getting him back to normal after a few days with his grandparents.

So that is Christmas through the years as I remember it. You, too, will have your memories. Happy ones, I trust. And I hope that this Christmas will be the happiest yet.

MARCH 24, 1955

"Distant fields are always green" is an adage as true to-day as it ever was. During the last ten years or so, some of our farm friends have been very unsettled. They were undecided whether to stay on the farm or sell out. Some felt they were getting too old for farming. There was too much hard work and a scarcity of farm help, most of it inexperienced, added to their troubles. Farm properties were fetching good prices. It might be a good idea to cash in on a good opportunity, move to town, get a smaller house, less work for tired Mrs. Housewife and likely there would be an easier job in town for Mr. Ex-Farmer. He would need something to fill in his time anyway.

So, some of these friends of ours did sell out, others are still sitting on the fence. So what happens? Extracts from recent letters tell their own story. "We so often wish we were still on the farm. It would be wonderful to get away from this 'convenient' noisy suburban area. There are so many noises: the everlasting hum of the air-conditioner, the fan on the furnace, constant murmur of traffic, roar of the planes taking off from a nearby airport and static interference on the radio or television as a nearby neighbour uses his electric razor.

Another letter: "I would trade this city job any day to be back with the cows and to hear the steady rustling sound of cows nosing the hay in their mangers. I am making good money at my present job, but I realize now that money isn't everything."

Then I meet and talk with a former farm-wife. In reply to my questions I get an answer something like this: "Yes, our house is very convenient, warm and comfortable even with a north-wester blowing. And of course there is far less work. But a house in a subdivision means living a life very different from what it was on the farm.

"Sometimes I stand at the open door, look along the street to other houses very like our own, and I long with everything that's in me for the good, clean country air, to be in a house that isn't hemmed in by other houses. I just have an almost unbearable craving to get out."

Partner said the heifer and calf were fine but he didn't know how he was going to get them into the stable. (My help is no longer appreciated.)

Then on that wonderful spring-like Friday, along came Johnny. He got the heifer tied up and also brought in a two weeks' supply of chop. And yesterday morning, the milk truck got through the lane without any trouble. Our snow fence is still up, so why wouldn't we count our blessings? The heifer might have calved on one of those terrible rough days, we could have been left high and dry without chop for the cows and the lane might have become impassable.

Not that we are enjoying the storm: it is a trifle drafty around here; even the cats find it warmer down in the cellar and we don't like the look of our coal bin. But we are banking on the theory that eventually all things come to an end, even storms.

Unfortunately that also applies to the coal. The question is which will last longer, the coal or the storm?

Actually, we are more concerned about what is taking place at Niagara. The forces of nature can be so devastating upon occasion, even more so than atomic power, and the occasions seem to be getting more frequent all the time.

Sometimes I wonder if floods, storms, cyclones and earthquakes are signs of Divine displeasure for atomic experiments, especially when phenomenal disturbances are worldwide in character.

So many changes, everywhere and in every walk of life. Even in the farmers' barns. I remember, years ago, when Partner was milking ten or twelve cows by hand I used to worry because after the field work was done he had so much to do at the barn. But he used to say, "Well, what are you worrying about? That's my recreation!" The children and I would be down at the barn feeding the calves and helping here and there. It was generally quite quiet and peaceful and we could talk back and forth among ourselves.

Now on the rare occasions when I go to the barn I notice quite a difference. There is the noise of the motor on the milking machine and the swish, swish of air as Partner puts the milkers on the cows. And a much louder swish as suction is released when Partner takes the milkers off. This, of course, is repeated with each cow that is milked. Then as the milker is being rinsed with cold water, there is a loud sucking noise as the cups drain the last bit of water from the pail.

And to cap it all, there is the radio going. Fine when Partner is alone but not so good when we have to shout to make each other hear. The barn isn't a peaceful place any more, and I never hear Partner say now that to milk is just recreation.

SEPTEMBER 15, 1955

The busy fall season is still with us. On most farms threshing is over but there are other jobs to do: pullets to house, cattle to change from pasture to stubble, fall wheat to sow, apples to pick and the other hundred and one jobs that have to be done before the leaves turn crimson and gold.

In the house, canning and pickling is still the order of the day; the aroma of pickling spices is wafted abroad and Mother surveys with satisfaction rows of green nine-day pickles, rich red beets and the deep yellow of mustard pickles. In fact a row of pickles can be a pleasing study in colour contrast.

The children of course are back to school, and mother must now do her own fetching and carrying. Surprising the number of parental steps that can be saved when the children are around. On many farms, the above picture holds true, while on other farms like ours, children have grown up and moved away. So now we do our own fetching and carrying, or in many ways fetch and carry for each other. On a farm where active farming is still carried on, modern machinery has taken the place of willing hands.

Taken the place, did I say? I wonder! A combine and a hay baler speeds up threshing and haying tremendously, providing there is no mechanical breakdown. Less manual work is now required for many other jobs but it seems to me the work involved is taking more out of the older farmer than it ever did.

Not physically perhaps — with a milking machine a man can milk fifteen cows as easily as he milked five years ago. But the tension is greater; the output of nervous energy is increased tremendously from the days when Dad and the boys loaded loose hay on the hayrack and milked the cows by hand. Agriculture science has progressed by leaps and bounds during the last twenty-five years, but I have yet to be convinced that the average older farmer is leading an easier life. Shorter hours, yes, daily chores lessened considerably — as long as everything goes all right.

But, a breakdown with the milking machine, combine or baler, or a power failure can take more out of a man in nervous tension than would the physical energy used for the same job the old-fashioned way. However, there is nothing that can be done about it, manual farm labour being practically non-existent. As a result, progress and invention go hand in hand

and it is probably only to the older farmer that adjustment comes a little difficult.

The younger generation naturally accepts modern methods of farming in its stride just as it accepts jet planes and fast-moving automobiles. Mechanized farming is also an attraction to the middle-aged businessman with a yen for the wide open spaces. To him farming with modern machinery appears deceptively easy. So he takes up farming as a sideline, or goes out of business altogether, buys a hundred acres in an unknown territory, spends several thousand dollars modernizing the house and barn and another few thousand on pedigreed cattle.

In a great many cases, a few years finds the businessman-farmer an older and a wiser man. As a result the farm is again on the market, the businessman having discovered by bitter experience that to the uninitiated, modern farm machinery merely substitutes one head ache for another. Ironically enough, if it were not for modern machinery, there would be fewer businessmen-farmers. If the would-be farmer thought he might have to milk cows by hand, clean out stables with a wheelbarrow and take hay and crop off the field the old-fashioned way, he might not be quite so keen on buying a farm.

But of course there are many successful businessmen-farmers. There is the executive type who can afford a farm manager and other help and thus indulge his hobby. Such farms are the show windows of agriculture — a very different proposition from the businessman who sets out to run a farm by himself, even if he has every piece of modern machinery he can get.

Well, I guess this is where I turn grandmother and leave farmers and farm methods, good, bad and indifferent, to take care of themselves. Dee, Arthur, David and Honey have just come in and I imagine I shall be required to do a spot of baby sitting — and dog sitting — while they go hunting tomatoes. Looks to me as if Dave has grown about two inches since we last saw him and that was only about two weeks ago.

How children vary. One wee niece, two and a half years old, weighs only about twenty-five pounds and yet is as healthy and active as a child could be. Excuse me I must rescue the cats and dogs. Dave has already made a bee-line in their direction. He is liable to love them to death.

OCTOBER 13, 1955

This is Thanksgiving Day. A big day for Canadian families. I imagine we are just as thankful as most people for 'the bounty of the earth,' but yet it is one season that we have never made a point of celebrating, that is to the point of having Thanksgiving dinner and all the trimmings. Partner and I were invited out to a turkey dinner, but we preferred staying at home to travelling the highways, crowded with slap-happy motorists.

Bob and Joy have gone to Cornwall for the week-end, but Dee, Art, Dave and another little boy were here yesterday. Also friends from the Guelph district and they all went home loaded down with apples — Greenings and Spys. I think between them they stripped the trees.

The apple crop this year is wonderful. In fact, when you look back, it has been a good fruit year all round. I suppose most house-wives, like myself, are finding it quite a job to locate even one empty sealer.

I am writing this column from a sunny south room upstairs. We have not yet started using the furnace because we find the south side of the house, with the sun streaming in, is warm enough while the kitchen stove keeps the north and west sides of the house quite comfortable.

After all, why bother fussing around with a furnace until you have to. So long as the furnace is all ready to go at a minute's notice, that is all that is necessary. It will get plenty of use later on.

Every time I go down cellar I look at the bulging bins — it doesn't seem possible we shall use all that coal before warm weather comes around again. In their new three-storey house (new to them, that is) Dee and Arthur have a stoker-furnace and they think they are going to like it better than the oil furnace they had in the other house — more economical, too.

So many ways to heat a house — and most people looking for a heating system that ensures the least possible amount of work. A far cry from the days when the majority of houses, country homes, anyway, were heated with only the kitchen range and a pot-bellied stove in the 'parlour' and perhaps a box-stove or Quebec heater in the dining room.

Those were the days when a pile of dry wood was our greatest treasure — preferably hickory, oak or maple; remember the lovely smell that came from burning hickory bark? Occasionally the house-wife would be faced with nothing but green elm or apple wood. And then the fire would smoke and smoulder and the oven wouldn't get hot and there would be frequent trips to the chip yard so as to get the potatoes boiled for dinner. Too many chips and sometimes the stove pipes would catch fire. Ah yes, those were 'the good old days'! Don't you sometimes look back and wonder how we ever survived? I do.

But every age has its problems. At present we are faced with diminishing farm incomes, increased cost of production, high cost of labour and essential services, speed on the highways and increased fees for hospitalization.

Apparently it is only a matter of time before some kind of Health Insurance will be inaugurated; whether at the national or provincial level remains to be seen. It, too, will have its drawbacks. But yet a uniform scheme of some sort will eventually have to be worked out. At present wage earners are pretty well looked after.

But what protection is there for the farmer and his family? True, they may subscribe to an independent form of hospitalization, but farm people seldom go to hospital if it can be avoided and hospital insurance doesn't cover the cost of illness in the home. And, as everyone knows, a person can run up big medical expenses without ever going near a hospital. Except on a farm, this creates a situation whereby patients, instead of staying at home, go to hospital as the only means of collecting insurance. It is one reason why our hospitals are over-crowded. A national health scheme to assist with the financial home treatment of patients would be a step in the right direction.

Two years ago, when Partner broke his collar-bone, there was naturally a big doctor's bill but not one cent could we get from insurance as Partner was not in the hospital. He felt he should stay home and keep an eye on things. There must be hundreds of similar cases. I remember one time during the depression, a doctor said this: "The rich can afford to pay; the poor are looked after; but the middle-class person pays his account without assistance, often as a result of selling cattle he should keep or raising a mortgage on the farm."

Well, Health Insurance belongs to the future. Now supposing we look back a year. Just about this time Hurricane Hazel hit Ontario. Remember Raymore Drive, and the International Plowing Match, and all the instances of major and minor damage in so many localities? By comparison, we have every reason to make this a Happy Thanksgiving week-end.

Part VII

Summing Up

1956–1962

February 2, 1956

Well, I might as well make a confession, and get it off my chest. We finally gave in — shall I say to mass hysteria — and had a television set installed. So, for the last few weeks, it has been a time of discovery, picking and choosing programs we like and finding our way around among the different channels. So far, we have enjoyed it very much and find it a good form of relaxation. That, of course, was our primary object in putting it in.

We can have entertainment now and still enjoy the comforts of home, and it is fun seeing people we know flashed on the screen. There have been quite a few. But as most of you very well know, TV is more than entertainment. There are excellent educational programs well worth watching. Partner, of course, gets a kick out of telecast sports. I, too, enjoy watching the hockey games.

Like everyone else, except where there are children, we do not turn our set on during the day. And we shut it off when we have callers, unless there is something they especially want to see.

One thing kept us from putting in television for so long: we could not see how we would ever find time to watch it. So what happened? It doesn't make much difference to Partner at all, except that he does a little less reading. His work, of course, is done before there is very much that he wants to see. But I had to rearrange my work considerably. Thus I left my ironing until evening and then watched television while I did it. I got my backlog of mending done the same way. In fact, for the first time in weeks, my workbasket is actually empty!

Arranging time for typing and writing was a little more difficult but that, too, I finally managed and have accomplished more than I did before. So it looks as if we denied ourselves the pleasure of television for an unnecessary length of time. One thing I cannot, and will not do. That is, sit hour after hour and do nothing but watch television. And it isn't necessary. A person can knit, sew, mend and watch a program without any trouble. That is for those who have bi-focal glasses or can work without glasses at all. I don't imagine it would be possible for people who need glasses for close work only.

There has been a little extra activity down at the barn this week. It just looks as if we are meant to keep cows, no matter what. One day Partner sent a cow to the stock market. The next day one of our heifers produced a calf, and the calf was a heifer. So we still have as many head of cattle as we had before.

You know, that is one thing I notice about farming: when one door shuts another one opens. For instance, a few weeks ago we were still shipping cream but our egg supply was down. Last week Partner bought another calf. That meant we stopped shipping cream. But our egg supply increased, so the scales were still just about even. But the drop in egg prices may soon change the picture.

Well, I suppose most farm people have been following proceedings at the Convention of the Federation of Agriculture in Hamilton. The reports and suggestions given by those at the top are thought-provoking to say the least. Obviously, it isn't enough these days to consider one branch of activity. Farming, industry, immigration, highways and zoning regulations are all tied in together. *And* national health insurance. Directly or indirectly it all affects the farmer and he must find the best way to adapt himself to changing conditions, which may be quite the opposite to that of his neighbour.

For instance, we had a middle-aged couple in here yesterday, still very active with cattle and crops. Recently the farmer found it impossible to obtain reliable hired help. The barnyard had to be kept clean and he could not keep pace with it alone. So off he went and bought a manure loader and a second tractor. Now he has enough equipment to keep him independent of hired help: a small threshing machine, baler, loader, horses and two tractors, and as many beef cattle as the farm will accommodate. But think of the capital tied up in all that equipment.

Another thing, this man believes in early to bed and early to rise. I mention that because there is some criticism about late-rising farmers. That is the result of labour-saving equipment. At one time farmers had to be up early to have the milk out ready for the truck to pick up. Now with milk coolers in general use, milk cans are left in the vat ready for the trucker when he comes. The morning's milk doesn't go until the next day. It is better that way as it gives the milk time to get properly chilled — an important factor in the production of pure milk.

So, if the farmer gets up later than he used to it is because there isn't the same necessity for him to beat the dawn every day. Which is just as well, otherwise how could farm folk take in so many late nights: farm forums, card parties and so on. Time was, when it was lights out for farm folk any time after 8:30 p.m. Nowadays that is the time when activity begins!

MARCH 15, 1956

M-m-m-m ... can you smell them? Yeast fruit buns in the making. I could almost eat them raw, they smell so good. This is my second attempt at buns after a lapse of several years, in which time I didn't make any at all. And at one time I made them every week. That was when the youngsters were at home and I found yeast buns more filling and less expensive than trying to keep the cookie jar full. I made this batch to-day because Bob and Joy will be in later and I know they will enjoy them,

Funny, how we get away from doing things. At one time I made all my own bread. I couldn't imagine my family being satisfied with baker's bread. Then one of the bread companies started canvassing for customers around here and I bought bread once a week to save baking so often. Eventually our family was reduced in number and it didn't seem worth while baking just for two or three. So the baker got another regular customer.

It was the same thing with butter. Even when we stopped making butter so sell, I always did a churning for ourselves every few weeks. The old barrel churn is still down in the cellar. Now we buy butter all the time. Butter — not margarine — I'd have you know!

But there were some things we never did do very well — not being born to it, as one might say. Curing pork, for instance. We tried several methods, but our side bacon was always hard and unappetizing. As for headcheese, the look and smell of a pig's head stewing away made me feel sick. After several attempts, we ended up by giving the head away after butchering. But I liked rendering lard. There was something fascinating in reducing all the cuttings to liquid grease and cracklings.

I was never much of a hand at making soap. Partner never wanted me to do it anyway because when he first came to Canada he lived on a farm where homemade soap was always used. It was very strong and very smelly and in winter-time his hands were raw and bleeding — which didn't make the milking any easier, and wouldn't have been allowed by the Health Unit in this day and age.

Porridge was another standby at Ginger Farm. Always porridge for breakfast, not the quick-meal porridge but real old Scotch oatmeal. That is another habit that fell by the way. Now it's packaged cereal. And in those days, we had tea at breakfast time. Now it's coffee; in fact, we wouldn't say thank you for breakfast without it or grapefruit. It was the youngsters who changed our habits. Bob took a liking to coffee when he was in the army, so when he was at home on leave I naturally made coffee for him and a pot of tea for ourselves. But that got to be too much of a chore, so finally we also drank coffee.

Maybe it's the weather has put me in a reminiscent mood. A few days ago, we had a real old-time storm and we are promised more of the same. The snow was swirling and blowing like fury, but not enough of it to pile into heavy drifts and it didn't interfere with road traffic at all. In the old days, the road past here was a county road, not a highway, and it was often impassable after a bad storm. Of course, no one ever thought of driving a car during the winter anyway. The old Flivver was jacked up on blocks for months at a time. Even when spring came the car couldn't be used because of the mud. Horses were all-important in those days and so were the trains.

Cattle and pigs were shipped to the stockyards by rail. Every station had its loading yard and farm stock was taken there by sleigh or wagon. Sometimes cattle were herded along the road on foot. I remember the first time Partner sent out a load of pigs by motor transport. We watched the truck go down the lane and thought it the last word in convenience for farmers! The second time we were not so sure. An old sow that was being shipped broke the side of the loading chute and got away. She was a contrary old dame anyway, so we finally ate her.

And then the chickens — hatched by broody hens. I remember having as many as fifteen setting hens at one time. When the chicks were hatched, we took half the hens away, keeping the ones with nice motherly dispositions. Sometimes they were too motherly and smothered some of the chicks during the night. Oh, the sick feeling when you found a number of poor dead chicks under a mother hen! Or half-grown chicks killed by rats, skunks or carried away by a fox. The time came when we got day-old chicks and a brooder stove. Later, it was started chicks, and then eight-week-old mixed chicks. Now we buy ready-to-lay pullets, which makes the work lighter as we grow older.

Such changes during the years! It sounds like a century ago, and yet it all took place in the thirty-odd years we have been farming. Sometimes when I speak of present conveniences, I wonder if I sound smug. Actually, we are anything but smug. It is just that as we look back, we realize how hard we and other farm folk worked, with few conveniences and so little of the comforts of life. But we are glad we went through that period; otherwise we wouldn't know enough to appreciate the warm, convenient and comfortable homes of to-day.

APRIL 26, 1956

Three weeks ago spring flowering bulbs were peeking through the ground. They are still peeking, no more and no less, for spring still tarries while the weatherman treats us to frosty nights and occasional snow flurries. Daughter was here Sunday, and she was reminding me that on April 17 last year she was in hospital and I had taken her some fresh-stewed rhubarb straight from the garden.

According to the date, it is now a week later and yet the rhubarb this year is no more than an inch above the ground.

Nobody minds a late winter, or fall, or even summer. But a late spring — that is harder to take. Everything within us and around us longs for the spring, for the rebirth of flowers and trees and shrubs.

Those who are well and active and busy about their day's work welcome the spring. But to those who are not so well, to the convalescents, to those who weary of the four walls of a house, to all such persons spring is doubly welcome. So for those people in particular we most sincerely hope that good health-giving days are not too far away. And when they come, make the most of them, friends. You who are house-weary, take time to be out of doors. 'Dust will wait but violets won't.' Get out and enjoy the sunshine — it is food for whatever ails you.

We are certainly hoping for a little warm weather because, as soon as he can play outdoors, our grandson is coming to visit us — all by himself. And it will certainly take the great outdoors to use up some of his surplus energy. So here's hoping, for his sake, and ours, too.

In the meantime, whatever the weather, we have plenty to interest us outside and the interest is likely to be maintained for some time. Surveyors from the Department of Highways are all over the farm, mapping out a cloverleaf for the No. 401, half of which will be on our farm. I suppose they know what they are doing, but it is all a mystery to us. One time we look out and we see from one to three cars and six or seven men. Half an hour later the cars may be gone and no sign of activity anywhere. Or maybe one car will be at the road. No men in sight, but by Rusty's insistent barking we know men are somewhere around — here, there, anywhere — we don't know.

Sometimes they arrive before 8:00 a.m., sometimes they don't show up at all. To keep track of them would be one grand guessing game. It is also necessary to forget sentiment once the surveyors get busy. First of all they bring in a card which says surveyors will find it necessary to enter your property and that "a valuator will arrange to make settlement in regard to damages." That is fine — as far as it goes. But can a valuator assess the worth to you, real or sentimental, of a tree or a group of trees?

We have evergreens on our property that were set out the first year we came. From little twelve-inch seedlings we have watched them grow to sturdy trees, twenty to thirty feet high. When Partner saw the surveyors working among the evergreens, he begged them to save the trees. He was assured the trees would not be destroyed unless it became necessary. With that he had to be satisfied.

Those trees took over thirty years to grow and could not be replaced by a similar growth for another thirty years. Also during our first year on the farm, we planted maples down the lane. Only a few of them lived. We treasured the survivors. It may be that one or more of them will topple under the official axe. We shall be compensated — in cash, maybe. But in other ways? Well, as I said before, we have to stifle sentiment, for that way leads to heartache.

In the meantime, Partner has his own guessing game and a little more work at the barn: a fresh cow and a new born calf to contend with. And then he comes to the house and we get talking about the contrariness of Nature's laws. Many times, when we were shipping milk to the dairy, we hoped for heifer calves to replace old cows going out. So what did we get? More bull calves than we wanted, of course.

One season we had twelve bull calves and one heifer. Another year, two little heifers and the rest bulls. Now with the idea of raising veal calves, we keep only two or three cows. So now what do we get? Heifer calves, no less. And last year, if you remember, the first cow to freshen after we sold most of our milking herd presented us with twin calves, and heifers at that. Sometimes it looks as if you can't win whatever you plan. Nature is liable to throw everything into reverse.

Which reminds me. A young couple in Toronto, Ted and Norma, have a very nice house cat. They are also expecting their first 'blessed event.' Norma thinks it would be unwise to keep a cat when the baby arrives. So when she was going home for a few days last week, she asked Ted to find a new home for the cat with some friends who had said they would like her. Ted, of course, delayed this little chore until the week-end.

Friday night he came home from the office to find Tabby proudly mothering four kittens. Quite an unlooked-for event. Seems to me some city folk need a little instruction about the facts of life! Poor Norma. She was worried about one cat, and now she has five.

AUGUST 30, 1956

Did you have any rain last week? We certainly had plenty. It rained and stormed intermittently all day Thursday. And if it wasn't raining, it was so dull you just wondered what might be coming next. Late in the afternoon, I wanted to go down to the post office, but every time I put on my hat and coat — crack, another storm started up. And since I am a coward insofar as weather is concerned, I decided to stay home.

Perhaps the slight earth tremors felt in the Ottawa district the day before were responsible for such persistent wet weather. It was pretty hard on the farmers trying to harvest their oat crops. Yesterday Partner and I took a run around the country and saw many fields half cut that had taken quite a beating. We even saw a field of wheat being combined — so badly down that only the weeds were showing. Something drastic must surely have held up the work on that farm for the wheat harvest to be so late.

We were glad the weather cleared Thursday night so we were able to watch the wind-up of the Republican Convention and to see and hear President Eisenhower's speech. What a wonderful reception he received and who could help liking the man? But he got Partner worried. Time after time he raised his arms above his head in acknowledging the cheers of the crowd. We always thought that to raise the arms above the head was the last thing a person with a heart condition should do. Perhaps we are wrong. One thing I noticed when he was speaking, at every opportunity he would glance at his wife and then smile his big, broad smile, just as if he were trying to reassure her by saying, "Don't worry, my dear, I'm all right!"

Of course, another excitement last week was Marilyn Bell's successful swim across Lake Ontario. I imagine fifty per cent of her admirers were hoping she wouldn't try again but since she did, naturally we all hoped she would win. It wasn't actually the swim that mattered so much, we just didn't want to see our plucky young girl defeated or hurt. You will notice I said 'our' — don't you think that is how almost everyone feels in Ontario: sort of possessive — we all want to claim that lovable young person as *our* Marilyn Bell.

Nearer home, our interest at the moment is in the highways — the old and the new. On the old highway — No. 25 — the provincial police are having quite a field day passing out tickets to speeding motorists. Partner was cutting weeds along the fence the other day and in a short while he saw four motorists given tickets. Another time I saw three cars stopped by the police.

Maybe it is just as well, for the traffic is really fast along this road. There is also a little activity on the 401 survey. We can see four men popping up and down like jack-rabbits across the field. We don't know what they are doing, as we had an idea the survey was completed some weeks ago. One thing is certain, we shall not be told to move off just yet as I noticed in the morning paper that work is only now starting from No. 27 across to No. 10 and will likely be completed in 1959! From No. 10, work will probably proceed in this direction but as No. 10 is about twelve miles from here, obviously farmers in this district can cool their heels for quite a while yet.

Just before the yellow panel truck came along to-day, I could see Mitchie-White away across the field hunting mice. He evidently didn't like being disturbed and came home in a hurry. It was the first time he had come to the house for about a week. That cat is the greatest hunter we ever had and because he is all white, we can see him such a long way off.

Well, we sent another veal calf to market last Monday and

it fetched top price. Wonderful! Then we got a new calf to take its place, so we still have only a little milk to separate. That reminds me — I picked up the last cream cheque at the creamery and it was over $21. It should have been about $3.50.

A mistake of course, and yet I could have cashed that cheque and no one been any the wiser. But what good would ill-gotten gain have brought us?

Incidentally, we don't need any super-markets in our town. Our local merchants have provided their customers with plenty of parking space, so now we can shop at home. Sure, we may spend a cent or two more here and there but at least it is going into the pockets of men who make our town their home, pay local taxes and take an interest in social services, churches and schools. What does anyone save by going to outside shopping centres anyway? It takes gas to get there, and if you have children along, it is doubtful if you get away without spending a dime or two giving the youngsters a ride on the big horse.

Ah-ha — I see another fellow getting a ticket on the highway … maybe he and his family are just hurrying home from a shopping centre!

MARCH 15, 1958

Note: Between the previous entry and this one, the Clarkes sold their farm to the Ontario government, which was constructing a cloverleaf to join Highway 25 with Highway 401. Gwendoline often looked back at life at Ginger Farm from her vantage point of town life in nearby Cooksville.

We are still in the deep freeze — definitely. At this moment it is ten below zero and there isn't a window we can see out of properly. That is because storm windows were not considered necessary over the plate glass. Which is quite true except in very severe weather. There is a part of each window that is not completely frosted. Through it we can see our neighbours having trouble starting their cars. The little girl next door left home a short while ago and then stood for ten minutes on a cold draughty corner waiting for the school bus.

The wind is howling around the house making weird noises, but inside the house we are warm and comfortable. It did occur to us this morning to wonder how much oil the furnace got away with during the nights we didn't set the thermostat back at all. Partner has a fire roaring away on the hearth right now and it looks and feels very cheery. So long as the rough weather doesn't outlast our food supplies, we shall be all right. Snow, so far, hasn't been any problem. The white stuff from our one and only snow storm is still lying around but no more has been added to it.

When I hear the wind, I keep remembering what it would be like on the farm. No matter what we did we could never keep the old house warm in a windstorm — partly because we were always afraid of fire. There were twenty-two lengths of straight smokepipe and four elbows running from the furnace to the chimney upstairs. Taking them down and cleaning them was quite a job, but for safety's sake it had to be done twice during the winter.

What a change in heating systems over the years. In pioneer days wood was the only fuel — pine stumps burnt on the open hearth after a tree had been felled. Then came the pot-bellied parlour heaters and the two-hole box-stoves that could be used for cooking as well as heating, split wood being used as fuel. From it we progressed to cookstoves, to soft coal and coke, and finally hard coal. And then there were oil stoves that would sometimes flare up and smoke the house out. In most homes there was also a one-burner 'Fairy lamp' lit for a while to take the chill out of upstairs bedrooms but taken away as soon as the children were warm and cosy in their beds under layers of patchwork quilts — after having undressed in front of the kitchen fire.

Electric heaters couldn't be used because in most homes there was no electricity. By day, children were dressed warmly with heavy underwear, and oversocks and gum-rubbers on their feet. They had to walk to school anywhere from half a mile to two miles. But at least they were on the move. As I watched our little neighbour-girl waiting at the corner in the biting wind I wondered which generation of children were the better taken care of.

Coming back to heating again. Wood for heating purposes is a thing of the past in most of central Ontario — except for fireplaces. Instead, think of the wide choice we now have in heating our homes. With coal — soft, hard or blower type. Heat can then be distributed through the house by forced air, hot-water pipes or radiant heat under the floors. Instead of coal we can have fuel oil or natural gas to run the furnaces, controlling it thermostatically by the turn of a dial in the hall.

It is all very wonderful, but I doubt if we really appreciate our modern heating systems — except when the power gives up the ghost. Then we feel hard done by and cry to high heaven and wonder why the Hydro Commission doesn't look after things better!

There used to be another type of fuel in common use out west when we lived there. I was reminded of this the other night on TV when a man was told to 'get a good fire going with buffalo chips.' Partner and I wondered how many people would know what he meant. We knew, because where we lived there was a good supply of 'cow-piles.' Cow-chips, I would have you know, were sun-baked dung that could be picked up from the pasture. Many is the time I went out after supper, carrying a sack and picked up our fuel supply for the next day. It was bone-dry, light in weight, and entirely odorless. But what a fire it would make.

APRIL 5, 1958

One who has at some time learnt to swim or to ride a bicycle never quite forgets the art. He may be out of practice but he doesn't forget. And that seems to apply to farming as well. Once a farmer always a farmer even if the hands are no longer actively engaged in doing farm chores. The interest is still there. That seems to be the way with Partner anyway. Why else should he take the trouble to ride in the cab of a milk-tank truck and find out for himself just what happens to the milk shipped in bulk to the dairies?

Just before we left the farm there was quite an agitation to induce dairy farmers to 'go tank' instead of shipping milk in cans. At the time it seemed to us like a tremendous outlay for equipment, more than a hundred-acre farmer could afford. But now the idea has really caught on and in some districts farmers shipping to local dairies are the only ones who continue to use cans, chilled in a milk-cooler before shipping.

One of our former neighbours is a milk-trucker and goes by here nearly every day so Partner arranged to ride with him on one of his trips. Partner already knew how bulk milk was handled at the farm but had no idea what happened at the dairy. Here is his account.

At the dairy where he went there was room for two tank trucks to back up into the building and stop at a given spot. Here a plastic hose was connected to the tank nozzle. A motor was then started which drew the milk from the tank and forced it into a vat on scales where it was automatically weighed. From there the milk went into the processing plant. While Partner was there three tanks, carrying about six tons of milk were emptied, washed and out again in about thirty minutes. And in that time Partner never saw one drop of milk!

As soon as a tank was empty a man dropped into it through a manhole at the top and thoroughly washed and scrubbed the inside of the tank. After he came out the tank was rinsed again. Then a sterilizing compound was forced into the tank and sealed. Then the trucker went to work, hosing and washing down the outside of his truck, and it was ready for the next day.

Waiting at the loading ramp there were also quite a large number of smaller trucks ready to pick up their daily quota of sani-seal packages and bottles to be delivered to the stores. Thus the whole process is accomplished with speed and efficiency and from the time the milk leaves the cows' udders at the various farms until it reaches your doorstep it is not once touched by human hands. Extraordinary, isn't it?

How different from a few years ago. Do you remember how often you found a certain amount of what appeared to be dirt at the bottom of a milk bottle? In fact a small percentage of sedimentation was allowed by the Health authorities as it wasn't thought possible that milk could be delivered 100% pure as it is to-day.

I also remember that if a new hired hand were engaged, among other questions he was generally asked, 1. If he could milk, and 2. If he were a 'wet' or 'dry-hand' milker. Partner never allowed wet-hand milking in his stable, for which I was very thankful. The very thought of it used to make me feel sick. But yet it was quite a common practice when we first started farming. A lot of farmers claimed it was better for the cows! Apparently little thought was given to the consumers, and that was before the days of enforced pasteurization. In the old days people must certainly have developed a sort of immunization otherwise tuberculosis and undulant fever would have been more common than they were. Remember, too, how children used to love to be around at milking time to get a drink of warm milk straight from the cow. Ugh — I used to wonder how they could drink it!

Yes, looking back over thirty-six years of farming it is extraordinary to note the changes that have taken place, and most of them a decided improvement from a sanitary point of view. But don't forget, all these improvements are reflected in the increase in our present day cost of living index. We pay for what we get, whether it is in the make and texture of a new dress or the improved quality of the milk we buy. The same applies to eggs. Remember when hens used to scratch for their living and the egg-yolks were dark and often smelt and tasted quite strong? The eggs we get now are light in colour, mild in flavour but the price we pay for them includes charges for shipping, candling, grading and sometimes delivering. All the farmer gets is the cost of producing the eggs, which includes the cost of raising the hens from chick-hood.

DECEMBER 27, 1958

Isn't it wonderful to be able to wish each other a Happy Christmas once again? Supposing we were not allowed to — supposing there were not any Christmas. Wouldn't it be ghastly if December 25 were just another date on the calendar? But it isn't, thank goodness, it is Christmas Day — the most glorious day of all the year, the birthday of the infant Christ. It is a day that means many things to many people. What we get out of it depends a lot upon what we put into it.

You hear so often Christmas isn't what it used to be. That is perfectly true; no one realizes and regrets it more than I. But still, underneath all the commercialism, the over-emphasis on Santa Claus, the showers of greeting cards given and received, the Star in the East never diminishes in brightness. It is there if we look for it. It points the way in our heart and inner consciousness to the wonder and joy of the Saviour's birth.

To me, Christmas now is something like the gift parcels we used to delight in as children. Very mysterious parcels, parcels with all kinds of labels and coloured ribbons. You shook the parcel inquisitively, but there was no sound. You carefully untied the fancy ribbons and tore off the outer layer of bright coloured paper. And what did you find? Only more papers, more ribbons and more labels — maybe even another box. You removed the second layer only to find the same thing again. This might be repeated several times until a package that started out in dimensions of twenty inches by thirty was reduced to a small box that could be held in the hand.

And what did the box contain? More than likely something that had been chosen with loving care, bought, perhaps, with nickels and dimes that had been saved for weeks. Something for Mother, Dad, big sister or brother; for Grandma, Gramp or baby sister. Maybe the mysterious wrappings were duplicated in all seven parcels. The tinsel and gilt, the gaudy paper and string; the unnecessary boxing created an illusion of Christmas. They were all there.

So, also, was the gift of love, often quite inexpensive and sometimes quite inappropriate, yet it symbolized all the desire of the giver to bring joy and happiness to loved ones in the family circle.

So it is, in a way, with our present-day Christmas. There are too many wrappings, many boxes within boxes, coloured labels plastered here and there, together with too much noise and ostentation. But yet if we have patience; if, as it were, we remove the papers one by one, eventually we come to the true meaning of Christmas. It is still there, just as it always has been, but a little harder to find among all the commercial wrappings.

The same applies to greeting cards. In our anxiety not to miss anyone who is likely to send us a card, we rush out and buy cards and stamps by the score. We send cards to people we hardly know well enough to pass the time of day with. We pore over last year's list, fearful of committing the social sin of forgetting someone, even though it be our next door neighbours to whom we can wish a Happy Christmas just by lifting the telephone receiver or calling a greeting as we see them going from their house to the garage.

So often greeting cards give me a let-down feeling. I like them, of course, they are so cheerful and Christmasey, I can't imagine the Yuletide season without them. But how often I have opened an envelope, sent by someone I haven't heard from for some time, and I have looked on the inside of the card, on the outside, inside the envelope again and what do I find — nothing but a signature.

What I like best is a simple card, with a short personal note. Then I feel I've got something. But how many of us have time to take this extra trouble? Most folk have so many cards to send, about all they can manage is to scrawl their names on the cards and write addresses on the envelopes. Who dares to be different? Very few. But wouldn't it be nice if we took the courage to ignore convention, cut out sending cards to casual acquaintances and spent more time on those to whom a personal message from ourselves might really mean something?

That is just my idea, of course, and one that I don't always live up to. Like everyone else I get caught up in a last-minute rush and cards are popped into envelopes regardless. The road to Heaven is paved with good intentions, and the Christmas season is littered with good wishes and loving thoughts, only the half of which are given expression. We all try to do too much in too short a time.

And here I am at the end of my column, and I haven't even said "Happy Christmas to you all." But neither have I sent you a greeting card without a message! This time you've got the message and not the card. Which would you rather have?

OCTOBER 1, 1960

Yesterday Partner was laughing at me. It was a cool day so I wheeled my sun-cot from the front porch to the back patio where it was more sheltered. Then the sun came out, bright and warm. There was no way of escaping it, so I went into the house and came out with a parasol. So there was I, holding a parasol up with one hand and writing with the other. Partner was sitting quite happily in a garden chair. He doesn't mind the sun at all. I wouldn't either, except that it bothers my eyes.

One thing is certain, I wasn't sitting in the sun last week! Our September heat wave was really awful while it lasted, wasn't it? On one of those ninety degree days. I was scheduled to speak at a W.I. meeting near Ginger Farm. I wished I could call it off, but of course I didn't. On the way over, I passed several farms where threshing was in progress and I thought to myself, what have I to grumble about compared with the women who are having to cook meals for the threshers?

Strange to say, that talk I had prepared was entitled 'Look Back in Gladness.' In it I was comparing present-day farm housekeeping to what it was thirty years ago. Now that hydro is available to farm folk we have electric stoves, refrigerators, plug-in kettles and so on. Very different from the days when getting meals for threshers meant either cooking on an oil-stove or bringing in chips from the backyard to make a quick fire in the kitchen range. Either way created extra heat. I couldn't have chosen a better day to suggest to my fellow W.I. members that they look back in gladness.

On the way home I stopped to pay brief visits to a few former neighbours. At one place a large swimming pool had been installed at the back of the house. About four adults and half a dozen children were having a wonderful time. But I am not sure that they were having more fun than our generation did at the 'ole swimmin' hole' down at the creek. I might add, this swimming pool had not been installed from the proceeds of farm income. Although still living in the old farmhouse, remodelled, this young fellow has a far more lucrative income than he ever got from farming.

A funny thing happened on my cross-country trip. I had to be given directions on how to get from one place to another — to farms we had known for thirty-five years. This was all on account of Highway 401. That is to say, people on certain farms now have to drive several miles to reach the next farm, because instead of a line fence the 401 is now the dividing line. It is slightly confusing until you get used to it. I also noticed a terrific increase in the amount of traffic on what used to be quiet country roads.

Well, Dee and the boys are home from the cottage and back to normal living. Dave is struggling once again with the mysteries of the 'three R's.' Not too enthusiastically, I gather. They were here Friday, well tanned and full of pep.

Incidentally, during the summer I noticed quite a number of letters in the press, for and against mothers and children spending the summer by the lake, leaving father to sweat it out down town, working all week then driving to the cottage for the week-end. Some letters made the women sound awfully selfish. But are they? Mothers of small children are not just sitting around all summer. There is work no matter where you stay. But at least the children have more freedom, get more fresh air and build up reserve strength against winter.

As for father, unless he is the helpless type, he would surely be happier alone than he would be coming home to a restless family, hard to control, with insufficient outlets for their energy.

It isn't possible for all families to have a country cottage but we feel that where it is possible it is definitely a good thing for everyone concerned. And living is cheaper. Dee was thrilled because in two months she saved $30 out of her housekeeping money. There were plenty of visitors but the visitors always helped with the work and with food supplies. That way no one was out of pocket.

Isn't the news concerning Hurricane Donna dreadful? Can you imagine a popular holiday resort like Florida suffering such disaster? And the end is not in sight. Donna is continuing on her way leaving millions of dollars of damage in her wake. We hope she doesn't head for Ontario or will have lost her punch before she gets here. Few of us will have forgotten Hurricane Hazel. She arrived in October. Some people are not the least weather-conscious. If they have planned a trip they go regardless. If we are away and a storm comes up we are always uneasy about what may be happening at home. I suppose that is the result of 'Hazel' and a couple of twisters before that.

OCTOBER 22, 1960

Yesterday we had our first rain in six weeks, and were the birds ever enjoying it. A dozen little juncos were having a grand time in a puddle near the back door and there were more varieties of sparrows around than I ever saw before. The lawn was black with starlings and the sunflowers were bending and swaying with the weight of numerous blue jays that came to harvest the seed.

As for the feeding station, juncos and sparrows were swarming all over it, inside, outside and on top of it. Yes, it was a great morning for the birds and I spent quite a bit of time watching them enjoy it. Ditto was the only one who was worried. Watching birds from inside the house wasn't her idea of fun. But you can be quite sure I didn't let her out while there were so many birds around.

Well, last week was a week to remember, and a week in which we were very glad to have a TV set. We wouldn't have missed the U.N. speeches for anything. We didn't always know when they were coming on so it sometimes happened

Partner would just nicely be starting into a job outside and I would call to him — "Come and hear Diefenbaker, or Macmillan," as the case might be.

They were wonderful, but we were stunned beyond belief at Khrushchev's violent and ill-mannered interruptions, which were only exceeded by his own speech on Saturday morning. How is it possible for the United Nations to make any headway while dealing with such an outrageous character? Most of the time I was listening to speeches in between canning and pickling — peeling a few onions and then running back to hear more.

Strange, isn't it, that we can be so intent on keeping up with our own little chores while the peace of the world is being verbally threatened? You would think making mustard pickle was frightfully important. And so it was, at the moment. That and canning grapes, plums, peaches and pickling beets, straight from the garden.

Before I was through, the house was reeking with the odor of vinegar and pickling spices. Partner thought I was crazy. "Why don't you give it a rest?" he said. "You don't have to get it all done in one week." He also offered to help. "Can't I peel the beets or something?" he would say. My answer was always the same, "Thanks, the best way you can help is to keep out of my road." Any woman will know what I mean. Slippery beets were hard enough for me to skin; I don't know how Partner expected his stiff, arthritic fingers to handle the job.

My goodness, did you ever know the days to draw in so fast? For the life of me I can't see what purpose daylight saving serves at this time of the year. There isn't any daylight to save anyway. We might just as well all be back on standard time and thus save a good deal of confusion.

Last week, if you remember, I mentioned Partner having a little extra wiring done. And have I been glad of that night-light in the hall. That started me thinking about entertaining, especially elderly folk. Have you ever wondered why people getting on in years are not too anxious to stay overnight away from home? One reason, I am sure, is because they are wakeful and restless at night, often hating to visit the bathroom at night for fear of disturbing the rest of the household, perhaps not quite sure where the light switches are and afraid to put them on anyway. A night light in the hall might help a lot.

And here are a few other suggestions. Put a clock in the guest room. A restless person naturally wonders about the time. He or she wakes up and wonders, is it just after midnight, or is it nearly morning? Sometimes it is want of a drink that keeps a person awake. Or perhaps longing for a little nighttime snack.

The remedy is simple. Fill a small thermos with whatever your visitors may like to drink. A small glass jar of plain cookies might also be appreciated. Generally speaking, a poor sleeper nearly always dozes off towards morning so assure your visitor it will be quite all right if she should sleep in. She might welcome a cup of tea first thing in the morning. Make sure of that overnight so as not to disturb her unnecessarily.

I say 'her' but it applies equally well to 'him.' Grandpa may have restless nights, too. At home he may have formed the habit of sitting in the living room for a while, maybe smoking a pipe. Not a good habit, but a man is surely entitled to do what he likes in his own home. Away from home, decency demands that his nocturnal habits be more restrained, and thus adds to his restlessness. His hostess, whether friend or relative, can make his stay a lot happier by giving a little thought to his creature comforts, and thereby lessen his fear of disturbing other folk at night.

JULY 22, 1961

This has been the craziest holiday week-end we ever knew. Dominion Day, as you know, fell on a Saturday this year and was ostensibly a holiday. We didn't expect any mail on that day but we got it just the same. And delivery men came around just the same — the baker, the milkman and so on. Local stores were all open, and business went on as usual except for department stores. Schools, of course, had already closed for the summer; teachers and students alike joyfully starting the long vacation. School being out meant families with cottages are now free to get away from it all — away to the lakes and beaches, to boating and fishing and living in sunsuits and swimming trunks. Now their number is legion with mothers willingly sacrificing the comforts of normal living for a few carefree months and odd week-ends at the lake.

With farm folk it is different. For them summer means more work and longer hours and often an influx of visitors. People who don't have a summer cottage to go to are only too happy to spend a holiday on the farm. And the children love it.

Last week we spent a day on a farm ourselves. It was good to be back among the cows, the pigs and the chickens and to sniff once again the smell of new-mown hay. It was close and oppressive when we left home, with a light rain falling, but as we approached Orangeville the clouds lifted and the air became delightfully fresh and invigorating.

That is what we notice more than anything — the change of air. We certainly noticed when we got home, too! Ninety degrees the next day and the humidity about as high as it could be with storms all around us. Poor Taffy was terrified, wouldn't leave me at all and refused to eat until the storms had passed over. I had every sympathy for him because I don't like storms either. Before and during a storm I feel awful. After the electricity has spent itself, or passed over, I feel like a different person.

One thing we can be thankful for — the recent rains have given the gardens a new lease on life. If only it would rain over the prairies and give the parched crops new life, too. Rain can work miracles. Shrubs here that didn't look too promising a few weeks ago are now making headway. The irises are past their best, but the rambler roses are in full bloom. In a couple of weeks we shall be enjoying peas and beans from our own garden — that is, rabbits permitting!

Back of our property there is plenty of wild bush and scrub land. It is a haven for birds and rabbits. The birds we welcome, but for the rabbits we have no love at all, especially as the wretched things are so tame. Even the baby rabbits will sit in the middle of the lawn with Taffy barking and the cat watching. They look cute, I must confess, but that's the only good thing I can say for them. They will probably be pretty busy this week-end because nearly everyone around here is away, except ourselves. And we are not moving around very much this weather — not with the humidity at 102! Dee and family left for the cottage Saturday. Art will be coming back, but Dee and the boys will be staying for the summer.

Why don't we join them? Well, it isn't through lack of invitations. We like being by the lake when we're there — it is a beautiful spot — but we don't enjoy the long drive back and forth. However, we may make it some day. I guess we are just old home-bodies anyway, especially Partner. Maybe I would go more if he would, but he enjoys his own home. I suppose I should be satisfied to have him so contented. He very rarely expresses a wish for anything more than we've got, but last week he did — and it didn't take me long to work on it. He said he wished he had a transistor radio; he would like to be able to keep up with the news — world-wide and political — any time we are on the road going somewhere, or even when he is working outside.

The very next day I went shopping for a radio, complete with carrying case. Now he can hoe the garden and have the radio hanging from a tree; we can also sit outside in the cool of the evening and hear all the latest in music, sports and news. Partner is very sports-minded. Last Sunday, he and Bob went to the Stock Car races at the Exhibition grounds. Partner enjoyed it, except for the fact that all around him young folk were guzzling the whole time: pop, hot dogs, chocolate milk and potato chips. Partner was appalled at the waste of money, especially at a time when there is so much talk of strikes and unemployment. When he told me, I was more appalled at what all this indiscriminate eating and drinking was doing to the stomachs of those concerned.

Here's my book-note for the week. I can highly recommend 'The Living Spirit' by Daphne du Maurier, author of 'Rebecca.' You can get it in a fifty cent paper-back.

JULY 29, 1961

Well, when I finished this column last week I was all set to go down to our local hospital for a day's sewing and mending. The W.A. meets once a week for that purpose. But my plans had to be changed in a hurry.

My nephew Klemi phoned from Malton. He had taken his girl friend there to board a BOAC plane for England. When they got there they were told the flight had been delayed, so Klemi wanted to know if I could put them up for the night. I made up a bed for Pam, but arranged for Klemi to spend the night at a motel just around the corner from here. That, too, had to be changed. When they arrived here it was to tell me that the BOAC had arranged accommodation for its passengers at the Lord Simcoe. So Klemi took Pam to Toronto, then came back here himself.

All the next day they were back and forth, keeping in touch with Malton for latest flight reports. I still don't know what the delay was all about, something to do with a strike, but it must have been on the other side of the water. Pam finally took off about eleven o'clock Monday night. Klemi came back here, returning to Peterborough Tuesday morning. He couldn't stay longer as he had his passage booked on a boat leaving Montreal Friday morning. It was all very confusing.

By the time they had gone, I felt as if I had been put through a wringer. It just shows how things you never expected to concern you at all can end up by disrupting all your prearranged plans. Just as a pebble thrown into calm water creates ever widening circles.

Thursday we did a little visiting ourselves. One call was to a farm, the home of an aged couple in semi-retirement. Their ages are eighty-two and eighty-three! The farm is a lovely spot, on top of a hill, well wooded and with an ever-flowing creek running through the ravine. Once it was a dairy farm, but now most of the land is down in pasture. However, there is still plenty of live stock around: two cows, two calves, three pedigreed dogs, about a dozen cats, a number of bantam hens and chickens and twenty-one goats!

The calves milk the cows, but six of the goats are milked by hand standing on a platform that brings them up to a convenient level for milking. The nannies and their daughters were in one pasture field, the males in another. In a stable, penned up by himself, was the old billy goat, father and grandfather to them all. He didn't have any horns but he sure had the longest beard I'd ever seen.

The farm is only a few miles from the centre of a residential and industrial development, and yet it is so quiet and peaceful. It would appear there are still occasional unspoilt beauty spots if one knows where to look for them.

From there we went on to visit Bob and Joy — and of course the two little fellows. There was plenty of activity going on there! I think there were at least ten or twelve youngsters playing around in the back yard when we went in to supper. I asked Joy how she could stand it. "I sometimes wonder!" was the answer.

From there we went to visit an old lady of eighty-six, convalescing from a heart attack. Staying with her was a friend from Powassan who is a reader of this column. Looks as if I had better watch my step — there is no telling who I am likely to run into!

Next day should have been a quiet day at home, but Partner managed to create a little excitement when he was mowing the lawn by backing into a low stone wall and falling over it into the driveway. Because arthritis makes him so stiff and awkward he couldn't get up. Two neighbours saw what had happened and came along and helped him to his feet. I was at the back of the house and unaware of the accident. Now Partner has a nice sore shoulder to carry around for a few days, so stiff I have to help him get his clothes off and on.

So that was our week, interspersed with plenty of rain, cold weather and hot news from Parliament Hill. The furnace still comes on at night. One night we saw Northern Lights. What kind of weather they indicate, I don't know. Art had a letter from Dee giving him a long list of things she wanted at the cottage, including a bag of coal! There shouldn't be too many mosquitoes and black flies anyway.

We still have quite a bit of summer visiting to do, but the trouble is to find nice days to take to the road — no sense in starting out in bad weather. So far, we have been lucky. However, the weather seems to suit the trees and shrubs, but the garden could do with less rain and more sunshine.

DECEMBER 9, 1961

We have been having a marvellous time this past week. Oh no, we haven't been on a trip, if that's what you are thinking. We haven't been any farther than our own basement. In fact that is exactly where we went, where we stayed and where we shall continue to stay for at least another week.

Oh no, we are not practising living in a bomb shelter. We are not in favour of that. Our one and only reason for practically living downstairs is for the purpose of clearing out junk! And believe me, it was necessary. A lot of the stuff downstairs was what we had brought from the farm — thinking we would have time to make use of it later on. Instead of that we added to the pile. Old clothes to cut up for braided rugs, some to make over for our grandsons. Stacks and stacks of magazines that contained 'interesting articles,' paper-back books, local newspapers, travelogues, maps and recipe folders.

I'm telling you, we could hardly navigate in our basement at all. More than that we could never find anything we wanted even if we were sure it was there.

One day I began to look around and wondered what would happen if either of us should pass to the 'Great Beyond'! That was when I determined to clean up — and Partner was only too glad to cooperate. Already he has burnt five bushel baskets full of junk — and the end is not in sight. We also packed a carton of 'better books' ready for a White Elephant Sale. I don't mean better in regard to the condition of the covers but to the reading matter — some of them are classics, some poetry, still of value to anyone who has the time and inclination to read them.

It has been a tiring job, and yet in a way, enjoyable. Readers of this column may be interested to know I came across many of the letters you have written to me over the years. They will not be burnt — at least not in my lifetime. They are stacked away in a big carton marked 'Fan Mail.'

Often when I take down a box I haven't any idea what I am going to find inside. One such box was about eight inches square. "Now what's in here?" I asked myself. You'd never guess. Love-letters, no less! Another box contained letters covering a two-year period from my much beloved mother who died in 1923 of cancer. I often wondered about mother — whether I had given her enough attention while she was still living, especially after I came to Canada. Thank heaven her letters reassured me on that point. Apparently I had written quite regularly and Partner and I together had supplied a little financial assistance. All her letters were pathetically cheerful, although I know she suffered terribly and was getting weaker all the time. You can imagine what those letters meant to me, bringing back many happy memories as well as sorrowful recollections concerning her last illness.

The box of love-letters I haven't had the courage to open yet. When I told Partner about them he said, "You had better burn those unread!" Now why should he say that? Do you suppose he thought they might contain reasons for regret, of unfulfilled promises or of dreams that didn't materialize? Anyway, they could boomerang for either of us as some are from Partner to me, others from me to him. At the moment I don't think I have the courage to open them anyway.

Not only that, I haven't time as I have yet to sort out my collection of writings. I have a printed copy of everything I ever had published, dating back to 1923, in papers, magazines and books, some of them published in England. Some of the clippings are pasted in scrap-books, others are loose or in the original paper or magazine in which they were published. When I was giving them the 'once-over' I couldn't believe I had written so much.

In his way Partner is as bad as I am for hoarding: he saves old nails, screws, bits of board, tools that need fixing, binder twine and odds and ends of paint. Some time we shall get it all sorted out. There will still be a lot of stuff left. An old edition (24 volumes) of the Encyclopedia Britannica, which we consider priceless. Also a huge Webster's Dictionary. Print and flannelette cuttings I refuse to throw out — I am hoping to make two quilts for the boys. Small glass jars make good containers for nails, buttons and so on as they don't need to be labelled — you know what you've got at a glance. Advertising letters come in handy for making carbon copies for anything I type.

Well, that's what we've been doing. Does it put any of you in the notion to go and do likewise? I'm telling you it'll be a grand and glorious feeling when the job is done! Try it yourself sometime.

December 23, 1961

A Happy Christmas to you all!

It is not yet time for our Christmas (glory be!) because this column goes to press three weeks ahead of the date that you actually read it. So you see what I mean when I say it is not yet time for our Christmas.

However, at this season of the year it is easy to anticipate. For that reason, I know that in every home where these Chronicles are read — and in thousands where they are not — there is at this moment a fever of activity.

There is probably a Christmas tree, gaily decorated and illuminated; parcels tucked away in secret places; Christmas cards galore bringing best wishes from a host of friends; and unexpected letters from some with whom we had almost lost contact.

There are oldish folk, a little tired and taking every chance they get for a quiet snooze, or maybe sitting quietly day-dreaming, remembering other Christmases so long ago.

And the children — who can know what this Christmas will mean to them? This season of mysticism — everything so mixed up in their childish minds: birth of the Christ-Child, annual visit of Santa Claus, the getting and giving of gifts. Don't you sometimes wonder what any child can make of it all? Do we take the right attitude in regard to children and Christmas?

Be that as it may, it is not my intention to moralize. I just want to say with all sincerity that I hope this will be for you the best Christmas yet, not necessarily in regard to gifts but because of the inner happiness that comes through close association with those we love.

That is what really counts, don't you think?

Has it ever occurred to you that memory is one of our greatest possessions? Without it the present would have little meaning, and inspiration for the future would be sadly lacking.

Naturally the extent of our memory depends upon age and experience. I remember the Christmases I spent in England as a child. My father died when I was a child and my mother took in dress making to support her five children, the youngest of whom was born three months after my father died but lived for only sixteen months. My mother had a hard life — there was no baby bonus or hospital insurance in those days. Everything we ate and the clothes we wore were all bought with the money my mother made by sewing.

But I can't remember a Christmas that wasn't happy. As children we hung up our stockings at the head of our beds on Christmas Eve. In the morning they were always full with nuts, an orange, homemade candy and a simple toy. We didn't have a Christmas tree and the holly and evergreens around the house were what we children had gathered from the woods. Our decorations were festoons of coloured 'paper chains,' the making of which kept us occupied for many happy hours before Christmas.

Christmas morning we were awake at dawn, exploring our Christmas stockings. Mother would come in singing and clapping her hands:

" 'Tis Christmas Day, 'tis Christmas Day, how happy we all should be with plenty of toys for girls and boys and a jolly big Christmas Tree!"

Then there was breakfast and after breakfast we stood around the old table piano singing carols to my mother's accompaniment. At noon we had a roast chicken dinner — the only time my mother could afford to buy chicken. For dessert there was homemade plum pudding with a sprig of holly on top. Somehow or other Mother always managed to have threepenny worth of brandy in the house for Christmas. This was poured over the pudding and lighted with a match. The dancing blue flames leaping up and around the pudding were a fascinating sight for us all.

Christmas night we nearly always had 'high tea' and friends in to share it. There was carol singing again afterwards. As I look back I can only hope that Mother got as much enjoyment out of Christmas as she gave to her family. I rather think she did, as she was that sort of person. She lived for others if ever anyone did.

After I was married, came to Canada and had children of my own, the memory of my mother was my greatest inspiration at Christmas.

December 30, 1961

Well, we have just come through an experience that comes every so often, generally once in two years. I am referring to civic elections. It got pretty hot around here last week —

phone calls, election cards in the mail or delivered by hand. Candidates calling and one neighbourhood meeting to see and talk with a would-be council member.

We went along with it all and got quite a kick out of it, until I was asked to act as a scrutineer. That little office I declined. I have done my share at that sort of thing; now I think I am entitled to sit back and watch others at it.

Partner always takes a lively interest in any election — civic, provincial or federal — but he never campaigns for any particular party. He likes to be free to attend meetings on either side, to ask questions and to express his views, which don't always coincide with those of the person running for office!

That doesn't mean Partner makes a habit of sitting on the fence. It just means that he has an open mind concerning the issues at stake. One thing neither of us can stand — that is apathy on the part of so-called electors. Partner will often say and do things just to start an argument that he hopes will make his friends and neighbours take more interest in what is taking place.

Really it is amazing the number of young married couples who don't bother to vote. But yet they have plenty to say among themselves about what the council does or doesn't do: why don't they give us better roads, why don't they bring the sewerage through, why are residential areas so often rezoned commercial, why are we taxed for improvements that are only of benefit to those living on the other side of the township, why shouldn't we have more improvements here? You have doubtless heard the same thing over and over. Then comes an election. How many of those who complain the loudest turn out to vote? You know as well as I do, but I do hope *you* are not one of the non-voting complainers!

Well, although electioneering and voting is to all intents and purposes a serious business, yet it also has its funny side. At a Ward meeting that we went to the candidate, in answer to a specific question, was trying to think in what year the present slump began.

Partner said with a laugh, "When the Conservatives got in!" He didn't really mean to make a loaded observation, it was just a quip to raise a laugh — which it certainly did.

At home, Partner and I had been arguing about the candidates and their policies and, as you know, it is generally taken for granted that a husband and wife will vote the same way. But Partner and I didn't — although Partner didn't know it until I told him. He was quite amused. Now I must see to it that he doesn't broadcast the fact, otherwise the neighbours may wonder whom they can trust — especially with the possibility of a federal election coming up.

Another matter around here that is providing plenty of discussion is a 'fall-out shelter.' Our doctor is building one in his own back yard. This doctor originally came from Central Europe. He has first-hand knowledge of the horrors of war and is quite convinced that Khrushchev means business, also that Canada is sadly lacking in defence preparations, therefore every man should take means to protect his own home and family. He said to me, "Mrs. Clarke, the situation has become so serious that only God can save us."

"And why not?" I asked. "God created mankind; why not place your faith in Him? Do you think He will be content to let what He has created be destroyed by an evil genius? Personally I would rather trust my Creator than the strongest fall-out shelter made by man."

Perhaps I am wrong. Perhaps in our flagrant disregard of Divine Law we are inviting disaster and the near extinction of the human race. A certain measure of punishment may be coming our way, but I cannot believe the Western world will be wiped out and the Communists allowed to triumph.

Well, my immediate problem is dishing up a hot dinner, which to-day is quite an adventure. Adventure? Yes. For the first time in years I've made a Yorkshire pudding. Will it be like what Mother used to make or a dismal failure? We love roast beef and Yorkshire pudding but I lacked the courage to try it. I'll add a postscript later.

P.S. — The pudding was quite a success!

JANUARY 13, 1962

As you know, every year on the Saturday before Christmas, the National Hockey League, puts on what is known as 'Young Canada Night.' To us it points up the changes that have taken place over a period of years.

When we first started listening to hockey broadcasts it was from a second-hand battery radio, with Foster Hewitt calling the game. Then came the year when, as a special attraction for Young Canada Night, Foster had his young son come to the microphone and take part in the broadcast. Bill was then about eight years old. Obviously Bill took a genuine interest in hockey, so the time came when he also became an announcer for the hockey games, not replacing his father but supplementing his activities. That is to say Foster broadcasts by radio and Bill on television.

This last Young Canada Night marked another milestone in the Hewitt family. Bill's young son also took part in the broadcast just as we remember his father did many years ago. No doubt it was a proud night for Grandpa Hewitt, and most certainly a family record in continuous broadcasting.

That brings back to mind the early days of radio. I remember, back on the farm, when we had our first radio. It was a big cumbersome affair, and of course it was battery operated. It had a number of knobs that had to be adjusted every time we turned it on, and then often it would squeal and whine until sometimes we couldn't hear any program at all.

Worse still were the times when the battery, without any warning, would give up the ghost. That necessitated a trip to town to get the battery recharged, and in winter a trip to town often meant going in by horse and cutter, or team and sleighs.

A few years later we got a smaller, more compact radio. We did get better reception but we still had to depend on batteries as it was long before the time we had hydro installed at the farm.

What a difference electric power makes in a home! Almost at once we got an electric radio — no batteries to worry about, just occasionally a tube would burn out and had to be replaced. Now radio and television sets have been improved to such an extent that only occasionally do they give any mechanical trouble. Which is marvellous when you think of the use — and abuse — they receive, with children turning the controls on and off, this way and that, with both radio and television.

What would happen if youngsters to-day were faced with the same conditions that were prevalent in the thirties: no television, and radios in only a few homes? Who is to say, which period encourages the better personalitites? Certainly children a generation ago were more creative and less dependent upon commercial toys and entertainment.

What would mothers of pre-schoolers do to-day without TV? In dozens of homes you hear the same story, "Come on, now, eat up your breakfast, then you can watch Popeye."

Television to young mothers is as good as a part-time babysitter.

Well now, for you people who read this column, Christmas is now a thing of the past. We, on the other hand, have another two days to go before the big day arrives. For you it is a time for catching your breath again. You can now collect all those lovely Christmas cards, put them into a box until the beginning of next December. Then you will bring them out once more and go through the same ritual all over again. That is all part of Christmas.

I was talking to Daughter this morning and she said they got their greatest kick out of taking the boys to do their own shopping. They each took money from their penny boxes to buy presents for Grandpa and Grandma and for their cousins, Ross and Cedric. Dee took them to Woolworths and they were allowed to choose the presents themselves. Dave had two dollars to spend but what he picked out came to just over four dollars so he went after his Dad to make up the difference! His father allowed him an extra dollar but also insisted that some of the things must be put back on the shelves. Naturally that was to make him understand the value of money.

We generally think that children have too many presents and take too much for granted. But apparently, given the opportunity, they get just as much pleasure out of giving as receiving. And that is something that should be encouraged.

Well, Happy New Year, everybody.

JUNE 2, 1962

It pays to have a bird feeding station. This past week besides the usual run of sparrows, robins and starlings, we have seen an oriole, a downy woodpecker, flickers, brown thrashers, dozens of red-winged blackbirds and a budgie bird!

At first I thought the latter was a blue bird. Then I remembered a neighbour had put her budgies out for an airing and somehow or other the cage door came open and away went the budgies. Our neighbour hopefully set the cage on a table but so far the budgies have shown no inclination to forego their new-found freedom.

Who can blame them? But how long can they survive, find their own feed and escape prowling cats who look upon birds as legitimate prey? Fortunately our Ditto does not bother much about hunting birds, but she will crouch motionless for ever so long out in the field watching for mice.

Well, I expect green thumb experts have been busy in the garden just lately. We are not experts, but we have been busy. In fact, Partner was up at Bob's for two days putting in shrubs for them as he and Joy decided to do a little landscape garden at the front of their house.

While Partner was away, the grass and dandelions at home really took a jump and I also had a new shrub for him to plant when he got home. It is a viburnum. I saw one in a friend's garden — she told me it had beautiful white blossom heads and a perfume that spread all over the district. That was enough for me. I love flowers that smell sweet as well as look nice.

One way and another it was a busy week. One day I was at a Press Club luncheon to hear Vida Peane tell about the plans that are being made by the Centennial Committee for celebrating Canada's Centennial in 1967.

Apparently it is something to which every organization should be giving some thought; in fact, many have made tentative plans already. Some are arranging to finance scholarships of various kinds: for science, music, medicine, literature and so on. Others are making a point of having local histories written and published, which I think is a grand idea. Too much history has already been lost, and so many lovely old buildings have been demolished to make way for modern industry and super-highways. We should at least have pictures and records to show these places at one time did actually exist.

The next night our doctor came in for a social visit and stayed until nearly one o'clock, arguing with Partner about politics and world affairs. He was born in Central Europe and had many unpleasant experiences during the Second World War, including going home one time after an absence of eighteen months to find his father had been taken away and killed by the communists. As regards Canadian politics, he contends that none of the political parties in Canada have a man to head the party who can really qualify as a true leader.

Then we got on to socialized medicine, to which he is naturally opposed not only for the sake of doctors but for the patients themselves. But he does think that medical benefits and hospitalization generally could do with an overhauling. That some patients are in hospital who shouldn't be there, taking up beds that are urgently needed by more serious cases still on the waiting list. With this I agree, because I know of several such instances. It is often less trouble for the family to have those chronic complaints in hospital than to look after them at home. And I can't see that socialized medicine is likely to help that situation at all.

Well, in a lighter vein, you often hear the expression, 'What you give you get in return.' It generally refers to some form of retribution as the result of a mean or unkind act. But you know it can be just the opposite.

For instance, Saturday I was doing some last-minute shopping, which I generally try to avoid. At the grocery store there was the usual line-up at the cash registers. At my desk I was second in line. Presently I turned around and there was a lady with just three items in her hands.

Well, you know how irritating it is to buy just a few things and then have to wait while customers ahead cash in with a whole cart-load of groceries. So I said to this lady, "You go ahead of me; you have so little."

At first she protested but in the end she accepted my offer. Then after she had cashed in, she turned to me and offered me her stamps. Then it was my turn to protest but she said, "No, you take them, I have no use for them." (I presume she was not a regular customer at the store.)

So you see what I mean, I gained a few stamps by being just a little bit considerate of another person. And I rather fancy we both felt glad things happened the way they did. It's the sort of thing that gives one a nice comfortable feeling.

CONCLUSION

It has long been a dream of my brother, Bob, and me to see our mother's Ginger Farm columns collected in a book — and now it has happened!

This would not have been possible if not for her scrapbooks. You may remember reading of her delight in unpacking a box and finding the scrapbooks she had kept over the years of writing about Ginger Farm. Some of these consisted of old school 'scribblers' into which she had pasted her weekly columns.

With these scrapbooks as the main source material, the preservation project began in earnest. The original columns were keyed in and stored by year on computer disks — over one and a half million words in total. After that came the difficult task of selecting the columns for this book that best represented the rich and colourful historical detail she poured into nearly thirty years of writing.

The sad part is, we were unable to find the article that Mother wrote as her farewell to her loyal readers. I am certain it existed, because I remember that she wasn't looking forward to writing it and was worried about what to say.

When Mother put her pen down, it was mainly because the farm itself had ceased to exist. Ginger Farm was under construction for the cloverleaf that was to connect highways 25 and 401. The barn and most of the other buildings were demolished. This meant that she was lacking in content to write about — something that was becoming difficult for her in any case as her memory and health began to slip.

She no longer had to cope with a young heifer getting through the fence for a greener pasture. All the cows were gone, even old Niger and Bessie, whose horns Bob used to be so wary of. There were no more chickens to pluck, and, thank goodness, no more threshing meals to prepare.

Yes, she enjoyed her new home — making her old-fashioned walnut furniture fit the new surroundings and fixing new curtains. Beyond that, what was she to write about? By now her readers were likely tired of hearing about her five grandsons. And as for the animals, only the cats Ditto and Tuffy remained. The demise of the column was not through lack of interest in current affairs; however, without the happenings on the farm, things just weren't quite the same.

Then, just two weeks after her last article was published, Art (my Partner) was killed in a single-car accident. I have always been thankful that she did not have to write that story for her readers.

Mother did continue to write short stories for *Farmer's Magazine* and attend her Scotch Block Women's Institute meetings. (A few years earlier she was thrilled to see her Halton

Pages of the Past articles, written for *The Canadian Champion* and the *Free Press*, published as a book.) She still had a purpose: five grandsons who needed mittens, which she knitted with doubled strands of recycled wool that seemed to stay dry a lot longer than the store-bought mitts.

She passed away in June of 1966.

Let me bring you up-to-date on some of the other people introduced to readers in Mother's columns. My father lived in their Cooksville home for just about two years after Mother's death and did a little babysitting for his neighbours, who in turn kept a eye on him to see that he was all right.

He finally consented to move into a retirement home. He remained keenly interested in everything, and nothing delighted him more than a trip to the farm at Tara near Goderich owned by Johnny, who had helped us so much on our farm in the war years. Grandpa lived to the age of eighty-four.

My brother, Bob, continued to work on heavy equipment in construction. His hobby of repairing the old Rumely tractors that he and his boys found was put to good use on special days at Kelso Agriculture Museum. He was often on the road taking his tractor and threshing machine there. Bob delighted in putting his equipment to work to show the children how it was done in the Olden Days. He lived to experience his wish to see the new century born, dying in January of 2000.

My nephew Cedric was married in the little old church still standing on the Kelso grounds. And speaking of weddings, a few years later he drove the bride of my other nephew, Ross, to the church on a Rumely tractor.

My parents would have been so proud of all of their grand-sons: Ross, Cedric, Jerry, Ed, and David. Three of them are in business for themselves. Another is a professor of geography, and the other is busy making sure that the heavy diesel equipment his firm sells is safe (along with his brother, he still repairs pioneer tractors and other equipment so they can continue to be shown to today's children as a glimpse of what it was like in the 1930s and 40s).

It was possible for us to bring Ginger Farm back through this book courtesy of the efforts of David's marketing executive Megan Cameron and a select group of willing students who entered the information and helped research the order of the columns, which previously had not always been accurately recorded. I am told that they enjoyed doing it because of the history but also because they developed a real affinity for my mother. So thank you, Megan. I am sure the other family members will all thank you, too, when this book is given to them on the occasion of my ninetieth birthday celebration.

Dorothy Walsh

CPSIA information can be obtained at www.ICGtesting.com
Printed in the USA
LVOW101633040613

336938LV00018B/744/P